GRAND STR 10 WO

A Guide to Great Power Politics in the 21st Century

Sven Biscop

BRISTOL
UNIVERSITY
PRESS

First published in Great Britain in 2021 by

Bristol University Press
University of Bristol
1-9 Old Park Hill
Bristol
BS2 8BB
UK
t: +44 (0)117 954 5940
e: bup-info@bristol.ac.uk

Details of international sales and distribution partners are available at
bristoluniversitypress.co.uk

British Library Cataloguing in Publication Data
A catalogue record for this book is available from the British Library

ISBN 978-1-5292-1750-6 hardcover
ISBN 978-1-5292-1751-3 paperback
ISBN 978-1-5292-1752-0 ePub
ISBN 978-1-5292-1753-7 ePdf

Cover design: Clifford Hayes
Front cover image: Clifford Hayes
Bristol University Press uses environmentally responsible
print partners.
Printed and bound in Great Britain by CMP, Poole

"Sven Biscop, who has spent his entire career analysing the European Union's strengths and weakness, is well-placed to help her to start thinking about a strategy. My recommendation can be summarised as: 'buy this book'."

Brendan Simms, University of Cambridge

"This book is both a conceptual treatment of grand strategy and a prescriptive argument about 21st century geopolitics. While I do not agree with all of its conclusions, I believe all readers will find it most stimulating."

Hal Brands, Johns Hopkins University and American Enterprise Institute

For Aberu, my husband

Contents

List of Abbreviations

A2/AD	Anti Access/Area Denial
AIIB	Asian Infrastructure Investment Bank
ASEAN	Association of Southeast Asian Nations
AWACS	Airborne Warning and Control System
BAKS	Bundesakademie für Sicherheitspolitik
BRI	Belt and Road Initiative
BRICS	Brazil, Russia, India, China, South Africa
CCP	Chinese Communist Party
CSDP	Common Security and Defence Policy
DCFTA	Deep and Comprehensive Free Trade Agreement
EAEU	Eurasian Economic Union
EaP	Eastern Partnership
EDF	European Defence Fund
EEC	European Economic Community
EMP	Euro-Mediterranean Partnership
ENP	European Neighbourhood Policy
EPC	European Political Cooperation
FONOPS	Freedom of Navigation Operations
GDP	Gross Domestic Product
GNA	Government of National Accord
IHEDN	Institut d'Hautes Études de Défense Nationale
INF	Intermediate-Range Nuclear Forces Treaty
INSTEX	Instrument in Support of Trade Exchanges
IPR	Intellectual Property Rights
ISIS	Islamic State of Iraq and the Levant
JCPOA	Joint Comprehensive Plan of Action
NAFTA	North American Free Trade Agreement
NATO	North Atlantic Treaty Organization
PESCO	Permanent Structured Cooperation
PLA	People's Liberation Army
PRC	People's Republic of China
R2P	Responsibility to Protect

SARS	Severe Acute Respiratory Syndrome
SCO	Shanghai Cooperation Organisation
SOEs	State-Owned Enterprises
SWIFT	Society for Worldwide Interbank Financial Telecommunication
TPP	Trans-Pacific Partnership
USMCA	United States – Mexico – Canada Agreement
USSR	Union of Socialist Soviet Republics
WHO	World Health Organization
WTO	World Trade Organization

Notes on the Author

Sven Biscop is Director of the Europe in the World Programme at the Egmont–Royal Institute for International Relations in Brussels and Professor at Ghent University. He is an Honorary Fellow of the European Security and Defence College (ESDC), and has been awarded the Cross of Officer in the Order of the Crown of the Kingdom of Belgium and the Grand Decoration of Honour of the Republic of Austria.

Preface and Acknowledgements

> Concerning the origination of plans and decisions: it is my conviction that no commander could normally take oath that a particular plan or conception originated within his own mind. Preoccupation with the concerns of command are such that it is impossible for any person later to say whether the first gleam of an idea that may eventually have developed into a great plan came from within his own brain or from some outside suggestion.[1]

I am only an academic, so the pressures of command on me are somewhat lesser, but like General Eisenhower I dare not claim credit for every idea in this book. I am a double-hatted academic, dividing my time between Ghent University and a think-tank, the Egmont–Royal Institute for International Relations in Brussels. That privileged position puts me in permanent contact with a wide variety of interesting people: students and faculty at my own and other universities; colleagues in think-tanks in Europe, the Americas, and Asia; and military officers, diplomats and officials working for the European Union, NATO, and their member states, and the various states represented in Brussels, the diplomatic capital of Europe. I am indebted to a great many colleagues from these various communities, many of whom have become friends, for sharing their insights. Our ongoing discussions serve to generate ideas and to sharpen my thinking. More often than not, the most stimulating discussions take place over a glass or a meal. We Belgians adhere to the dictum of Napoleon's foreign minister, Talleyrand: 'Good dinners make for good reporting'.[2]

Fortified though I may feel for being a member of this inspiring community, writing a book on the big topic of the grand strategies of and relations between the United States, China, Russia and the EU remains a risky undertaking. I certainly do not pretend to be an expert on all of these players and all of their policies. For a start, I speak neither Chinese nor Russian. The key primary documents, such as a national security strategy, are available in English, but I can only scratch the surface of the rich intellectual debate that is going on within both countries, of which the English-language publications by Chinese and Russian scholars offer but a glimpse. Fortunately, all roads lead to Brussels: all major think-tanks regularly send delegations to visit the EU, and there are ample opportunities to learn from such distinguished visitors. Similarly, an annual course in the summer school at the People's University of China in Beijing, and an annual seminar with the Institute of Europe of the Russian Academy of Sciences in Moscow, have provided me with the chance to interact directly with many Chinese and Russian scholars. In 2020, the coronavirus interrupted both, but I look forward to resuming intercontinental travel as soon as the situation allows. I 'zoom in' and 'team up' online when I have to, but nothing can replace face-to-face meetings. Contacts within the EU and with the US and the United Kingdom are, of course, plenty. I have attempted, furthermore, as much as time permitted, to consult sources in other languages than English; where I quote these directly, all translations are my own.

All of this still does not make me an economist, however, or an expert on climate change, nor does it render me knowledgeable on artificial intelligence or quantum computing. I am a political scientist and of necessity have devoted more attention to the dimensions of international politics that I know best: diplomacy and defence. That should not be read as a judgement of the relative importance of the issues, however. Before a state can even play an active role in international politics, it must establish a sound economy and create political stability at home. Alasdair Roberts suggests therefore that one should study domestic and international grand strategy together, for 'If there are two grand strategies – one foreign, one domestic – is either one of them really grand?'[3] Writing such a book would require one to be even more of a homo universalis. This book is not about how to establish a state's domestic power base; I write about how to use power in international politics once a state's home base is secure.

This book is also not a theoretical treatise. I have aimed to write a book that anybody with an interest in international politics can read. I have tried, therefore, to abide by the great historian Hugh Trevor-Roper (Lord Dacre): 'Life is short, and those who will not take the trouble to write clearly cannot properly expect to be read.'[4] Working at the interface of policy making and academia, I do not believe that the role of political scientists is to write learned papers that only other political scientists can understand. I too, like Michael Green, sometimes long for 'an era when social science was not yet hampered by impenetrable theories and methods or obscure postmodernist critique but instead sought to unveil the patterns of history and contemporary events in ways that would provide usable insights for policy'.[5] I use the concepts and theories of political science as a display case: they help display the issues and the connections between them. They should not act as wrapping paper that obscures the issues from view; when the complex knot is untied and the wrapping is thrown away, all too often nothing is revealed but an empty box. The issues are further illuminated by their history, and so I use many examples from history, not only to indulge my passion for history in general, but because one cannot fully understand international politics today without knowledge of what went before.

As an academic I remain an observer, and sometimes an advisor, but I have no intention of stepping onto the practitioner's patch. 'I was a professional diplomatist and they were professors of history. An absurd conflict of vanities was thereby introduced.'[6] The situation that Harold Nicolson, a member of the British delegation at the Peace Conference in Versailles in 1919, found himself in vis-à-vis the non-diplomats of the American delegation, is to be avoided. The professor's role is to generate ideas; if they have some merit, they will be picked up and become part of the intellectual context within which it is up to the decision-makers to decide.

'Faced by the mountainous heap of the minutiae of knowledge and awed by the watchful severity of [my] colleagues', I could have greatly reduced the risk of error inherent in a book about the big picture by, instead, 'tak[ing] refuge in learned articles or narrowly specialised dissertations, small fortresses that are easy to defend from attack'.[7] That is what I often do, like most academics. I have written, for example, on the technicalities of defence cooperation in Europe – European defence certainly is a 'small fortress', in more than one sense. One can only make sense of the details, however, if one knows the big picture, and that is what I have tried to draw in this book, assuming the risk as well as the responsibility for all errors.

I cannot list all the academics and practitioners from whose wisdom, over the years, I have benefited, but some stand out as deserving special thanks. Credit for the idea of structuring the entire book around ten characteristics of grand strategy must go to Thomas Renard, my colleague at Egmont; initially, I planned only to address these all together in an introductory chapter. Without my mentor, Emeritus Professor Rik Coolsaet, I would never have written any book, and our regular dinners have contributed a lot to this project as well. Through our exchanges, Jan Joel Andersson, Bruno Angelet, Valerie Arnould,

Ilana Bet-El, Jo Coelmont, Bart Dessein, Geoffrey Edwards, Zhongping Feng, Daniel Fiott, Marc Franco, Tobias Gehrke, Bastian Giegerich, Eva Gross, Judith Heimann, Jolyon Howorth, Paul Huynen, Emil Kirchner, Heinz Krieb, Tania Latici, Alexander Mattelaer, Costanza Musu, Marc Otte, Barry Posen, Lars Schümann, Luis Simón, Rupert Smith, Marc Thys, Nathalie Tocci,Serge Van Camp, Johan Verbeke, Bert Versmessen, Richard Whitman, Nina Wilén, Patrick Wouters, Jing Yu and Rui Zhang have all nourished my thinking.

As always, I warmly thank my two employers, the Egmont Institute and Ghent University, for allowing me the freedom to pursue my interests and even pay me a salary for it. The Belgian foreign ministry deserves due credit for funding an independent think-tank like Egmont. I am very grateful to its current director-general, Hugues Chantry, who assumed his post in the middle of the 2020 lockdown, for his trust − and for his sense of humour. Stephen Wenham from Bristol University Press showed great enthusiasm for this project from the very start, and I greatly appreciate his warm encouragement.

Finally, the one I can never thank enough is my husband Aberu, who shows infinite patience while I have far too little. Leaving sunny Taipei for rainy Brussels, just to marry me, was the surest demonstration of true love. I dedicate this book to him.

Sven Biscop
Brussels, 1 May 2021

Introduction: No Peace from Corona – Why Grand Strategy and Great Powers Remain Important

This will change everything. When in early 2020 the coronavirus spread around the world, and one state after the other succumbed and ordered society and the economy into lockdown, this was understandably the first reaction of many. For the middle classes in the affluent countries of the world, COVID-19 was the greatest disruption of their existence since the Second World War. Confined to my Brussels apartment with my husband, without visitors, and resolved to avoid online meetings as much as possible, I suddenly had a lot of writing time – indeed, almost nothing but writing time. But I too wondered for a moment whether the book project about grand strategy and the great powers that had been gestating in my mind for a few years still made sense. Soon enough, though, I concluded that in the realm of international politics, the relations between states, COVID-19 might not actually change all that much, precisely because it was a worldwide disaster. And so I sat down to write.

Had the coronavirus struck some great powers but not the others, it could have been a gamechanger, creating an opportunity for the powers that escaped to increase their wealth and influence at the expense of the others. But there was no escape. The coronavirus caused a symmetric crisis: it hit everybody. How hard depended in the first instance on the power of each and every state: the resilience of its health infrastructure, the speed and resolve of its crisis response, the scale of its economic recovery package. National leaders who delayed, putting up a show of insouciance or omnipotence, put their countries at risk. The later they acted, the more people died, the greater the economic and societal disruption, and the deeper the depths from which to recover. Many weak states anyhow have but limited capacity to protect their citizens,

1

even in normal times. The longer-term consequences of the corona crisis obviously are asymmetrical, therefore – but only because the poor (people and states) end up even poorer while the rich hold their own.

The great powers of the early 21st century – the United States, China, Russia and the European Union – can mobilise more resources than anyone else. The coronavirus could not bring down a great power that responded adequately; only their own domestic mistakes could. All four initially mismanaged the crisis. Some kept up that mismanagement longer than others: in the autumn of 2020, China was already well underway to economic recovery when the others were hard hit by the second wave of the pandemic. Effectively though, all four great powers were internally shaken and economically weakened by the pandemic. But all four can invest what it takes to recover and will maintain their power. Initial mismanagement did lead to internal political contestation, but the authoritarian regimes in Russia and China remained firmly in place. In the EU, member state governments and the Brussels institutions gradually regained confidence and legitimacy as they grappled with the pandemic. Even in the US, where presidential elections took place as planned on 3 November 2020, President Donald Trump only narrowly lost the popular vote to Joe Biden, in spite of continuing to deny the severity of the pandemic (even after catching the coronavirus himself: having been cured, in Trump's mind that apparently settled the issue for the rest of America too).

Between the great powers, there was no clear winner or loser, and the balance of power between them basically stayed the same. The nature of their relations did not change either. The pandemic could have prompted a great cooperative effort. That would probably have allowed the great powers to overcome the crisis faster and to assist other countries earlier and much more effectively, to the benefit of the global economy as a whole. But the trend since the turn of the century has been one of increasing rivalry between the great powers. As the coronavirus neither wiped out the power of the 'big four' nor altered the balance of power between them, and as no strong joint humanitarian impulse emerged, rivalry continued unabated. Rather than overturning this trend, the pandemic became one more dimension in which great power rivalry played out. The powers variously threw conspiracy theories at each other, launched disinformation campaigns, struggled for influence in the World Health Organization, and courted their own and foreign public opinion by disbursing aid and engaging in 'mask diplomacy'. Between the US and China in particular mutual accusations became intense. President Xi Jinping had to prove to the Chinese public that he was in control and had to make them forget the initial cover-up of the outbreak in the city of Wuhan. Trump too had to make his audience ignore his initial dismissal of the pandemic as a 'Democrat hoax' and tried to shift the blame to China.[1] An internal Chinese report warned that as a result of the growing tensions, anti-Chinese sentiment was at its highest since the violent repression of the Tiananmen student protests in 1989.[2]

One of the aims of this book, however, is to demonstrate that great power politics can take other shapes than rivalry too. Trends do change, and the strategies of the great powers do evolve. The starting point of the book is that, given the discrepancy in power between the current 'big four' and the other states, it is still the great powers that to a very large extent shape international politics. Simply defined, a great power is precisely that: *a state with the ambition to make decisions and the resources to take action with a global impact.* In the early 21st century, these are the United States, the established power; Russia, the declining power; China, the rising power; and the European Union, which is not quite sure whether it wants to be a power. How they interact with each other and the world will determine the course of international politics in the first half of the 21st century. Understanding their grand strategies is crucial, therefore, to understand the world, and that is what this book sets out to do.

A strategy consists of ends, ways and means. *Grand strategy concerns the vital ends that a state has to achieve in order to assure the survival of its chosen way of life, for which if necessary it will mobilise all instruments (the ways) and resources (the means) at its disposal.* The US, the EU, China, and Russia: Are their ends mutually exclusive or can they co-exist? Will they pursue their ends in a confrontational or in a cooperative way? Do they have the means of their ambition? Will they sustain a certain rules-based order that they can all subscribe to? This book seeks to offer a nuanced analysis of the competition and cooperation between today's great powers. I cannot but write from a European perspective, as a citizen of Belgium and the EU, based in Brussels. But I have attempted to understand the grand strategy of each of the great powers as they see it themselves: what are they aiming to achieve in the world as they perceive it? Against that background, I then offer an assessment of the effectiveness of their strategies: are they achieving what they themselves set out to do?

The book pursues the narrative through ten chapters, under the heading of ten keywords that together capture the essence of grand strategy:

(1) Simple – a grand strategy that is too complicated to explain will not be implemented.
(2) Competitive – the other party has a strategy too.
(3) Rational – religion, ideology and emotion are bad counsellors.
(4) Allied – you need allies but cannot always choose them.
(5) Comprehensive – you need political, economic and military power.
(6) Creative – strategy is an art as much as a science.
(7) Agile – a strategy that does not adapt fast becomes unstrategic.
(8) Courageous – dare to act, or not to act, as your interests demand.
(9) Dirty – you have to act in the world as it is.
(10) Proactive – nobody will defend your interests for you.

These ten characteristics all work upon each other; effective strategies will exhibit most of them. Altogether, the ten chapters will cover the key external policies of the great powers.

In the eleventh, concluding chapter, I adopt a more normative perspective, in accordance with my think-tank background, and suggest four precepts for a less confrontational grand strategy, in order to maintain a peaceful and stable world order. Somewhat immodestly perhaps, these recommendations are addressed to all of the four great powers – usually, I purport to know better only as far as the EU is concerned.

★★★

It is very tempting to develop a black and white picture of great power politics. Surely great powers cannot be but adversaries? If China is rising, it must be seeking world domination. If Russia is declining, it must be plotting revenge. The 'other', be it gaining power or losing it, is always dangerous, and easily vilified. The xenophobic fear of the 'yellow peril' from China is never far away.[3] The idea of Russia as a country that can take more pain than others and must therefore be doubly watched is vivid.[4] Similarly, others everywhere see American machinations, for it must be that the US will not refrain from anything to maintain its dominant position. Europe then either is a mere puppet of the US or, alternatively, a cynical free-rider on American military might which, behind a façade of lofty rhetoric on values, pursues only its own economic advantage.

At times, near fantastical projects are ascribed to the other great powers. Michael Pillsbury's 'hundred-year marathon' will undoubtedly become a classic in the genre.[5] He claims that in the 1950s, shortly after the establishment of the People's Republic in 1949, China developed a secret plan to overtake the US in 100 years – though not so secret that he could not unveil it and turn it into a thesis for a bestselling book. Iain Johnston has demonstrated that Pillsbury's work is largely based on a single book by a Chinese colonel, which he not only misreads, but does not even quote directly.[6] That is unfortunate, from an academic point of view, but also dangerous, because scaremongering will not help anybody make better strategy. Many Chinese policies and actions do present major cause for concern; designing a strategy in response demands clear-headed thinking. Adding imaginary conspiracies to the plot only muddles the water. The US did not secretly plan at the end of its civil war, in 1865, to become a super power by 1945. That is the position the US, and the Soviet Union, ended up in at the end of the Second World War, because of the circumstances they encountered and the decisions they made. Exactly how China would conquer the world, short of a great power war from which there would very likely only be losers, this and other conspiracy theories never make quite clear, by the way. One assumes that the US and the other powers will not just surrender their global influence and subordinate themselves, nor will they simply fade away.

But alleged proof of outlandish plots is not necessary to provoke criticism and fear of the other powers. Achieving what 'we' have already achieved, and acquiring equal strength or – heaven forbid – surpassing 'us' in some domains, is sufficient. We are warned that in manufacturing, technology and finance, China is now in a genuinely competitive position with the other powers.[7] In areas of artificial intelligence, quantum computing and green technologies, China even has an edge over the US and the EU (while Russia is lagging behind in innovation). But is that necessarily problematic? Thanks to China's new-found wealth, the direst poverty is slowly disappearing and a relatively prosperous middle class is growing. Beijing is also investing in military power, however. China certainly has gained a freedom of action that it did not have before, and pursues its interests more assertively, and at times even aggressively. For sure, the other powers have to make a greater effort now to safeguard their own interests. One should take care, however, not to present everything that another power does as illegitimate. The 'other' is not just a 'predator';[8] it has legitimate interests too.

'But the integrated nature of the Chinese Communist Party's military and economic strategies is what makes it particularly dangerous to the United States and other free and open societies', writes General H.R. MacMaster, former national security advisor to President Trump.[9] The 'other' has to be presented as fundamentally different from 'us'. Yet does not every great power seek to craft an integrated military, economic and political strategy? Comprehensiveness is indeed one of the essential characteristics of strategy. Often, however, other powers are blamed for undertaking perfectly legal and legitimate actions simply because they do not fit in our plans. Can one judge the same action differently depending on who is behind it? The opening of a Chinese navy base in Djibouti in 2017 caused many to cry out, as if it were a threat to world peace. Yet the US, the UK, France and others already had bases there – to defend world peace, presumably. Americans and Europeans must not encourage China to open more navy bases, of course. But only a balanced judgement of the other powers' actions can produce good strategy.

There are crucial differences between the great powers, each of which has its chosen way of life. Most notably, the US and the EU are democracies; China and Russia are authoritarian states. For a democrat, the many aspects of Chinese and Russian domestic policies that violate the Universal Declaration of Human Rights definitely are reprehensible. Even though their own record is not exactly perfect, Europeans and Americans can legitimately criticise human rights violations by other states. Less obvious is whether democracies can and must seek to change the system of government itself in non-democratic states. The Universal Declaration includes the right to take part in government through free elections, and one may be convinced that democracy is the better system – but the active promotion of regime change is a recipe for permanent instability and strife. Furthermore, the fact that a state is authoritarian does not mean that it cannot have legitimate interests. If one aims for stable great power relations, mutual respect is required, as is the acceptance of the others for what they are, even if one does not like all that one sees. Americans and Europeans have a moral duty to condemn human rights violations. But the US or the EU will not change China's or Russia's way of life – only the Chinese and the Russians can do that, and vice versa.

Since Xi came to power in 2012, China has definitely become more repressive again, after a period of gradual relaxation. Russia too, under Putin, has moved in the direction of more authoritarianism. But the question is, as Fareed Zakaria wrote, whether that in itself makes them a vital threat.[10] Even if China or Russia would become democracies, they would still be great powers pursuing global interests – in the realm of grand strategy, that is the determining factor, not that they are authoritarian states. Surely, even to a democratic China the US would not simply say: 'Congratulations – let us cut the cake in two now, and divide the world between us.' From the strategic point of view, the primary concern is not how states organise themselves internally, no matter how much they misbehave, but how they behave in international politics, in their relations with other states.

When one observes their international behaviour, the differences between the great powers appear far less great. In every conversation I have had with American officials or scholars, they immediately push back against the idea that the US can in any way be put into the same basket with China or Russia. Yet, says Graham Allison, 'Despite their many differences, the United States and China are alike in at least one respect: both have extreme superiority complexes'.[11] I agree with Hanns Maull that the US and China

> sometimes resemble mirror images of each other. Both share a sense of national exceptionalism and see themselves as the natural centre of world politics. Both support the notion of international order in general, with significant differences concerning the details, but both are profoundly ambivalent about, if not entirely opposed to, accepting that the principles, norms and rules of international order apply to themselves as much as they do to others. Both have unilaterally violated these principles when they considered this necessary to secure their own vital interests.[12]

The same applies to Russia; only the EU can be said to adhere more sincerely to the rules-based order, though not all of its member states always fully comply with it either. Unfortunately, many powers bend the rules or simply ignore international law when that suits their purpose. But a breach of the law by one power does not justify another to do the same; and respecting the rule of law at home is no excuse for violating it abroad. One should, in any case, equally condemn all violations.

What is different is the international environment, the constellation of power: since about the turn of the century and for the first time since the Second World War, there are, once again, several great powers. No single one of them has sufficient power to dominate international politics by itself. The US no longer is the only great power, as it appeared to some for a while after the end of the Cold War. China has achieved some incredible successes, including in some areas in which Americans and Europeans assumed they would forever be in the lead. Russia and China both behave assertively, sometimes aggressively, and for the first time since the Cold War the US and the EU are at the receiving end again of other powers' strategies. That rankles, understandably – but that emotion should not be the basis of

American and European strategy, nor should a quest for status and the satisfaction of outwitting the US and the EU become an end in itself for Chinese and Russian strategy. Strategy is about the rational pursuit of interests; emotions only get in the way.

The reality is that in international politics the great powers all use similar methods to pursue their grand strategies, each with the aim of preserving its own way of life. To safeguard one's way of life, certain conditions have to be fulfilled: these are the state's vital interests, in the political, economic and security spheres. Every state requires secure borders, markets, natural resources, and so on. Grand strategy is not about discovering the sinister plans of the other great powers, but about trying to understand their grand strategies, from their point of view, so as to continually improve one's own. That is not easy, and one will never fully know the strategy of the other, but with a bit of empathy one can often know enough for one's own purposes. Winston Churchill's dictum on Russia is well known: 'I cannot forecast to you the action of Russia. It is a riddle wrapped in a mystery inside an enigma.' The next sentence is rarely quoted, however: 'But perhaps there is a key. That key is Russian national interest.'[13] One need not agree with how another power defines its interests, but one has to understand it. That requires a sober analysis, avoiding both alarmism and wishful thinking, in order to design effective strategies to respond and to anticipate while reducing the risk of an escalation of tensions.

As one power pursues its interests, it will for sure intrude on the interests of another, since the powers all compete for markets, resources and influence. But the fact that one's interests are in competition with those of another power does not necessarily mean that the other power is a rival that has a strategy *against* you or is actively looking for confrontation. And, of course, interests can also coincide, and other powers can seek to work *with* you as a partner for cooperation. Every state puts its own interests first – for Xi Jinping it is 'China First' as much as it was 'America First' for Donald Trump. The question is how broadly or narrowly those interests are defined.[14] If China were only an adversary, then why are Europeans and Americans buying Chinese smartphones and laptops? Why, if Russia is nothing but an adversary, is Europe importing Russian energy? And if the US is Europe's ally, then why under Trump did it impose tariffs on Europe's trade? International politics is too complex to yield to simplistic explanations. The great powers compete and cooperate with each other at the same time, all the time: that is inherent to international politics. Rivalry, on the contrary, can be avoided, for it is the product of a conscious choice by some of the powers. Great powers can thus be, as the EU said of China, partners, competitors and rivals all at once.[15]

★★★

Great power politics is not all that matters. If humankind does not mitigate the consequences of the climate crisis, nobody will be able to maintain their chosen way of life. The coronavirus temporarily distracted from the urgency of the climate disaster. As factories closed and planes and automobiles (the trains are alright, climate-wise) stayed motionless for months, the outbreak even led to some transitory reduction of pollution. But the corona crisis interacts with the climate crisis. Already weak states have crumbled further, the struggle for scarce resources has become even fiercer, and existing tensions within and between states have intensified. So rather than doing away with the causes of war, the virus has exacerbated them. United Nations Secretary-General António Guterres' call for a universal ceasefire in the face of the pandemic was the right thing to do, but it was only to be expected that it would mostly be ignored.[16] In many instances, violence actually increased, where one party perceived a temporary advantage while its opponent was weakened by the outbreak. New wars broke out, even, such as between Armenia and Azerbaijan over the enclave of Nagorno-Karabagh. For the middle classes in the richer parts of the world, the coronavirus was a rude shock that upended their daily routines. But in many places the pandemic actually produced more of the same: more poverty, more wars and more refugees. Dying of hunger or dying of COVID-19: it is not a choice that an academic in Europe has to face.

While humanity is working on solutions for the climate crisis, global health, poverty and energy scarcity, it is important that great power rivalry does not create blockages or, in a truly worst case scenario, that we do not kill each other in a great power war first. Furthermore, without the active involvement of the great powers, the solutions to global problems may perhaps be found, but the chance would be smaller. And it would certainly be unlikely that such solutions could be effectively implemented unless the great powers actively cooperated, given their share in the global economy (and global pollution) and their influence in international organisations.

Not just the great powers, but states in general remain the key players in international politics. Only states have the authority to enter into commitments on behalf of their citizens, and states control the instruments and resources needed to act on the international scene.[17] The corona crisis highlighted that ultimately only the state has the responsibility as well as the means to protect its citizens. Countries with 'big government' – where the state already played a more interventionist role in the economy, such as China but also the members of the EU – might even have an edge on the US when it comes to managing recovery after such a crisis.[18] States have also created the many international organisations that play a big part in international politics. These organisations are instruments of the states, therefore; they act within the mandate that their member states decide upon and with the budget that they confer upon it. The EU is the exception that confirms the rule: it is a supranational organisation in which states have pooled their sovereignty in specific policy areas, mostly domestic, but including international trade. In those areas, the EU is not an instrument of its members but an international player in its own right, unlike other multilateral organisations.

Non-state actors play a part too: corporations, non-governmental organisations and philanthropic foundations, as well as private security companies, irregular armed forces and terrorist organisations. But the increased role of non-state actors does not mean that we have arrived in a 'non-polar' world, in which there are no more 'poles' or great powers, as some pretend.[19] Non-state actors, in reality, can act only where the state allows them to, or is too weak to stop them. The big players in information technology, for example, wield a lot of influence, but only because governments have refrained from regulating their affairs more closely (and from taxing them appropriately). Contrary to what many believe,[20] the advent of cyber space does not change the predominance of states: in cyber space, the tactics change, but the nature of strategy and of relations between states does not. When humankind successively conquered the seas, the air and space, each brought new opportunities and new vulnerabilities, and each immediately became a theatre for cooperation and competition between states. In cyber space, private individuals or organisations can cause a lot of damage. But in this sphere too, states are still the main players, either acting directly or allowing private players to act from their territory. Some states seek to compensate for their lesser power in other domains by acquiring cyber capabilities.[21] But more than anybody else, it is the great powers in whose hands cyber instruments have become powerful tools – and weapons.

Some states have more power than others, including, as Maull points out, 'certain supranational organisations', that is the EU.[22] These are the great powers, whose decisions and actions have global impact. That is undoubtedly the case of the US and China. The Russian Federation, in comparison, is less powerful; unlike the Soviet Union, it mostly has deep impact in its broad neighbourhood. Forays into Venezuela or the Central African Republic cause a lot of nuisance to the US and the EU, but for lack of economic means, its relations with most of Latin America and Africa do not run that deep, while in Asia Russia avoids causing nuisance to China. Nevertheless, by virtue of its military power and its position in the multilateral architecture, and because it aspires to the same status as the Czar's empire and the Soviet Union, Russia must be taken into account as a great power. By contrast the EU, though it defines itself as a global player, shies away from the language of power. The Union certainly has global economic and, to a lesser extent, political impact; taken as a whole, the military power of its member states is second only to that of the US (though is not one whole and, consequently, has far less impact). The EU too, therefore, must be counted among the great powers. Countries like Japan, India and maybe Brazil might gradually increase their global role. But in the medium term, no other state or organisation is likely to acquire both the ambition and the resources to join the ranks of the great powers.

★★★

Historical comparisons immediately come to mind. A context in which a handful of powerful states has global impact in some ways resembles the late 19th century, for example, when European empires controlled the world.[23] But today's world also has similarities with the interbellum period between the two world wars, when non-European great powers, the US and Japan, entered the scene, and a first attempt was made to order international politics through the League of Nations, the forerunner of the UN. I share Sir Michael Howard's 'confession of faith': there is no way to understand international politics without studying its history.[24] At the same time, one must take into account Sir Hew Strachan's warning, that 'history is not just a repository from which we can cherry-pick enduring truths'.[25] Harold Nicolson went even further: 'People who study the past under the conviction that they themselves would automatically behave better in the present are adopting a dangerous habit of mind'.[26] Throughout the book, I will quote examples from the history of international politics, to illustrate how grand strategy has worked, or failed, in the past; not to draw direct lessons or recommendations for the present and the future, but to deepen our understanding.

History is long and complicated, so one can always find an example to prove any point. But perhaps one universally valid lesson from history is this: nothing is inevitable. The international environment may make one or the other choice more likely, but governments and people always can, and must, make choices. Those who, based on historical examples, convince themselves that the emergence of a rising great power must of necessity lead to war with the established great power – the so-called 'Thucydides trap' – stop looking for ways to keep the peace.[27] Graham Allison himself, who popularised the notion, has emphatically rejected such inevitability: 'Is war – real bloody war – inevitable? No. To repeat: no.'[28] The problem is that the frame of the 'Thucydides trap', which is now widely used, inherently assumes that every rising power questions the existing order of things.[29] It is logical, as Xuetong Yan states, that 'A dominant state's main interest is to maintain its position in the world, while that of a rising state is to gain more international power.'[30] But that does not necessarily entail that the latter seeks to dethrone the former or to overthrow the existing world order; a rising state may also gain more power within the current system. It is, of course, impossible for every great power to be forever on good terms with every other power; so great power relations will usually involve a degree of rivalry – but rivalry does not have to be the dominant pattern.

★★★

> Americans at that time [1945] – or at least we in Berlin – saw no reason why the Russian system of government and democracy as practised by the Western Allies could not live side by side in the world, provided each respected the rights, the territory, and the convictions of the other, and each system avoided overt or covert action against the integrity of the other. … What caused the change … may possibly never be clearly understood by any of us.[31]

This is how in 1948 General Eisenhower looked back, somewhat puzzled, at the beginning of the Cold War between the US and the USSR. His sentiments were later echoed by Marshall Zhukov: 'Much was said in the most heart-felt expressions about the desire to consolidate for ever friendly relations between the countries of the anti-Fascist coalition. This was said by the Soviet Generals, the Americans, French and British, and all of us wanted to believe it would be that way.'[32] Is the world heading for a new Cold War-like confrontation, between the US and China? Some claim that it has already started, and actively feed a new 'red scare'.[33] The line of the Committee on the Present Danger, created during the Cold War and revived with the help of Stephen Bannon, President Trump's former Chief Strategist, is that 'as with the Soviet Union in the past, Communist China represents an existential and ideological threat to the United States and to the idea of freedom'.[34] Others, like Hal Brands, are surprised that a new cold war has not started yet, since 'Hegemonic powers are not supposed to tolerate, much less assist, the rise of challengers: they are supposed to fiercely and even violently resist'.[35] The same author even argues that the US should start thinking about covert operations again, like when it 'sought to undermine or topple unfriendly regimes during the Cold War'.[36] Joshua Shifrinson, on the contrary, argues that one must not automatically assume the worst on behalf of rising states, but take into account the constraints and opportunities that they face.[37]

What has acted as a brake is that, unlike the US and the USSR, the American and Chinese economies are closely interwoven. The reason why an escalation of the tensions between Washington and Beijing into a systematic, all-encompassing rivalry would be so enormously damaging is precisely because it would cut off natural interconnections in trade, investment, science, education, and many other areas. It would push the global economy into an even deeper recession than the corona crisis has already caused, and disrupt international politics as both sides would seek to force other states to align with one or the other. Is a new cold war really in the interest of the US and China? It would certainly serve neither the EU nor Russia, who would play a secondary role in a bipolar confrontation. Rather than looking out for their interests, the US and China would try to push them into the role of vassals. Unless China itself would provoke its enmity, the EU definitely does not agree with Stephen Walt that 'Europe's future is as China's enemy'.[38]

Starting a new cold war is easy enough; avoiding it is more difficult. It requires putting aside emotions, and applying reason. Is there any reason, actually, why a citizen of the US, the EU, China or Russia should fear the other great powers? The great powers use legal ways to influence, and illegal ways to subvert each other's policies. But no great power is envisaging war with another, because as Sir Lawrence Freedman writes: 'Once the possibility of escalation to nuclear use is introduced, prudence affects all types of conflicts.'[39] The great powers have different political systems, but none is truly aiming to convert the other to its own way of life. Economic competition can be fierce, but it is inherent to our economic system and therefore not disruptive. Technological advantages can be gained, but in the end it is impossible to restrict technologies to those that have invented them.[40] Nuclear weapons are a case in point: the US expected to maintain a nuclear monopoly for many years after it built the first nuclear bombs in 1945; just four years later, the Soviet Union successfully tested its own bomb.

Sitting behind my desk in Brussels, in my mid-forties, I probably do not really believe that I will not be able to live out my life in peace. That should not lead to complacency, but to optimism; and that, the belief that something can be achieved, is the starting point of any proactive strategy.

1

Simple: But Not Easy

A persuasive grand strategy usually is simple. A grand strategy is a mission statement rather than a manual. The core of grand strategy is a view of the state's role in international politics, the few large ends that it sets out to achieve, and a broad idea of how to go about that. The details are for the geographic and thematic strategies that should follow on from a grand strategy. With a bit of effort and goodwill, a grand strategy can be elegantly expressed in a few brief pages, though few states manage that. 'I didn't have time to write a short letter, so I wrote a long one instead', the saying, often attributed to Mark Twain, applies to the drafters of strategy as well (though academics are not well placed to criticise others for writing too much).

That, ideally, a grand strategy is simple does not mean that it will be easy to bring into practice. 'Everything is very simple in war, but the simplest thing is difficult', said Clausewitz, by which he meant difficult to implement.[1] Clausewitz had served in the Napoleonic wars. Field Marshal Erich von Manstein, who served in the Second World War, similarly concluded that 'in war the simplest thing often turns out to be the most difficult. Not in the decision as such, but in its unfailing implementation mostly lie the true difficulties.'[2] These statements apply to grand strategy in war and peace. If the grand strategy itself is already too complicated to explain to those who have to implement it, it is most probably not a very good strategy, and will likely never be implemented as intended at all. If, conversely, a straightforward strategy based on a simple idea is well communicated, it will serve to inspire those charged with its implementation, and provide them with a sense of purpose and the resolve to achieve it. 'Action at the service of a strong and simple idea', thus Charles de Gaulle summed up his policy in the Second World War.[3]

In addition to good ideas, grand strategy requires clear language. Sir Lawrence Freedman stresses that strategy is meaningless without it: 'Not only does strategy need to be put into words so that others can follow, but it works through affecting the behaviour of others. Thus it is always about persuasion, whether convincing others to work with you or explaining to adversaries the consequences if they do not.'[4] Referring to one of his famous wartime speeches, Sir Winston Churchill once upbraided an official who had submitted a badly-worded document by asking him to imagine that he would have said that 'hostilities will be engaged on the coastal perimeter', instead of: 'We shall fight on the beaches'.[5]

A good example of a simple, and successful, grand strategy is in fact that of the allies in the Second World War.[6] After the US entered the war on the side of the UK in 1941, both allies settled on a grand strategy that could be summarised in two words: Germany first. Japan could be contained, and even allowed to advance further if needs be, because it could threaten neither the British nor the American homeland. But Germany could and, were it to conquer Britain, that would deprive the allies of the base from which to launch the liberation of Western Europe. Therefore Germany had to be defeated before the allies could turn on Japan. At their 1943 conference in Casablanca, Roosevelt and Churchill added two more words: unconditional surrender. That made it crystal clear to both Germany and Japan when the allies would end the war. The US and the UK also created a simple structure with a clear line of command to implement their grand strategy. The Combined Chiefs of Staff brought together the service chiefs of the two countries' army, navy and air force, who under the leadership of the president and the prime minister ran the war. This grand strategy provided a clear goal and sufficient flexibility at the same time: 'With a few themes always at the fore and a grasp of context, there was a framework for taking in new developments and for exploiting new opportunities.'[7]

A seemingly simple grand strategy can cover many interpretations, however. US strategy towards the Soviet Union during the Cold War could be summed up in just a single word: containment. But very soon after its inception by US diplomat George Kennan, different decision makers began to understand the strategy in very different ways. Containment could mean pushing back against Soviet expansionism where it mattered most – the world's industrial centres of Western Europe, Japan and the US itself – by applying mostly political and economic instruments. Or, at the other extreme, it could mean pushing back, and even rolling back, Soviet power everywhere, including by force of arms. The former understanding was closer to Kennan's own thinking; the latter was held by people like Paul Nitze, his successor as director of the State Department's policy planning staff, and the inspirator of NSC68, the National Security Council document that defined a worldwide scope for containment.[8] Nevertheless, agility is one of grand strategy's necessary characteristics, and containment, for better or for worse, did inspire US policy for several decades. Clearly, it was a simple, powerful idea.

★★★

Grand strategy is so simple that, as Edward Luttwak states, all states have one, whether they know it or not.[9] For in one sense of the term, grand strategy means the level of strategy that concerns interaction between states, and all states have relations with other states. Every state seeks to preserve its chosen way of life – that is the ultimate end of grand strategy, for which the state can mobilise all instruments (the ways) and all resources (the means) at its disposal. To that end, every state must safeguard its vital interests – those that guarantee the survival of its way of life. 'The need for strategy never sleeps', as Colin Gray put it.[10] States may choose not to state their grand strategy explicitly, and may therefore not codify it in a high-level public document – something which Luttwak anyway considers to be 'a very modern and rather dubious habit'. Some states may not even *think* explicitly about strategy, and may thus not really have a clear strategic concept in mind at all. But, over time, every state develops its own habits and practices: its broad ways of looking at the world, and of approaching its relations with other states.

However, Luttwak rightly adds that 'All states have a grand strategy, but not all grand strategies are equal'. States with a less developed strategic concept will be less able to defend their interests when confronted with more purposive states, who have a clear idea for themselves of what they want to achieve. Not thinking about strategy is a strategic choice too, therefore, which carries its own consequences. As Alasdair Roberts notes, 'an inept strategist is still a strategist, just as a bad writer is still a writer'.[11] The less developed the grand strategy, the more reactive the approach. A state with the ambition to proactively shape events and developments will need to define an explicit grand strategy specific to its purposes, which it can then choose to publish or to keep secret, in whole or in part. These are the three functions of grand strategy: to read and react to the world, to act in it, and to communicate with it.

First, strategy helps a state to react to the future as it unfolds. When I lecture for practitioners (military officers, diplomats, senior officials), nearly every time someone in the audience will stand up and assert that strategy is useless, because unforeseen events will forever force you to change your strategy anyway. Some authors have proclaimed the death of grand strategy, on the assumption that strategy 'works best on predictable terrain', which in today's fast-moving world no longer exists.[12] The function of strategy is not to predict the future, however; that has never been predictable. Foresight is important: one can and must extrapolate from past trends, and assess the capabilities and intentions of the other players, in order to understand the environment in which one pursues one's own strategy.[13] But in the end, as Gray always stressed, there is no such thing as a foreseeable future.[14]

Things are happening all the time. The question is: what is important for *me*? A state that has a clear strategic vision and knows its ends and its interests has a grid to read the world. It can more easily and more quickly determine whether new events and developments affect it or not, and, consequently, whether it needs to react or not, and how. One could argue, therefore, that the more unpredictable the terrain, the more grand strategy matters.[15] Obviously, if new events completely overturn the assumptions on which a strategy rests, one must adapt it. But not everything that happens must divert a state from its chosen course of action. Moreover, such agility when the situation demands it is not the same as systematically improvising without any prior idea of ends, ways and means. Improvisation usually takes more time, for one has to start the policy-making process from scratch every time around, and that means taking chances, as one acts from an unprepared position. And yet some assert that 'policy made on a case-by-case basis will be at least as good, and likely better, than policy derived from grand strategic commitments'.[16] It *might*, of course, because one can always get lucky, or the other players may have an even worse strategy. Adolf Hitler's strategy was so reckless that it should have failed from the start, when in violation of the Treaty of Versailles he reintroduced conscription (1935) and reinserted German troops into the Rhineland (1936); his own generals kept warning him against taking so much risk. But the strategy succeeded because the other powers at the time acted so meekly. 'He is very good, but is he lucky?', Napoleon supposedly asked of his generals.[17] But nobody is lucky all the time, so it is always wiser to act on the basis of strategy, even an imperfect one, than without one. 'Strategy cannot usefully be regarded as a quest for perfection', Gray points out; a state only needs a 'good enough strategic performance' when compared to the other players.[18]

The second function of strategy is to help a state to shape the future: it sets an agenda for action. A grand strategy does not have to imply grand objectives. A state with less power may be content with limited ends, or choose to pursue them only indirectly, through an alliance or an international organisation. Even a powerful state facing severe threats may focus on preventing further deterioration of a bad situation, as Freedman notes; ultimately, the simple end of grand strategy always is survival.[19] A great power, however, is a state with the ambition and the resources to act globally, and will thus acquire global interests to defend. But even that does not mean that every great power pursues revolutionary ends; a great power too may settle for evolutionary ends, and incremental action. Freedman explains that 'as a practical matter strategy is best understood modestly, as moving to the "next stage" rather than to a definitive and permanent conclusion. The next stage is a place that can be realistically reached from the current stage.' He adds, 'This does not mean that it is easy to manage without a view of a desired end-state. Without some sense of where the journey should be leading it will be difficult to evaluate alternative outcomes.' Without a clear sense of purpose, a state can only ever be reactive; that will not suffice for a great power to safeguard its interests. Great powers often define both intermediate ends, therefore, and broader ends to be achieved in the long term. Indeed, Freedman characterises strategy as 'an ability to look up from the short term and the trivial to view the long term and the essential, to address causes rather than symptoms, to see woods rather than trees'.[20] Or, as Richard Betts puts it, more modestly, one should 'distinguish grand strategy concerns as ones that are long-term or at least transcend a particular incident'.[21]

Strategy's third function (in spite of Luttwak's doubts) is to communicate one's ends, to the public, to allies and to adversaries. Every state needs domestic legitimacy and support, and will therefore explain its grand strategy to the public. In a democratic state, the public will want to know what its taxes are being spent on, and may vote the government out of office if it is not satisfied, though international politics rarely determines the outcome of elections, except in times of grave international crisis. Parliament will want to exert its control over the executive, however, and thus needs to be convinced of the strategy. Even an authoritarian state needs a degree of buy-in from the public, and it too can be swayed by strong currents of public opinion. A grand strategy also signals to one's allies and partners in which areas they can expect which type of cooperation – and in which areas they ought not to count on a contribution, so as not to raise false expectations. Finally, a public grand strategy is a signal to potential adversaries as well, indicating the red lines that will trigger action if they are crossed. Naturally, states never publicise their entire strategy in every detail; some part will always be classified, in order not to give away one's plans. In wartime in particular, most of strategy will be kept secret, though even then a state will want to signal an idea of its war aims to the public as well as to the enemy. For those who had read Hitler's *Mein Kampf*, his grand strategy ought not to have come as a complete surprise.[22]

★★★

If grand strategy ought to be simple, the first rule of crafting strategy is simple as well: know thyself. As the ultimate end of grand strategy is to preserve one's way of life, a strong internal consensus is necessary on what the essential aspects of that way of life are. Next, a state must forge consensus on the country's role in international politics: What kind of player does it want to be in order to safeguard its way of life? What is the main mode of its grand strategy? A state can be mostly reactive or quite proactive; it may be satisfied with the role of faithful ally of a bigger power, or seek a strongly independent role. It can see itself as a mediator and a bridge builder in multilateral cooperation, or aspire to become a regional power and dominate the politics of its neighbourhood. States may focus their efforts on a limited number of specific policy areas in which they have particular expertise and a strong interest, or pursue a 360-degrees strategy. A very few states will identify themselves as great powers with global interests and ambitions.

States develop such a concept of their broad ends, and thus of their vital interests, over long periods of time, together with a general way of looking at the world and of dealing with other states. This can be called a state's strategic culture, which Gray defines as: 'The persisting (though not eternal) socially transmitted ideas, attitudes, traditions, habits of mind and preferred methods of operation that are more or less specific to a particular geographically based security community that has had a necessarily unique historical experience.'[23] This broad orientation may be shared by the public, but it mainly reposes in a state's strategic establishment: the politicians, diplomats, military officers and civil servants who prepare, decide and implement strategy, together with the specialised academics and journalists that contribute to the strategic debate. These various players may be very alive to the strategic tradition that they are operating in and actively discuss it, or it may rather be something in the back of their minds that they do not think about much, but every state has a strategic culture. Not in every state is it strongly held, though. Volatile and fragmented domestic politics, a less cohesive strategic establishment, and a weak diplomatic service and armed forces can result in a strategic culture that is but faintly held, and that will not likely inspire any proactive strategy.

The US has a strong strategic culture, but during the first two years of the 2017–2020 Trump administration, it unusually presented the image of a very fragmented strategic establishment to the world, in particular when it came to Russia. When at a meeting in Helsinki in July 2018 Donald Trump openly sided with Vladimir Putin and against his own intelligence community, and denied Russian interference in the 2016 presidential elections, he provoked public push-back from many parts of the US strategic establishment, including from within his own Republican Party. Cohesion around the views of the president was gradually restored, as the secretaries of state and defence and the national security advisor were (several times) replaced, while many management positions in the administration were left unfilled when people resigned or were fired. Even so, tension remained between a strategic establishment that had been raised in a very anti-Russian strategic culture and the more sanguine views of the president.

Strategic culture is shaped by history. Some countries' contribution to history, like my own, Belgium, has mostly been to provide the great powers with the battlefields on which to fight their wars. A state on such a territory will think differently of itself and the world than a state that has been fortunate enough to escape conflict, such as Sweden, which has not had to fight a war since the times of Napoleon. Geography plays a part too, because a state's location implies specific opportunities and vulnerabilities that will influence its outlook – this is geopolitics. Both history and geography influence strategic culture, but they do not determine it, for the same historical experience or geographic location can produce different strategic choices. A state that has fallen victim to invasion can subsequently seek a military alliance or opt for neutrality. A state that feels secure in its home base can see that as an opportunity to withdraw from international politics and develop an isolationist culture, as the US did even after its participation in the First World War, or as a chance to pursue an interventionist strategy on other continents, which gradually became the US approach after the Second World War. Over the centuries, British strategy, for example, has fluctuated continuously between strong engagement on the European continent and a focus on overseas empire building. Brexit, the 2016 decision to leave the EU, signalled a return to abstinence from continental politics, but the realities of fending for itself in a world of great powers may yet force Britain to reengage with the European continent. 'Global Britain' (the slogan of the incumbent Conservative government) and Britain as part of Europe are present side by side in the UK's strategic culture.

The US is unique among the great powers in the sense that is has not seen war on its continental territory since the Civil War of 1861–1865, and no foreign invasion since the War of 1812 against the UK (when British forces burned down the White House). That may explain why the 2001 terrorist attacks on Washington and New York were such a shock to the strategic establishment and the public at large. It may also help to understand some of the differences between US and EU strategic culture. Simplifying: in the American experience, war takes place on another continent; the US sends in troops, which defeat the forces of evil and return victorious. In the experience of the majority of EU member states, war takes place on their own territory, and causes such death and destruction that the victors are not necessarily much better off than the defeated. That has led to a European strategic culture that is much more reticent to the use of force.

Since it develops gradually, strategic culture also evolves slowly, unless a severe internal or external shock forces an abrupt change upon a state. A revolution may bring to power an entirely different regime with a totally new idea of the role of the state in international politics. The threat of war, the collapse of markets or the exhaustion of natural resources may likewise render a state's existing orientation obsolete.

The EU differs from the other great powers, which are states, because it is a composite entity, consisting of 27 member states each with their own strategic culture. The EU as such is not a state, but it is not just an organisation of states either; it is something in between, a state-like organisation. That is because unlike other international organisations, the EU is a supranational union, in which member states have pooled sovereignty. Ian Morris describes it as 'simultaneously the dullest and most daring trick that statesmen had ever attempted'.[24] Joining the EU can be compared to moving into an apartment building. Inside one's own apartment, one can do as one pleases, within certain rules and as long as one does not overly disturb the neighbours. About the building as a whole, however, one still decides, but only as part of a collective decision by all the owners; one cannot decide to replace the elevator or to renovate the roof by oneself. (Nor, if one decides to move out, can one take the elevator or the roof along, as the UK has discovered after Brexit.) One better participate in the meetings, tedious though they may be, for decisions are taken by majority and are binding even if one does not attend. In the policy areas in which its members have totally or partially pooled sovereignty, the EU is a player in its own right therefore, either instead of or in cooperation with the member states. Thus the EU is also developing its own strategic culture. It is actively building it even, and has created the European Security and Defence College for that purpose, which offers courses to diplomats, military officers and officials from all member states.

The challenge is that the EU 'does not know itself': not only do the member states hold very different views about what kind of player the EU should be in international politics, they also view the future of the EU itself differently. Some wish to see the EU develop into a federal state, the 'United States of Europe';[25] others still regard the Union primarily as a market rather than as a political player. The crucial fact is, though, that in the EU, for the first time in history, the states of Europe have united voluntarily. In the past, all attempts to unite Europe by force (by Louis XIV, Napoleon, Wilhelm II, and Hitler) failed. It has even been argued that it was precisely the absence of a Europe-wide empire since the fall of the western Roman Empire, and the competition between states that this gave rise to, that explains Europe's rise compared to other parts of the world.[26] Today, however, the EU already is a state-like organisation; the Union is still evolving and its end-state may not be clear, but it will not soon fall apart, just like the United States will not fall apart any time soon.

★★★

Every state has a strategic culture, but not all states think explicitly about strategy and craft a grand strategy. At a minimum, each state, no matter how limited its strategic objectives, ought to monitor its environment, in order to identify the threats and challenges to its interests (though some states may not even do that in any profound manner). Threats are risks that imply the possibility of violence (terrorism, civil war, invasion) and may therefore require the threat or use of force to avert them. Challenges can also be life-threatening, but do not involve the use of force and can therefore also not be solved by armed force: subversion, climate change, epidemics, poverty, weak state structures.

A state that does seek a proactive role and decides to produce an explicit grand strategy will of necessity perform a more profound analysis of the environment, in order to decide which courses of action are feasible. In an explicit grand strategy, a state will set more specific ends, and identify the broad instruments (the ways) that it will apply to achieve them. On that basis, the necessary resources (the means) can then be allocated, though, of course, a state will take into account which resources can reasonably be made available when defining the strategic ends. This is a balancing act: ends that obviously surpass the means will never be met; but a state that is not willing to commit a minimum of means will not reach its ends either. Starting from the grand strategy, more detailed strategies for specific geographic and thematic policy areas will be developed, which are then put into action. The results of action must be assessed in terms of effectiveness and efficiency: to which extent did the state achieve its stated ends, and at what cost? This must be a permanent loop: states ought to continually finetune, change or abandon specific geographic and thematic strategies as required by their results.

Having an explicit grand strategy, published in whole or in part, does not yet guarantee that it will drive a state's actions. It goes too far, though, to say, as Richard Betts does, that grand strategy is but 'a description imposed by observers on the record of statesmen, a notional description of an administration's goals that isn't actually followed …, or a claim made in hindsight rather than a conscious and coherent plan of an administration in advance of action that is actually implemented'.[27] Sometimes a state does feel obliged to come out with a public strategy without being intrinsically convinced of it. I once received a telephone call from the head of policy planning in the foreign ministry of a large EU member state. You will have seen, he said, that my government has just made a public statement that the EU needs a new strategy – now we have to decide why we took that position. Would I be willing to join a brainstorming at his ministry to discuss that? Of course, I would. Everything depends, therefore, on a state's leadership and its administrative structures. Have the political, diplomatic and military leadership made the strategy their own? Has it been incorporated into the instructions and procedures for the administration and the armed forces? Have responsibilities been delineated and is there a reporting structure? Adopting a grand strategy is not enough; a state must then organise itself to implement it.

Here again, this is more challenging for the EU, as a state-like organisation, than for the other great powers. EU member states have pooled their sovereignty in specific international policy areas, notably trade. But foreign policy and defence constitute an exception: in these areas the EU as such is not a player (yet) but still operates on an intergovernmental basis; member states take all decisions by unanimity. As a result, both deciding on strategy and organising to implement it are complicated. So far, the member states mostly feel little or no ownership of EU strategy, which consequently does not drive their national foreign policies. Even within the EU machinery, not every branch feels bound by it. Inevitably, translation into more detailed sub-strategies, policies and action is haphazard. Very often still, the member states prefer to act by themselves instead of as a union. The reality is, however, that the sovereignty of the individual member states has become more and more circumscribed. Sovereignty entails the capacity to take your own decisions and to implement them. No EU member state has the resources any longer to consistently act alone on the global stage, certainly not when the other key players are continent-sized great powers. They mostly retain but negative sovereignty: they can in all freedom decide not to do something. It is only where member states have pooled sovereignty in the EU, and thus achieved the same scale as the great powers, that they have the capacity to act. Since the heyday of imperialism in the 19th century, it has been clear, in fact, 'that to be a truly great power, continental scale was essential'.[28] As the EU's High Representative, Josep Borrell, put it, referring to the Sino-American rivalry: 'Pooling sovereignty around currency is much less difficult than pooling sovereignty around defence or foreign affairs ... But today we have to do it because we are living in a new bipolar system.'[29]

The best grand strategy will fail if the strategies and actions that follow from it fail. Or in military terms, grand strategy cannot deliver results if the operations and tactics are faulty. Vice versa, however, a series of isolated policies and actions, however successful by themselves, will rarely yield durable results if the overall strategy is mistaken. Knowing how to do something is not the same as knowing what you are doing. If the problem is the strategy, the solution cannot be 'technological' improvements at the level of implementation, but must be political, as Arthur Schlesinger observed of the American war in Vietnam.[30] Sir Arthur Harris, chief of the Royal Air Force's Bomber Command during the Second World War, put it sharply in his memoirs:

> The Germans never make a small mistake, because they are cautioned against all small mistakes in their manuals, without reference to which they seldom do anything whatever. But they can always be relied upon to make all the imaginable large and catastrophic mistakes, together with a good many that only a German can think out.[31]

Thus they lost the war. Grand strategy has a multiplier effect: much more can be achieved with the same instruments and resources if they are put to use to implement a sound strategy; but much more can be lost if one makes the wrong strategic choices.

Unlike the overall orientations of a state's strategic culture, within its broad confines an explicit grand strategy can and does change more quickly and more often. A change of government can bring a change of strategy. Indeed, many states systematically review their grand strategy for every legislature. A regular review process ensures that at least once every four or five years, grand strategy is on the political agenda, the assessment of the environment is updated, and the validity of the ends tested. New events and developments may sometimes necessitate shorter-term change, but a four- or five-year time horizon is a minimum, since the ends of grand strategy are rarely such as can be achieved immediately. Many democratic states do not look much beyond this horizon, beyond the next elections. If the ends become too distant and too abstract, they can indeed lose all meaning for practical policy making. At the same time, a longer-term view can strengthen the sense of purpose, and thus the resolve to stay on track over time. In his famous Fulton College speech, Sir Winston Churchill called for 'constancy of mind, persistency of purpose, and the grand simplicity of decision'.[32]

Today's great powers all regularly publish grand strategic documents. In the US, every president is obliged by law to submit a National Security Strategy to Congress for every term in office. Since the turn of the century, these relatively short and very readable documents have become powerful tools of communication, which can mobilise as well as antagonise. The 2002 edition, for example, the strategy of the first George W. Bush administration, put forward pre-emptive military strikes as a key instrument, and in Iraq in 2003 that is exactly what the US did, invading the country on the grounds (which were afterwards disproved) that it was developing weapons of mass destruction that posed an imminent threat. In China, the Secretary-General of the Party's report to the five-yearly congress of the Chinese Communist Party (CCP) lays out the grand strategy. Length and readability are of less concern: at the last congress, in 2017, Xi Jinping spoke for three and a half hours, and the written version ran to 66 pages. In Russia there is no fixed regularity, but the state published a National Security Strategy in 2000, 2009 and 2015. The EU published a grand strategic document for the first time in 2003 and, despite several attempts by groups of member states to put a review on the agenda, followed up with a second strategy only in 2016. There is a general feeling that too much time elapsed between the two strategies, but still no system to ensure a regular strategic review is in place.

★★★

The central 'simple idea' that has informed the grand strategies of the current great powers undoubtedly is competition. Great powers cooperate and compete at the same time, but since the first decade of the 21st century the US, the EU, Russia and China have come to see each other in more antagonistic terms, not just as competitors but also as rivals. All have gradually put more emphasis on the competitive dimension of great power relations. In the early 2000s, the EU still focused nearly exclusively on cooperation, which remains the primary mode of its grand strategy, but it too has moved in the same direction. The trend in great power politics is an increase in great power rivalry.

An early public manifestation of this trend was to be found in Russian strategy. Speaking at the 2007 edition of the Munich Security Conference, which every year convenes the American and European strategic establishments, Putin strongly condemned what he described as the US attempt to create a unipolar world: 'one centre of authority, one centre of force, one centre of decision-making'. The 'uncontained hyper use of force' by America and its allies, according to Putin, had resulted in a world in which 'no one feels safe'; and 'of course such a policy stimulates an arms race'. Putin also condemned North Atlantic Treaty Organization (NATO) expansion and the basing of American troops in the new allies.[33] Although Putin did not reveal (or threaten) any particular response, this speech was widely seen as a turning point, marking the end of more or less constructive relations between Russia and the US and its European allies.

The next year, 2008, saw a war between Russia and Georgia. When on 7 August Georgian President Mikheil Saakashvili sent troops into the Russian-supported breakaway province of South Ossetia, which had declared its independence in 1990, Moscow reacted with force of arms and advanced into Georgia proper, until French President Nicolas Sarkozy brokered a ceasefire on 15 August. Russia subsequently recognised the independence of South Ossetia and Abkhazia, another province that had seceded from Georgia in 1992. For the US strategic establishment, this confirmed that Russia was now set on a path of confrontation.[34] Europeans were divided, however; in Western Europe in particular, many felt that Saakashvili had needlessly provoked Russia, and the EU and Russia quickly returned to business as usual. The stickers with the Georgian flag that the Brussels office of the German Marshall Fund, an American think-tank, distributed did not find many takers.

Europeans were forced to review their position when in 2014 Russia invaded Ukraine. The EU and Russia had made Kiev proposals for closer association that were mutually exclusive, the former offering a

Deep and Comprehensive Free Trade Agreement (DCFTA), the latter membership of its Eurasian Economic Union. Ukraine ended up in an impossible situation. The country, which had always looked both east and west, was forced to make a choice that it should not have had to make. Under Russian pressure, Ukrainian President Viktor Yanukovych went back on his initial decision to sign the DCFTA with the EU, triggering widespread protests. The EU brokered a deal with the opposition, but then Yanukovych unexpectedly fled the country. Next, Russia invaded and subsequently annexed the Crimea, and fomented a separatist armed rebellion in eastern Ukraine. Stalemate has reigned ever since.

Moral outrage at the first attempt by one European state to change the borders of another European state by force of arms since the Second World War was justifiably great. The oft repeated American assertion that such naked aggression has no place in the 21st century sounded rather hollow to non-Americans, however, given the illegal US invasion of Iraq – also in the 21st century, though not in Europe. Europeans did (and do) worry about Russian intentions, however, and together with the US continue to deploy forces at the borders with Russia by way of deterrence (NATO's 'Enhanced Forward Presence'); European defence spending has been going up since 2014 (so Putin rather than Trump can claim credit for that). The US and the EU also maintain economic and visa sanctions against Russia. And yet, the Union never entirely gave up on cooperation. In its current grand strategy document, the 2016 EU Global Strategy, the EU pleads for 'selective engagement': to 'engage Russia to discuss disagreements and cooperate if and when our interests overlap'.[35] Such compartmentalisation of relations, disagreeing on one thing and cooperating on another, serves to prevent further escalation.

Russia published its strategic outlook in a National Security Strategy in 2015.[36] Most of the document was actually devoted to internal challenges for Russian citizens, such as health, demography and living standards; strong emphasis was also put on preserving 'traditional Russian spiritual and moral values'. In the realm of international politics, two objectives stood out. First, 'consolidating the Russian Federation's status as a leading world power ... in a polycentric world', that is a world of multiple great powers (or multipolarity), the emergence of which Russia saw as 'being accompanied by an increase in global and regional instability'. Second, 'developing the potential of regional and sub-regional integration and coordination' with the former Soviet republics. Read together with the intervention in Georgia and the invasion of Ukraine, this could be understood as recreating a sphere of influence: a zone in which Russia would be the only external power allowed to interfere. Close alignment with Russia should act as a guarantee against 'the practice of overthrowing legitimate political regimes and provoking intrastate instability and conflicts', a reference to western support for the 'coloured revolutions' that brought to power democratic regimes in Georgia and Ukraine. Thus one could see an aspiration to create a Russian-dominated buffer zone, against the military build-up of NATO that the document explicitly identified as 'creating a threat to national security'.

The picture that emerges is one of a Russia that is confident and ambitious yet feels threatened at the same time.[37] Russia's way of looking at the world has not changed much since Soviet or even Czarist times, in spite of the great domestic political changes. Russia has always 'construed itself as a nation that, as a fact of its very existence and identity, has almost always been surrounded. To hypervigilance at the border, therefore, can be added hypersensitivity to those who live across it'.[38] One could rather say that during the first two decades after the end of the Cold War, Russian strategic culture slumbered; now, the strategic establishment has revived explicit strategic thinking, and has translated it once again into a proactive grand strategy. In its ends and ways, that strategy continues the main orientation of the grand strategies of the Romanov empire and the USSR, but resources are much more limited. During its two decades of strategic slumber, Russia has lost much of its great power status, which it now seeks to regain.

Russian grand strategy focuses on the US as the main competitor. US grand strategy, however, while reciprocating the antagonistic view of Russia, has shifted its main focus to China, because of its rapid emergence as a great power. This shift materialised during the two terms of President Barack Obama (2009–2016), who sought to draw down America's engagement in the wars in Iraq (since 2003) and Afghanistan (since 2001, when the US invaded the country as an act of self-defence against the al-Qaeda terrorists harboured by the Taliban government). In a 2011 article, Secretary of State Hillary Clinton popularised the term 'pivot to Asia' for the strategy of the Obama administration, which maintained a balance between cooperation and competition.[39] The US strengthened its bilateral military ties with its Asian allies and sought to include them in a new regional free trade area, the Trans-Pacific Partnership (TPP), but it also attempted to engage China. The tone changed when Trump entered the White House. His 2017 National Security Strategy framed great power relations as a nearly exclusively competitive interaction.[40] The starting point was the assessment that 'China and Russia challenge American power, influence, and interests, attempting to erode American security and prosperity'. Because the premise that 'engagement with rivals and their inclusion in international institutions and global commerce would turn them into benign actors and trustworthy partners' was seen as having 'turned out to be false', the US changed course: 'An America that successfully competes is the best way to prevent conflict'. America was portrayed as 'the most just and prosperous nation in history'; to protect it, the US must 'ensure that American military superiority endures'. Relations with China became increasingly tense; in 2018 the US started imposing tariffs on imports from China, thus launching a trade war.

US strategic culture has long included American exceptionalism, the idea that 'America's values, political system, and history are unique and worthy of universal admiration', in Stephen Walt's definition, and that therefore the US 'is both destined and entitled to play a distinct and positive role on the world stage'.[41] What Trump added is the feeling that the US has been taken advantage of, by its rivals as well as by its allies, that international organisations are being exploited by other states, and even that the US has underinvested in its security – although in 2019 the US accounted for 38 per cent of global defence spending.[42] Under Trump, the shift of focus to China and to the competitive dimension of international politics accelerated. The US had begun to talk of great power competition already in the final years of the Obama administration, however.[43] What changed was that the US itself became more assertive, and at times antagonistic, in dealing with great power competition, but simultaneously reduced its engagement in other dimensions of international politics, in particular multilateralism, blocking or withdrawing from the World Trade Organization (WTO), the World Health Organization (WHO) and TPP. The focus on China and its identification as a rival, rather than just a competitor, can count on a strong bipartisan consensus. If a Democratic administration will likely mean a change of language, and perhaps of tactics, it is far less clear to which extent the substance of grand strategy would change.

The evolution of US strategy was, of course, a response to the rapid emergence of China as a great power. For many observers, with hindsight the main event of 2001 was not the '9/11' terrorist attacks on the US, but China's accession to the WTO. A second turning point was the 2008 financial crisis, which left China relatively unscathed, allowing it to play a key role in restarting the global economy while the US and the EU were hit hard. Arguably, this acted as a catalyst for a more active Chinese grand strategy.[44] China now is pursuing its interests in every country of the globe; and it definitely has acquired the ambition to have a global impact. Its growing confidence and assertiveness in international politics can be witnessed in its grand investment in connectivity, the Belt and Road Initiative (BRI), which extends to Europe, but also in its de facto annexation of the South China Sea, by stationing military forces on various islands and constructing military bases on artificial features. Internally, this has been accompanied by growing repression, by a clampdown on the Uighur population in Xinjiang province, and by consolidating China's hold over Hong Kong by eroding its autonomy. Neither the US nor the EU recognise Chinese claims over the South China Sea; the US and a number of EU member states underscore that position by regularly sending their navies and air forces through the area on 'freedom of navigation operations' (FONOPS). Both Washington and Brussels also condemn human rights violations in China, and in March 2021 adopted relatively limited sanctions; the US trade war with China was driven primarily by overall strategic concerns, not by human rights considerations.

Xi Jinping, who became general secretary of the CCP in 2012 and president in 2013, set forth his grand strategic view at the 19th party congress in 2017.[45] By 2049, the 100th anniversary of the foundation of the People's Republic (PRC), China aims to have become a 'fully developed nation'. In international politics, the end is to be 'a global leader in terms of comprehensive national power and international influence'. Unlike Russia, Xi saw growing multipolarity as a source of opportunities rather than threats, noting that 'relative international forces are becoming more balanced'; he even offered 'socialism with Chinese characteristics' as a model for 'other countries and nations who want to speed up their development'.[46] His ambitions included the military sphere: Xi aimed for the People's Liberation Army (PLA) to be 'fully transformed into a first-tier force' by 2049. At the same time, his emphasis on the fact that 'a military is built to fight', and that the PLA should 'regard combat capability as the criterion to meet in all its work', seemed to indicate that the armed forces still had some way to go.[47] As expounded by Xi, this grand strategy did not identify the US as a threat, but China's global ambitions rankled the US most of all.

As China went through domestic political upheaval, its strategic culture evolved as well (much more so than in the case of Russia). Under the Qing dynasty (1644–1912) China reached its greatest territorial expansion, adding Taiwan, Tibet and Xinjiang to the empire. From the middle of the 19th century, China's great power status eroded, as the country was shaken by large-scale uprisings such as the Taiping rebellion, and incursions by the other great powers.[48] Large swaths of territory were lost to Russia and Japan, while the UK, France, and others (even Belgium) acquired extraterritorial concessions in many Chinese cities. The Republic of China that succeeded the empire in 1912 consequently developed a defensive strategic culture, aimed at undoing what the Chinese officially call the 'century of humiliation'. That remained the basic orientation of the PRC, which quietly shelved its initial commitment to fostering world revolution. 'Hide your strength, bide your time', was the watchword of Deng Xiaoping, who assumed control after Mao Zedong. Now that China has achieved great power status again, in an incredibly short period of time, it has started to pursue a very proactive grand strategy, but within a strategic culture that is still marked by the urge to defend and consolidate Chinese sovereignty and territory (as China defines it), as it has been for more than a hundred years.

'Let China sleep. For when she wakes, the world will tremble': the quote, ascribed to Napoleon, is probably apocryphal. More to the point, because based on much closer observation of China, is Philippine President Manuel Quezon's statement to General MacArthur in 1941, even as the Japanese army was about to storm his last stronghold on the Bataan peninsula: 'My great fear is the Chinese. With their increasing militarism and aggressive tendency, they are the great Asiatic menace. They have no real ideologies, and when they reach the fructification of their military potential, I dread to think what may happen.'[49] If China's newly proactive grand strategy proves successful, and resources keep pace, China's strategic establishment may develop a more activist strategic culture as well, which might give rise to an ever more ambitious and possibly even expansionist grand strategy. Or China's strategic culture may precisely act as a break on too ambitious grand strategies that might provoke a harsher confrontation with the other great powers than China would wish for.

The EU, in contrast with the three other great powers, is still only attempting to create a common strategic culture, by involving its member states in joint actions (becoming by doing), and in writing a single grand strategy (I learn to think, therefore I become). As it is doing so, the increasing great power rivalry forces the EU to reorient its strategic thinking at the same time. The European Economic Community that preceded the EU (1957–1993) was an international economic player, but had only limited actorness in the political and none in the military field. It developed the inkling of a strategic culture centred on the wish to prevent conflict and to cooperate with other states and organisations. This, and the perception of the end of great power rivalry in the first decade after the end of the Cold War, shaped the EU's first grand strategic document, the 2003 European Security Strategy.[50] Its title, A Secure Europe in a Better World, indicated its idealistic orientation, captured in the basic idea that 'The best protection for our security is a world of well governed democratic states'. The EU aspired to create democratic states by offering its neighbours close association in return for reform, and by strengthening 'effective multilateralism' and building 'strategic partnerships' with the key players at the global stage.

Only in 2016 did the EU adopt its next grand strategy, the EU Global Strategy. The failure of the Arab Spring, the wave of uprisings that started in late 2010, to democratise the Middle East and North Africa (except for Tunisia); the Russian invasion of Ukraine; and the rapid rise of China led the EU to take the competitive dimension of international politics more into account, but without positioning itself as a rival to the other great powers. Instead of joining in the rivalry, the EU sought to contain it. Proclaiming 'a rules-based global order' to be one of its vital interests, the EU set out 'to promote agreed rules to contain power politics and contribute to a peaceful, fair and prosperous world'. Among its priorities, the Global Strategy did include the protection of Europe itself and the need for 'strategic autonomy' in defence, as well as building 'cooperative regional orders' and 'effective global governance'. The EU called this approach 'principled pragmatism'; the US dubbed its 2017 strategy 'principled realism' – similar terms covering very different grand strategies.

★★★

The US is seeking to maintain its position in international politics as the most powerful of the great powers. China, having become a great power again, is aspiring to a position that it feels is commensurate with its growing power. Russia continues to seek compensation for its lost great power status. The EU is seeking a distinctive role as a great power that abstains from great power rivalry. These are 'simple' ends that are likely to remain the grand strategic ends of the four great powers for many years to come. The trend is that the great powers, with the exception so far of the EU, use ever more competitive ways to pursue these ends, and even resort to active rivalry against each other. But increasing rivalry is not inevitable, and these 'simple' ends should not obscure the fact that complex choices have yet to be made about the ways of pursuing them.

The powers can still opt for more cooperative ways. The US can maintain its position by keeping China in check and recruiting allies against Beijing, or by investing in the provision of effective global governance and making itself attractive again as a leader for many states. China can increase its position by hollowing out and pushing against international law and international organisations, or by making a greater contribution to their success. Russia has sought compensation mostly through force of arms and by undoing other states' projects; it could focus more on its own projects and increase their attractiveness. A change of leadership in any of the powers could easily lead to the introduction of new preferred ways of doing things (as one hopes Biden's victory will in the US); then again, a new leadership might opt to step up the competition (in Russia, for example, where nobody in the EU or the US knows who would succeed Putin). Everything depends on how the great powers react to one another's moves. The main reason why even a simple grand strategic idea is never easy to implement is that the other party has a strategy too – grand strategy is indeed competitive.

2

Competitive: The Other Players Have a Strategy Too

When a state adopts a strategy to increase employment or to prevent pollution on its own territory, it has no rivals. Of course, certain citizens, employers, trade unions or pressure groups may have other ideas and try to thwart the government's plans. But there is no other state or entity with the legal authority to adopt an alternative strategy for the same issues on the same territory. In domestic politics, every state reigns supreme. If another state does try to interfere, that constitutes an act of subversion, which will likely result in retaliation.

International politics, in contrast, is inherently competitive: states operate alongside each other in the same geographic theatres, international organisations and thematic policy areas, each pursuing its interests through its own grand strategy. The competitive nature of grand strategy is probably its most obvious characteristic, and yet it is often forgotten that the other players have a strategy too, or they are underestimated. 'Always remember, however sure you are that you can easily win, that there would not be a war if the other man did not think he also had a chance': Churchill's quote applies just as much to peacetime grand strategy.[1] Great powers and other states alike, when designing strategy, must take into account not only the limitations imposed by their own resources and the constraints of the environment, but also the fact that other players will be pursuing a proactive grand strategy of their own. As General Montgomery, frustrated with the state of planning, wrote to General Alexander prior to the allied landing in Sicily in 1943: 'I have been ordered to invade the mainland of the continent of Europe on the 30th August. In the absence of information to the contrary, I must assume that some resistance will be offered by the enemy.'[2]

States cannot be but competitors, as they seek influence, partners, markets and resources in the same countries and organisations. Such competition is natural; economic competition, moreover, is inherent to capitalism. Normal competition can turn into rivalry, however, if one state perceives foul play by another. A state that does not apply reciprocity, bending or evading the rules that other states observe, or that seeks to fence off markets and resources for its own exclusive use, may provoke the active rivalry of its competitors. So will a state, of course, that launches into rivalry itself and uses subversion and aggression to pursue its interests. Rivalry means that states actively work against each other, aiming to undo the strategy of the other; ultimately, this can escalate into war. Natural competition can just as well motivate a state to improve its own performance instead of undermining another state, though. In fact, interests coincide as much as they clash, so states can also be partners when cooperation serves their interests better than confrontation. Partnership can be cemented into an alliance: the promise of mutual assistance in case of aggression by a rival. Grand strategy does not only reach its ends via zero-sum games; states can also create win–win situations.

★★★

In the history of international politics, competition between the great powers usually took place in a setting of multipolarity. At almost any point in history, among the many states there were a few great powers with global reach (as global as was possible at any particular time). Usually, none of these great powers was powerful enough to dominate the others, so a shifting pattern of cooperation, competition and rivalry emerged. Such a multipolar world, in which several poles or powers operate with or against each other, is what constitutes normality in international politics. During the Cold War, the rivalry between two 'superpowers', the US and the USSR, who outclassed all other states, dominated international politics. But this bipolar world was an exception.

Unipolarity, when there is but a single great power without peer competitors, is even rarer. In Europe, the Roman Empire was for centuries the only great power – in fact the only state – until the fall of the empire in the west in 476; but even the Romans faced great power rivals on their Asian borders, such as the Parthian (247 BCE–224) and Sassanid (224–651) empires.[3] Within the Europe-wide empire, the Pax Romana was maintained, but not without brutal repression of repeated uprisings – 'They make a desert and they call it peace', as the Roman historian Tacitus quoted one of Rome's enemies, the Scottish chieftain

Calgacus. The history of Europe from 476 until the end of the Second World War provides endless examples of multipolar competition and rivalry. The heyday of the British empire, from the mid-19th to the mid-20th century, is often described as the Pax Britannica, but Britain was only one of several great powers, and there was hardly a year in which a punitive expedition had not to be sent against insurgents within or intruders from without the empire. This was the age of gunboat diplomacy, but it was distinctly multipolar. China for most of its history faced peer competitors on its northern borders; some of them actually conquered China and established their own foreign, non-Han dynasties, most notably the Mongol Yuan dynasty (1271–1368) and the Manchu Qing dynasty (1636–1912). In modern history, perhaps the first two centuries of Qing rule could be described as a unipolar era in Asia, until the European great powers entered into direct competition and rivalry with China.

The fall of the Berlin Wall in 1989, and the dissolution of the Soviet Union and the end of communist rule in 1991 meant the end of the Cold War, and of bipolarity with it. To many it appeared that 'history' had ended too, as most famously expressed by Francis Fukuyama, in the sense that no other system of government seemed capable of surpassing parliamentary democracy, which therefore more and more states would adopt.[4] Another way to put it would be that the way of life adopted by the states of Western Europe and North America would increasingly serve as the inspiration for other states. Some went further and argued that the end of the Soviet Union not only heralded the spread of democracy in domestic politics, but also meant unipolarity in international politics, with the US as the sole superpower.[5]

That turned out to be an illusion, however. Once it had overcome the chaotic transition that followed the demise of the Soviet Union, during which its ambitions in international politics were limited, the Russian Federation returned on the global scene as the great power that it had never really ceased to be. Moreover, Russia embraced capitalism, but not democracy: the successor to communism was an authoritarian state. In the same period, China rapidly emerged (or re-emerged, when seen from a long-term historical perspective) as a great power. Alarmed by the tottering communist regimes in central and eastern Europe, the Communist Party of China (CCP) reacted violently against pro-democracy manifestations on Tiananmen Square in 1989, and remained firmly entrenched in power. China too adopted capitalism, but a state-led variant that it later dubbed 'socialism with Chinese characteristics'. The end of the Cold War also saw the European Economic Community (EEC) evolve into the EU, which quickly began to seek its own distinctive role in international politics. Thus, not only did the 'western' way of life not become a model for the rest of the world, but international politics also quickly returned to normal as multipolarity reasserted itself. The US' unipolar moment was but a moment indeed.

In fact, the world had been multipolar for much longer already, even during the latter decades of the Cold War, if one assesses all three dimensions of power: military, political and economic. In military terms, the Cold War was a bipolar era: no other state could challenge the superpowers or even dissuade them from their planned course of action. Because the superpowers convinced or forced many other states to ally with them, leaving only the group of non-aligned states to steer an independent course, in political terms the era was bipolar too. In economic terms, however, the US and the USSR eventually lost their lead over the other states. In his classic 1988 work on great powers, Paul Kennedy stated that 'it is plain that there already exists a *multi* polar world once more, if one measures the economic indices alone'. In the book, Kennedy quotes US president Richard Nixon, speaking in 1971 already, to the effect that

> there now existed five clusters of world economic power –
> western Europe, Japan, and China as well as the USSR and
> the United States. 'These are the five that will determine
> the economic future and, because economic power will be
> the key to other kinds of power, the future of the world'.[6]

In economic terms, international politics has been multipolar since the 1970s, and in more general terms since the 1990s. The world has not really 'returned' to multipolarity in the 21st century, therefore, as it is often described. Rather, multipolarity just became more visible, as Russia and China, and to a lesser extent the EU, began to pursue their interests more assertively. This led to more intense competition and, eventually, to rivalry.

★★★

From 2007–2008, multipolarity could no longer be denied, in the face of Russian assertiveness in its near-abroad, China's surge in influence after it emerged quite unscathed from the financial crisis that hit the US and the EU, and the inability of the US to prevent or to undo Russian and Chinese actions that it condemned. One reason why the multipolar nature of international politics was not immediately obvious until then is that the US strategic establishment resisted the use of the term itself. Effective unipolarity would have suited the US very well, of course; some American thinkers went so far as to prescribe American unipolar dominance, for a multipolar world would be far more dangerous in their eyes.[7] Natural as it was for many strategists to cling to the notion of unipolarity, it was also unwise to deny the multipolar facts on the ground. One may wish for unipolarity, but basing one's strategy on such wishful thinking is hazardous. Partly this was a reaction to Russia, which often presented a multipolar or polycentric world as an objective of Russian grand strategy (as in Putin's 2007 speech mentioned in the previous chapter); Moscow probably enjoyed irritating the US merely by mentioning the term. Under the Trump administration, the US swung the other way and multipolarity became a driving concept of US grand strategy. For Trump, the new term to be excised from the strategic lexicon was not multipolarity but multilateralism, that is the notion that one can deal with a multipolar world by promoting cooperation between the powers – Trump preferred to focus on competition. But many in the Democratic party too in effect see relations with Russia and China mostly through the lens of competition and rivalry, and the Democrats too have come to adopt a more transactional approach to multilateralism.

The fact is that polarity is but a factual description of reality, without any moral judgement attached to it. International politics is unipolar or multipolar, just like a state has small or large armed forces: that is neither good nor bad. How the great powers – single or plural – use their power, and how a state uses its armed forces: that can be judged from the point of view of morality, or effectiveness. Creating a multipolar world cannot be an objective of grand strategy, therefore: one power may assist another power in its rise, but it has to be rising in the first place – one cannot create another great power. In a world that really is unipolar, the sole great power may have as its grand strategic objective the upholding of its position, and try to prevent other powers from rising. But in a multipolar world, attempts to create unipolarity can only lead to war, since no great power will ever willingly abandon its position of power.

It is often pretended that in the 21st century international politics is becoming bipolar again, with China replacing the Soviet Union as the second pole opposed to the US. One should remember, however, that bipolarity came about because at the end of the Second World War the European great powers, as well as China, were exhausted, victors and defeated alike. They were in no position to play a global role (though that did not stop France and the UK from trying, and from undertaking futile wars to hold on to their colonial empires).

Those were exceptional circumstances. In the 21st century, economic, military and political power are much more evenly distributed.

According to the World Bank, the US in 2018 had a GDP of $20.544 trillion in current dollars; China of $13.68 trillion; the EU-27 (without the UK) of $13.058 trillion. Of the great powers, only Russia lagged far behind at $1.657 trillion; it was indeed behind Japan ($4.971 trillion), the UK ($2.855 trillion), India ($2.718 trillion), Brazil ($1.855 trillion), and Canada ($1.713 trillion). In terms of GDP per capita, Russia and China were in the same league, however: 2018 World Bank figures in current dollars were $62,886 for the US, $35,616 for the EU, $11,288 for Russia, and $9,779 for China. Since 2000, China's share of global GDP has grown from 3.64 per cent to 16.04 per cent. The US share, in the same period, shrank from 30.78 per cent to 24.26 per cent, and the EU's from 25 per cent to 22 per cent; Russia's share grew from 0.78 per cent to 1.96 per cent. These figures do not bear out the widespread idea of American decline: the US, and EU, economies have continued to grow, just more slowly than the Chinese.[8] The important conclusion is that, in economic terms, there clearly are three great powers that are in a class of their own compared to all other states, and that will therefore not lack the resources to pursue a grand strategy with truly global scope. In the future, the relative economic strength of the US, the EU and China vis-à-vis each other may vary, but they will remain the world's largest three economies by far. All three face their own economic challenges, which the COVID-19 pandemic increased, but it is highly improbable that anyone of them will collapse, in view of the resources that they can mobilise. Russia is not in the same league, but not so far behind that it too cannot afford a proactive grand strategy.

In military terms, there clearly are four great powers.[9] At the start of the 2020s, Russia retains the world's second-largest nuclear arsenal (6,490 nuclear warheads) and 900,000-strong active armed forces. It has continued to modernise its forces, and has improved the morale of the troops by shifting from a mostly conscript-based force to a mix of professionals and conscripts. Large-scale manoeuvres and operations in Ukraine and Syria have demonstrated the operational effectiveness of the Russian armed forces, though this probably does not extend to the 250,000 conscripts. The defence budget, however, is affected by the rise and fall in energy prices, on which Russia is highly dependent; when state revenue has dropped, plans have had to be postponed. In 2019, the Russian defence budget stood at $48.2 billion. The Chinese defence budget for the same year was $181 billion, for active armed forces of 2,035,000 soldiers, and 290 nuclear warheads. China is lagging behind, however, in terms of operational effectiveness: the Chinese forces were much behind in modernisation, and still have a considerable way to go; the same applies to training for modern operations; and few soldiers have operational experience. China has been rapidly modernising its nuclear arsenal, however.

The Russian and Chinese defence budgets are dwarfed by the US budget of $685 billion in 2019, for 1,379,800 active troops, and 6,185 nuclear warheads. No other power comes close to the US capability to project its military power around the world and to undertake large-scale operations. The total numbers for the 27 EU member states are impressive too: a defence budget of $214.8 billion and 1,356,450 active troops. But these are 27 separate armed forces, of mostly small size, each with their own ministries, staffs, academies, supply organisations and so forth. As a result, the operational effectiveness of Europe's forces is limited: the spear has a very long shaft but a small tip. Nevertheless, as several thousands of European troops are deployed on operations each year, the armed forces of several EU member states are among the most experienced in the world. Of all EU member states, France has the most operationally effective army; it is the only nuclear power in the EU, with 300 nuclear warheads.

There are other nuclear weapon states: India (140 warheads), Israel (90), Pakistan (160), North Korea (30), and the UK (200). Saudi Arabia ($78.4 billion in 2019), India ($60.5 billion), the UK ($54.8 billion), Japan ($48.6 billion), and South Korea ($39.8 billion) also have major defence budgets. But they lack the scale to be global players in the military sphere, whereas the great powers are active worldwide on a permanent basis, or have the potential to be.

In political terms, the world is not becoming bipolar either. Bipolarity would imply that the interactions between just the US and China would somehow set most or all of the agenda of international politics, and that a large group of states would align their strategies with both or either of them (depending on whether Washington and Beijing cooperate or compete on an issue).[10] The EU is of course closer to the US than to China or Russia; the latter in turn is closer to China than to the other two (but not as close as Europe and America are); but fundamentally, all four great powers pursue a distinctive and independent grand strategy. Furthermore, regional powers like Brazil, India and Japan also pursue their own regional and, in specific geographic or thematic areas, global strategies. The US and China have interests in nearly every country of the world, but so does the EU (and in specific regions, Russia). Washington and Beijing have a stake in many tensions and conflicts in different parts of the world, but for the most parts these have neither been triggered by their rivalry nor are they being instrumentalised by them. Tensions and conflicts in the Caucasus, North Africa, the Middle East, the Gulf and the Horn of Africa, for example, are a product of regional rivalries or internal strife. The US has intervened in many cases, while China has until now played but a limited role; Sino-American rivalry plays little or no part. In the Ukraine crisis, the US and the EU have allied against Russia; China again has been more or less absent. Recurring tensions over the border between China and India also follow their own dynamic, quite independent from China's tensions with the US. Talk of a 'G2' (analogous to the G7, the group of seven major industrialised countries) or a 'strategic dyad' shaping the world is off the mark, therefore, and is rebutted by China itself.[11]

★★★

This picture might change if the rivalry between the US and China escalated into a new cold war, that is if Washington and Beijing decoupled their economies and systematically undermined each other's strategies. Fortunately, Biden's election victory made this scenario far less likely. Were it to materialise, this would still be a cold war different from *the* Cold War, because at heart international politics are more likely to remain multipolar rather than to become bipolar. The two other great powers, the EU and Russia, have little appetite for a bipolar confrontation in which they would be reduced to the role of supporting actors. The Europeans have been there before, and the EU seeks to avoid a repetition: 'We, Europeans, cannot accept the idea that the world should organise itself around a new Sino-American bipolarity which would come to replace, after a 30-year transition period, the Soviet-American bipolarity that, literally, divided Europe', said the EU's High Representative, Josep Borrell, shortly after coming into office in late 2019.[12] Both Washington and Beijing put pressure on the EU and its member states to align with their strategies, but most capitals prefer not to make that choice. The EU is deeply economically intertwined with both the US and China, and it seeks to maintain relations with both while safeguarding its own economic sovereignty.[13] Moscow for its part aspires to a multipolar world and sees itself as one of a concert of powers that would preside over it.[14] After the Ukraine crisis and the resulting dispute with the US and the EU, Russia did move closer to China, but for the Russian strategic establishment the thought of ending up as a mere adjunct power of China is beyond the pale.

Many other states too would rather sit on the fence than get caught in a Sino-American confrontation. That includes America's allies in

Asia, much though they reject China's territorial claims and its assertive ways of pursuing its interests. Even as these states seek safeguards against domination by China by deepening security ties with the US, they also want to avoid confrontation with China, which for many is their largest trade partner.[15] 'China is a reality on the doorstep', as the prime minister of Singapore put it.[16] Neither the US nor China should count on allies rushing to their side, therefore: other states have far too great an interest in maintaining open global trade and investment relations with all great powers to undertake any action that could bring a new cold war closer. Hence one must conclude with Xuetong Yan that a US strategy of containment against China, like the one it pursued against the Soviet Union, is no longer possible: China is already far too integrated into global political and economic relations.[17] Consequently, forcing a choice upon real and potential allies and partners would risk alienating many of them.[18]

Both democracies and non-democracies prefer to avoid taking sides in any Sino-American dispute. A potential new cold war would therefore also differ from the Cold War in the sense that it would not be an ideological confrontation. For sure, the US and China have chosen their own way of life, and have very different political systems. China, however, as we will see in the next chapter, does not seek to export its ideology, unlike the Soviet Union, which built up communist regimes and parties across the world.[19] Indeed, one could ask whether, behind the façade of communist symbols that the CCP hangs on to, there is much ideology left at all in a regime that has adopted state capitalism and mainly wants to stay in power. Actually, the proselytising impulse is probably stronger in the US. American exceptionalism has always had a strong missionary component: the idea that the US is not just a model for others to emulate, but that it should actively export its model. But even the American strategic establishment, if it leaves its rhetoric behind, probably realises that the US has little or no actual leverage over China's domestic form of government. As Yan remarks, rather than about ideology, Sino-American rivalry is about material interests; it can be extremely intense, but it does not directly concern regime survival.[20] More generally, it seems that ideologies overall no longer have the mobilising power that they had during the Cold War: 'The age when worldviews served as motor and motivator of great power conflicts is over.'[21]

Most states, in sum, much prefer multipolarity, because it offers more flexibility: a state that can play off four great powers against each other has more options than one that must choose sides among two superpowers, or try to stay non-aligned. In fact, this applies to many members of the strategic establishment in China itself, one of the putative poles of a new bipolar world. Whenever I ask Chinese officials or academics whether they think China would be better off in a world without the EU, the answer always is a somewhat grudging: no. Not because they necessarily like the EU that much, but because they prefer the extra options that a game with three (or four, counting Russia) great powers offers as opposed to a world in which China alone would be facing the US, as the only peer competitor. That does not prevent China from playing EU member states off against each other, when that suits its interests, of course. Nor is it entirely good news for the EU, which does not want China to see their relations as a mere instrument to counterbalance the US rather than as a useful relationship in its own right.[22] But it does go to show that in a multipolar world the great powers have, to a certain extent, a stake in each other's fate.

★★★

Multipolarity as a pattern of great power competition is not new, and neither is globalisation – the interconnectedness of the world.

> The inhabitant of London could order by telephone, sipping his morning tea in bed, the various products of the whole earth, in such quantity as he might see fit, and reasonably expect their early delivery upon his doorstep; he could at the same moment and by the same means adventure his wealth in the natural resources and new enterprises of any quarter of the world, and share, without exertion or even trouble, in their prospective fruits and advantages

wrote John Maynard Keynes in 1920;[23] read 'smart phone' for 'telephone', and you have a pretty accurate description of today. The difference is, of course, that many more people in many more countries have a smart phone now than had access to a telephone in the interbellum. International connections have always shaped people's lives – Roman coins have been found in China, for example – but more people now directly take part in these connections, for education, for work and for pleasure, instead of being mere objects of them. That said, many also remain excluded from the benefits of globalisation, and their rancour against what with reason they see as an impersonal force is understandable and, more often than not, justified.

Globalisation does not only mean interconnectedness; it has also produced increased interdependence, in particular between the great powers, and thus has an impact on their relations. By 2021, the EU and China were each other's first trade partners, the second being the US, while the EU and the US had the world's largest trade and investment relationship by far. The EU also was Russia's first trade partner, before China; vice versa, Russia ranked fifth among the EU's trade partners. That too was an enormous difference with the Cold War, when the American and Soviet economies were almost totally separate: 'economically speaking, the Soviets did not need to be contained; they contained themselves by refusing to join the world economy', is Odd Arne Westad's insight.[24] China, in contrast, is today an integral part of the world economy. Even the Pentagon relies on Chinese suppliers for certain key components of ammunition.[25] That has (justifiably) spurred a drive to increase defence industrial autonomy, but it illustrates the degree of economic intertwining between the great powers. Evidently, decoupling the American and Chinese economies would be possible if one or the other side wanted to, but only at an enormous and perhaps crippling cost to themselves and to the global economy as a whole. Complex global supply chains in every sector of the economy criss-cross many states, so a Sino-American decoupling would have immediate disastrous effects for every state on the globe.

Giovanni Grevi has coined the term 'interpolarity' for this situation: a multipolar world of highly interdependent great powers.[26] When in the wake of the coronavirus outbreak, all great powers were hit by an economic recession, some undoubtedly hoped to gain some advantage by getting out of the slump earlier than the others. But in the main, all great powers had an interest in the basic recovery of the others, since their own economies could not otherwise take off, given their importance for each other's imports and exports. Xi Jinping's announcement (at the 19th Central Committee of the CCP in October 2020) of a new focus on a 'dual circulation economy' in the 14th five-year plan (for 2021–2025), that is on boosting domestic consumption, exactly proved that China is still very much dependent on exports. Interpolarity does not only exist in the economic sphere; the great powers are also dependent on each other's active cooperation to solve global challenges, such as COVID-19 itself, and the climate crisis and all its consequences.

These various dimensions of interdependence may act as a brake on competition and rivalry, and stimulate cooperation between the great powers. But history shows that interpolarity does not guarantee that competition will not turn into rivalry or escalate into war. In 1914,

Norman Angell's widely commented notion of 'war as a great illusion' turned out to be an illusion itself: contrary to his optimistic scenario, economic interdependence did not prevent war. As Angell himself had in fact feared, 'powerful forces of interest, conviction, prejudice and passion' prevailed.[27] The Great War was not inevitable, though. The clash of interests between the great powers of the day could have been resolved peacefully, as indeed it was on many occasions before 1914. But too many members of the strategic establishment in too many of the powers came to see war as the best solution.

★★★

Gradually, all the great powers came to recognise that 21st century international politics is multipolar. But for decades, their strategic thinking had been shaped by bipolarity. Although formal bipolarity ended with the Cold War, and the world had in many ways been multipolar two decades before already, the strategic establishments were still getting used to the change even as the world entered the 2020s.

Of the great powers, the EU had to make the greatest adaptation. After the Second World War, the European states initially sought to create an alliance among themselves, aimed at first against the possibility of a resurgent Germany and then, as the Cold War started, against the Soviet Union. The US strongly supported European defence cooperation, because initially it was wary of a permanent military commitment on the European continent. Washington pushed hard for the European Defence Community, which would have merged the armed forces of Belgium, France, Italy, Luxembourg, the Netherlands and West Germany into a single European army, thus rearming Germany without recreating the German armed forces (which, so soon after the end of the war, was still very sensitive). When in 1954 that project failed, the emphasis shifted to NATO, which had been created in 1949. The US thus ended up taking the lead of the defence of Western Europe anyway, through NATO, while European integration assumed a mostly economic focus through the EEC. As NATO allies, the Western European states played their assigned role in American grand strategy. There was little need for, nor did the US encourage, explicit strategic thinking on the part of the Europeans; it sufficed to translate NATO guidelines into their national defence plans. Mutatis mutandis, the same applied to the central and Eastern European states whom the Soviet Union forced to join the Warsaw Pact. The EEC as such developed a strategic culture, if it can be called that, which centred on its technocratic expertise to conclude trade and association agreements with other countries. Alongside the EEC (rather than as a part of its institutional set-up), its members did create European Political Cooperation (EPC), in 1970, to consult each other on foreign policy but, as a purely informal mechanism, its impact remained limited.

When from 1993 the EU finally brought European cooperation in the fields of foreign trade, foreign policy and defence policy under one roof, it had to create integrated European strategic thinking almost from scratch. The EU's strategic culture, as seen in the previous chapter, is still very much developing. In part, the EU is hampered in this by its very success. Thanks to European integration, EU member states still compete, like provinces of a state compete for subsidies, contracts, investments and so on, but it is very rare for them to be rivals who actively work against each other. Actual war among EU member states has become a practical impossibility: making war upon another member of the single market and the Eurozone, who is governed by the same political authorities, would amount to making war on oneself. Perhaps even more importantly, war within the EU has simply become unimaginable. Within the Union, military power plays no role, therefore: whether a member state can convince the others of a proposal does not depend on how many tanks it can put into the field. (Which in the case of Belgium is just as well, as the last Belgian tank has long been deposited in the Royal Army Museum, where it can be admired for a small fee.) Instead of foreign policy, EU internal politics has become a kind of domestic politics, more akin to relations between the constituent parts of a single state than to relations between sovereign states.

As a consequence, however, less bandwidth is available for actual foreign policy, and many EU member states have forgotten how to think strategically about power and its uses. Yet in the world around the EU, rivalry between states is still rife, and some states do not hesitate to use military power to pursue their interests. Moreover, because internal EU politics is closer to a process of state formation than to international politics, it is unlikely to inspire other states to set out on a similar far-reaching project. The mere existence of the EU model has not had the impact on other states that many had hoped. The Russian invasion of Ukraine, the wars in North Africa, the Middle East, and the Gulf, and increasing tensions between the US and China forced the EU to start to adapt fast. The EU had little choice. Brussels was glad that the Cold War was behind it, and sought to avoid a new cold war between the US and China; it could not at the same time expect the US to behave as if the Cold War were still ongoing and solve Europe's security problems in its stead. But forging a composite entity into a resolute strategic player inevitably takes a long time. The

EU entered the 2020s with strategic establishments, plural, for which the member state capitals remained the centre of gravity, its adaptation to multipolarity far from finished.

Even the US has had to adapt to multipolarity. For a while it seemed to the American strategic establishment that the entire world had become its sphere of influence.[28] To the armed forces, fortified by the rapid operational tempo and precision strikes that they had demonstrated in the first Gulf War (1991) and the intervention in Kosovo (1999), it appeared that no adversary could come even close to the US.[29] This illusion of unipolarity and military invincibility produced a hubris, as Joseph Nye called it, that led the US to overextend itself and, in 2003, to invade Iraq even as it was still fighting the war in Afghanistan.[30] Both regimes were quickly defeated, but rather than victory, initial military success produced a political and military stalemate that lasted into the 2020s. Military superiority alone proved insufficient to realise the US' strategic aims (which in neither war were clear in the first place). At the same time, the unbridled and illegal use of military force in the case of Iraq provoked resentment on the part of many other states, partners and rivals alike.

In 2014, the Russian invasion of Ukraine proved to Washington that Moscow did not need to be a peer competitor of the US to exercise a lot of nuisance power. But the rude awakening to the reality of multipolarity was caused by the rapid rise of China, which, unlike Russia, had become a peer competitor, equalling the US in the global reach of its political and economic (if not in its military) power. Yet even in the military sphere, although to this day the US remains the strongest military power by far, its technological superiority over the other great powers has markedly declined. They too have acquired precision-strike capabilities, and have built up so-called A2/AD (anti access/area denial) zones, for example in the Russian enclave of Kaliningrad or in the South China Sea, where advanced weapon systems could make penetration by US forces potentially very costly.[31] A2/AD is a new term for an age-old defensive strategy: great powers have always sought to construct defensive works to deter adversaries while enabling their own offensive operations, from the citadels that Vauban built for Louis XIV to the Maginot Line that traced the Franco-German border in the interbellum. The novelty of A2/AD lies only in the fact that it disproved the US assumption that its technological edge was so great that its competitors would never catch up. Alas, history shows that every new offensive weapon generates its defensive response, in a never-ending cycle of lethality.

At the grand strategic level, the emergence of China left the US searching for a new approach. Unless competition and rivalry were to be seen as ends in themselves, Washington had to ask itself the questions posed by Hal Brands and Zack Cooper: 'What, exactly, does America seek to achieve vis-à-vis China? Should US leaders indefinitely contain Chinese geopolitical influence? Force the "breakup or mellowing" of Chinese power? Pursue a grand bargain with the Chinese communist party?'[32] At the start of the 2020s, there was a bipartisan consensus between the Democrats and Republicans in the strategic establishment that the priority was China, but the strategic ends and ways were far from fully developed.

★★★

The US may have felt challenged by China's rapid rise, but behind the façade of unity and assertiveness, many in the Chinese strategic establishment felt challenged too. In the first years of the PRC, its grand strategy was mostly implicit. 'What they had was a set of instincts, a sense of where they wanted to wind up and how', writes Sulmaan Wasif Khan.[33] The original leadership never shed the feeling of being 'haunted by chaos', as in the title of Khan's book, and that fear of internal and external enemies overthrowing the regime has persisted to this day. Hence, after the internal upheaval of the Mao years had subsided, Deng's maxim of 'hide your strength, bide your time', and China's insistence to present itself as a developing country rather than as a global player. But when it became one of the world's three biggest economies, it became impossible to avoid the much more exposed position of a great power. As China acquired global interests, it became involved in global problems. Its traditional stance of sitting on the fence in any crisis, letting the other powers do the dirty work of managing security problems while taking care of its economic interests behind the scenes (a stance which it presents more attractively as 'non-intervention'), became difficult to maintain in each and every instance.

Since the 2008 financial crisis at the latest, China has been adjusting not so much to multipolarity, as to the fact of its own great power status. It has discovered that power does not only create attractiveness on the part of other states, but also greed (though that can be put to good use), as well as fear and push-back. This only increased when under Xi's leadership from 2012 onwards China adopted a more assertive stance than ever before since the death of Mao. So assertive indeed that some in the Chinese strategic establishment considered that it became counterproductive. As we saw in the previous chapter, at the beginning of the 2020s China's actual strategy was no longer fully in line with the defensive strategic culture that it developed over the last two centuries. Whether strategic culture will act as a brake on strategy, or strategic practice will end up changing strategic culture, the adaptation to great power status will confront Beijing with difficult choices yet.

Alone of the great powers, perhaps Russia did not face any difficulties adapting to multipolarity, because it had simply never ceased to think of the world in terms of competition and rivalry. International politics in the 21st century could be seen as confirming Russia's image of itself: 'always the target of aggression, caught forever in a cycle of foreign predation, peace only as calm before the next storm'.[34] But, as seen before, Russia feels threatened and confident at the same time. In the words of Dmitri Trenin:

> Russia is alone, but it is free to move. Its geographical position in the north and centre of the great continent of Eurasia both allows and compels it to have a 360 degrees vision of its gigantic neighbourhood, from Norway to North Korea, and from Murmansk to Mumbai. It has the two powerhouses of the continent, the EU and China, as direct neighbours, and it does not have to choose between them.[35]

Nevertheless, the reality of an ever more powerful China, and its limited economic power as compared to the other great powers, meant that Russia too could not look forward to the 2020s without any apprehension.

★★★

Of today's great powers, only the US has a secure geopolitical position. Bordering on the Atlantic and the Pacific, on Mexico and Canada, and having become self-sufficient in terms of energy, it faces no direct threats to its own territory or to its connections with the world. The EU, in contrast, faces an assertive Russia in the east, which some member states fear might threaten EU territory itself; in the south, an arc of instability from Morocco to Iran threatens negative spill-over effects for the EU's connectivity as well as for its own territory. Russia has seen its traditional buffer in the west diminish as a result of NATO and EU enlargement, in which it sees the hand of the US; just like the EU it faces an unstable southern flank. More ominously, though less talked about by Russia, China's presence in the Russian far east and in the former Soviet republics in Central Asia and the Caucasus is ever growing. China considers its eastern seaboard and maritime communications vulnerable to American blockade; the alternative overland routes to the Indian Ocean and to Europe pass through unstable regions, including – from Beijing's point of view – China's own western provinces, where it suppresses its Uighur citizens.

The vulnerable geopolitical position of China, Russia and the EU could strengthen the perception of threats and inflame competition and rivalry, in particular with the other great powers. The US could see its secure geopolitical position as a base from which to engage in such rivalry. Since grand strategy is inherently competitive, the danger of exaggerating the threat that the others pose to one's interests is ever present. Preventing normal competition from escalating into rivalry demands a cool head, putting aside emotions and prejudices for a sober calculation of what one's interests require – grand strategy is rational.

3

Rational: Reason Trumps Ideology, Religion and Emotion

Making strategy is a rational process: an objective analysis of how much power one has, and how much power one's competitors and rivals have, determines which ends are feasible. Strategists make mistakes, of course. Their assessment of the environment can be wrong, they can misread the strategies of the other players and under- or overestimate their resources, they can fail themselves to commit the resources required and implement what they decided. Or they can be outwitted by the strategists of another state. If the premises of a strategy turn out to be false, or a competitor or rival is more successful, strategy must be revised through the same rational process. 'But governments and people do not always take rational decisions. Sometimes they take mad decisions, or one set of people get control who compel all others to obey and aid them in folly', Churchill points out.[1] History is full of examples of leaders who allowed religion, ideology or emotion to trump reason, overreached, and failed.

Philip II, Catholic King of Spain from 1556 to 1598, trusted in divine providence rather than heeding his advisors who warned of the lack of resources to make war simultaneously on protestant England, the rebellious protestant provinces of the Netherlands, and the 'infidel' Ottoman Empire. The results of this overreach were dramatic. The Spanish armada sent against England was sunk in the Channel (1588). The northern Netherlands, the United Provinces, became an independent republic and a great power, and would enjoy a 'golden century' (not least thanks to the influx of refugees and wealth from what remained of the Spanish Netherlands on the territory of current-day Belgium, I cannot refrain from pointing out). The Ottoman conquests were but briefly delayed before the empire continued its expansion.[2]

Truly catastrophic was the result of Hitler's decision to invade the Soviet Union, after having failed to defeat the UK. Launching operation Barbarossa (22 June 1941) was logical within Hitler's own ideologically determined worldview; the destruction of bolshevism had been his avowed aim since the publication of *Mein Kampf* in 1925.[3] But the decision was not rational when looking at the reality of a two-front war and the limits on German resources. Yet in December of the same year, after the Japanese attack on the American fleet in Pearl Harbour, Hitler even declared war on the US as well. The clearer it became that the war could not be won, the more the Nazis ignored the realities of the balance of power and appealed to 'fanatical will' as the way to victory. Millions of dead later, the red flag flew over the Reichstag in Berlin. The Japanese decision to go to war with the US was an even more glaring example of irrational strategy.[4] Japan had actually concluded that a war against the US could not be won – and then convinced itself to ignore its own evidence and went ahead anyway, vainly hoping that a single knock-out blow against the American fleet could decide the issue. As a result, Germany and Japan were not only militarily defeated; both countries suffered near-total destruction. Resources do not lie: one has them, or one hasn't. Quoting De Gaulle: 'Optimism suits those who have the means for it.'[5]

It is not impossible to craft a rational strategy in pursuit of ideological or religious ends. But the more otherworldly the ends are, the less likely those who proclaimed them will be to compromise on them, even when reality imposes limitations on what can be achieved. Under US President Lyndon Johnson, faulty decision making in 1963–1965 produced an escalation of the war in Vietnam, where eventually half a million American soldiers would be in the field.[6] The US did not lack in resources, but Washington's ideological lens could only see the Vietnamese communists as puppets of the USSR. It failed to see that their ends were local – an independent and united Vietnam – and therefore posed little or no threat to the US. In reality, therefore, the US had limited interests at stake, and ultimately had to abandon its war for the wrong ends; whereas for the Vietnamese communists everything was at stake – so they persevered and won.[7] The attempt by ISIS to create an 'Islamic state' in the Middle East is a 21st century example of how religious zeal can produce irrational ends.[8] By stating its objective (in 2014) of overthrowing the existing states in the region and establishing a 'caliphate', while also undertaking terrorist attacks in Europe, ISIS provoked the creation of a broad and powerful coalition against it. By suppressing and murdering Muslims whom it considered unfaithful to its own interpretation of Islam, it lost public support with much of its potential constituency. Hitler preferred to go down in the ruins and take Germany with him rather than surrender. For the ISIS leadership, the apocalypse that in 2019 predictably ended its rule over the territories that it had conquered in Iraq and Syria was likewise the only acceptable alternative to victory. But its sheer audacity had created havoc in the region; in spite of the powers arraigned against it, defeating ISIS was a difficult enterprise. This testifies to the truth of another Churchill quote on rationality: 'Madness is however an affliction which in war carries with it the advantage of SURPRISE.'[9]

These examples ought to serve as a warning: when a strategy is not based on reason in the first place, and disregards the realities of power, one must be really lucky, or one's competitors very incompetent, in order not to fail.

★★★

The current Russian grand strategy of creating a sphere of influence in the former Soviet republics is grounded in history, and not only because these states were once part of the empire and the USSR.[10] In the absence of obvious defensive barriers, Russia has sought to expand westwards as soon as it had the means, in order to create a buffer zone large enough to absorb any aggression from another European power. The invasions by Sweden's Charles XII (1709), Napoleon (1812) and Hitler all penetrated deep into Russian territory before they were defeated precisely because of this strategic depth: no army was large enough to successfully wage a campaign on such a large front and be sustained so far from its home base. But the Nazi invasion devastated the Soviet Union. After the Second World War, the creation of satellite states controlled by Moscow in the countries liberated by the Red Army (and the annexation of the three Baltic states) was to provide insurance against Russia ever having to face such a threat again. Most of this buffer disappeared when after the Cold War the central and Eastern European states chose to join NATO and the EU, including the Baltics, the only former Soviet republics to do so (and the only ones that had been independent states throughout the interbellum). This outcome went against the basic tenets of Russian strategic thinking.

Russia cannot realistically hope to undo EU and NATO enlargement, but it does attempt to weaken their cohesion by divide-and-rule tactics, cosying up to some of their members' governments while pressuring others (in particular those who depend on Russia for their energy supply). Moscow also engages in subversion, corrupting politicians and officials and spreading fake news. Large-scale military manoeuvres on the borders with NATO and EU countries further serve to impress and deter them. Moscow does want to prevent further EU and NATO enlargement. It actively seeks to dissuade the other former Soviet republics in eastern Europe and the Caucasus from building close relations with, and certainly from joining, NATO or the EU. The risk of more states escaping what Russia regards as its sphere of influence is far from imaginary: the US had advocated NATO membership for Georgia and Ukraine in 2006–2008, but the European allies resisted. The Russian military presence on Georgian and Ukrainian territory now effectively blocks any future membership bids: neither NATO nor the EU will invite a member that is not in full control of its territory. Russian forces have also been present in Transnistria, a breakaway region of Moldova, since 1992. Originally the troops were deployed as peacekeepers in the framework of an agreement with Moldova; a 1994 agreement to end the operation was never ratified by Russia, which retains some 1,500 troops there. The foreign policies of Armenia and Azerbaijan are dominated by their continued dispute over the territory of Nagorno-Karabakh, over which they fought a war in 1991–1994. A second war over the enclave broke out in September 2020; in November Russia brokered a deal cemented by the deployment of Russian troops. EU or NATO membership is obviously not on these countries' agenda. Belarus, finally, has closely aligned its strategy with Russia ever since independence and seemed a stable fellow traveller. Until, that is, in September 2020 large-scale protests erupted against the fraudulent re-election of President Alexander Lukashenko. NATO and the EU are well aware, however, that any hint of a membership offer would only complicate the position of Belarus.

What Russia fears is not that NATO or the EU are building up strength and recruiting new members in order to confront it militarily. NATO is a defensive alliance and has no designs on Russia, nor has the EU; that would definitely run counter to the strategic culture of the Europeans. The threat that Russia perceives is more ideological: that the transition to democracy in its former satellites and in the former Soviet republics of Georgia, Moldova and Ukraine might yet inspire Russia's own citizens to try and force democratisation upon Moscow. The demonstrations that erupted after the failed poisoning and subsequent imprisonment of opposition leader Alexei Navalny in February 2021 only confirmed those fears. 'Western enmity was not a matter of what a Western actor was *doing*, but what the West was portrayed as *being*', says Timothy Snyder.[11] Russia therefore attempts to undermine the European democracies in order to reduce their power of attraction as a model for its own people. This is also why even as Russian strategic documents depict NATO as a threat, Russian official discourse at the same time portrays the West as decadent and weak, in order to convince Russian citizens of the superiority of the Russian way of life; the orthodox church is mobilised for this purpose too. The legalisation of same-sex marriage in many European countries is singled out as an example of this alleged decadence, and discrimination of the gay and lesbian community inside Russia has become an instrument of its strategy. (I remember a speaker at the Russian Academy of Sciences in Moscow extolling Russia for holding in trust Europe's traditional values until the time that Western Europeans would come back to their senses – not suspecting that one of his co-panellists was an atheist married to a man himself, as I subtly pointed out when speaking next.) Culturally, Russia actually is very much a European country. A visitor from any European capital will immediately feel at home in the galleries, theatres and concert halls of Moscow. Perhaps it is exactly because of this kinship that the Russian regime fears the influence of Europe.

While it does try to weaken the democracies, Russia cannot hope to convert them to its own authoritarian model. Unlike the communist ideology during the Cold War, which had a worldwide appeal, Russia's present-day narrative may influence the way people in the democracies perceive it, but it is highly unlikely to convince them to abandon democracy for the Russian model. Quite the contrary, the result of Russian propaganda and disinformation campaigns in Europe has been, in the assessment of Sir Lawrence Freedman, 'that Russian officials were not believed about anything, even when telling the truth. Russian propaganda played extremely well in Russia but badly everywhere else, which had the effect of increasing Russia's sense of isolation but not its influence.'[12] In the case of Ukraine, Russia went so far as to invade the country to forestall further democratisation and closer relations with the EU, but that was a failure: the invasion made full NATO or EU membership impossible, but also ensured that the majority of public opinion turned against Russia.

Seen from Brussels or Washington, Russia's confrontational stance may seem costly in the absence of any hostile intention on their part. But for Moscow, strained relations with the EU and the US, economic sanctions, and the (relatively limited) resources spent on military interventions do not weigh up against the domestic benefits of the strategy. President Putin has to a large extent built his internal legitimacy on the image of the strong leader who can rattle Russia's 'rivals' in the West.[13] The regime cannot promise its citizens much economic progress, hence the focus on 'Russian' values, nationalism, and a confrontational foreign policy, in particular towards the EU. In Snyder's analysis:

The point was to choose the enemy that best suited the leader's needs, not one that actually threatened the country. Indeed, it was best not to speak of actual threats, since discussing actual enemies would reveal actual weaknesses and suggest the fallibility of aspiring dictators. ... Russia's real geopolitical problem was China. But precisely because Chinese power was real and proximate, considering Russia's actual geopolitics might lead to depressing conclusions. The West was chosen as an enemy precisely because it represented no threat to Russia. Unlike China, the EU had no army and no long border with Russia.[14]

Leaders like Putin count on Europe being the 'polite' great power, who will not demand tit for tat. Stalin thought in this way too: 'At the notion that this execution could provoke nasty repercussions in western public opinion, Stalin had probably smiled to himself and thought – just as he was to say on a similar occasion about the people of the West: "Nichevo, vsyo proglotyat – Never mind, they'll swallow anything".'[15]

The more Russia's confrontational strategy gets tied up with the domestic legitimacy of the government, however, the more difficult it becomes to forge a compromise, even when that would suit Russia's interests more than persisting in rivalry. On Ukraine, for example, one could argue that Putin has manoeuvred Russia into a dead-end street: having presented the crisis as a symbolic and almost domestic issue on which no compromise is possible (because Kiev was the capital of the first Russian principality, Kievan Rus, in the 9th century), he would struggle to retrace his steps. Many Russian scholars, disappointed with the results of Russia's bonds with China, have started to plead for a normalisation of relations with the EU. But that cannot be done unless a compromise is found over Ukraine.

The importance of maintaining an image of success in great power rivalry has also led Russia into commitments further afield for which the cost-benefit calculus is more doubtful. Russia firmly committed to support President Nicolás Maduro of Venezuela, for example, including with military aid, when in 2019 the national assembly declared his election invalid and declared Juan Guaidó to be the acting president. Russian loans and arms exports were at stake, but the primary objective probably was to cause nuisance to the US in an area of traditionally strong American influence. The Trump administration took the bait and reacted firmly against Russian interference, allowing Putin to profile himself just as he wanted.

However, Maduro also alienated all of Venezuela's neighbours, who saw an influx of refugees escaping the country's economic and political crisis. Moreover, once the Venezuelan people began to turn against Maduro, Russia could not hope to maintain him in power indefinitely, just like it could not prevent Ukrainian President Yanukovich from losing his grip on the country once he lost public support. Russian engagement in Venezuela thus seemed to be lacking long-term ends. It might have thwarted short-term American plans; but in the end, Venezuela is hardly a vital interest of the US – was it worth the costs on the Russian side? Similarly, in 2017 Russia used the unexpected request for support from President Faustin-Archange Touadéra of the Central African Republic to build a military presence in another country in crisis, where French influence had long reigned supreme. Russia gained concrete advantages in terms of arms exports and natural resources, in addition to disturbing European and American calculations. But once more one must question whether Russian strategy had clear long-term ends in sight in a country that remained torn by civil war.

The Russian military intervention in the civil war in Syria, which started in 2015, was successful in its much more concrete aim of ensuring that President Bashar al-Assad stayed in power, thus guaranteeing Russian interest in the country, including access to the navy base in Tartus. Although Europeans and Americans had intervened in the Libyan civil war in 2011, they refrained from direct intervention in the Syrian conflict because the Assad regime was supported by Russia and Iran. Only when ISIS emerged victorious from the chaos in Iraq and Syria did they create a global coalition to defeat it, in 2014. Russia had an obvious interest in the destruction of ISIS too; Moscow feared its power of attraction over Muslims in its own southern districts. Perhaps joint American-European-Russian action against ISIS might have created a degree of understanding, which could have influenced their divide over Ukraine that same year. But with rivalry being the dominating frame, such a joint undertaking was impossible. The most that could be achieved was a minimal exchange of information in order to ensure that Russian and coalition operations against ISIS would not get in each other's way and risk incidents. Meanwhile, Russia has remained one of Syria's few partners, and Russia alone does not have the resources that reconstruction of the country requires.[16] Russia's more open-ended interference in another Mediterranean country, Libya, also offered the promise of more concrete advantages. After the American and European military intervention in 2011, the civil war continued, now between the various forces that had first united to defeat Qadhafi. Europeans and Americans kept their distance, allowing Russia (and others) to move in. By intervening on the side of Field Marshal Khalifa Haftar, Russia perhaps hoped, if Haftar came out on top, to gain another navy base on the Mediterranean shore.

Putin, bolstering his domestic power through a forceful foreign policy against what he has portrayed as Russia's American and European rivals, has made some brilliant tactical moves, but the strategic ends have not always been clear. The need to fan the flame of rivalry for domestic reasons has begun to transform tactical flexibility into a dogmatic antagonism – and dogma is impervious to reason. Russia appears to grasp any opportunity to thwart American or European plans even when the long-term cost-benefit assessment of such action does not seem to be in its favour. The direct expenditure in resources may be limited, but as dogmatic rivalry reduces the available strategic options, the opportunity costs are high. And if Russia ends up the sole associate of regimes that are shunned by almost everyone else, that hardly seems a strong basis for Russia's global influence.

★★★

As it is for Russia, so for China too foreign policy is of vital importance to the domestic legitimacy of the regime. The legitimacy of the CCP is largely based on its economic success in lifting people out of poverty – a goal which is far from completely achieved. The Party has to ensure ever rising economic prospects, and demonstrate that it assumes responsibility for people's wellbeing, also in terms of the environment and health (an image that got severely shaken by its initial attempt to cover up the outbreak of the coronavirus in Wuhan in late 2019). If the CCP fails, it may lose 'the mandate of heaven' (like successive imperial dynasties in earlier times), and see the people revolt against it. In this sense, although China is an authoritarian state, all leaders since Deng Xiaoping (Mao's successor) are aware that they are accountable to the people.[17] In its foreign policy, China prioritises the pursuit of economic interests, therefore, and it goes about that in a very pragmatic way. Whereas Russia cloaks its foreign policy in the language of rivalry, China talks of 'peaceful rise' and 'harmonious development', and by and large cooperates with any state, regardless of its political system or its allegiance to other powers. According to Ian Johnson, Deng 'abandoned even the pretence of communism for a pragmatic policy of "crossing the river by feeling the stones" – an ideology that basically means that anything goes as long as the economy develops and the party stays in power'.[18] Venezuela is a case in point: officially, China, like Russia, supported Maduro from the start; but behind the scenes

Beijing soon hinted to Guaidó that naturally it would gladly work with him were he to prevail, if he would guarantee China's economic interests. This was not a new attitude: the PRC soon appraised that its diplomacy did not gain from breaking off relations with any state or from letting relations with one state impinge on those with another.[19] The most telling example of this pragmatism is that in 1972 China welcomed US President Richard Nixon and embarked on a course of cooperation with the US against the USSR.

Ideology thus plays little or no role in Chinese foreign policy. Xi does present 'socialism with Chinese characteristics' as a model for other states, but in reality it holds no appeal to the democratic world. The specific Chinese model of authoritarianism can only offer inspiration to states that are authoritarian already, and even then its applicability, apart from the economic aspects, is limited.[20] Xuetong Yan points out that the Chinese government itself has not referred to Marxism as a guiding principle for its foreign policy since Deng initiated the reform and opening-up policy in 1978, because its core idea of class struggle inevitably contradicts the principle of 'peaceful development'.[21] Instead, Yan says, China has adopted 'economic pragmatism'. In other words, China still abides by another famous motto of Deng: 'It doesn't matter whether a cat is black or white, as long as it catches mice.'

The crucial exception to China's overall pragmatism is any issue that in Beijing's view concerns its territorial integrity. Whatever China terms a domestic issue – notably the situations in Hong Kong, Tibet and Xinjiang, and the future of Taiwan – it is not willing even to discuss with other states, not even when it blatantly breaks international law, as when it lays claim to the entire South China Sea. Instead China pursues its goals very assertively. No state disputes that Hong Kong, Tibet and Xinjiang are part of China. But the EU and the US, among others, do insist that human rights must be respected and, in the case of Hong Kong, the terms of the 1997 handover of the former British crown colony to China (under the principle of 'one country, two systems', Beijing pledged to respect Hong Kong's way of life for 50 years). Nobody, however, recognises China's de facto annexation of the greater part of the South China Sea. The more China stirs domestic nationalist feeling about the South China Sea (based on alleged ancient claims that are actually entirely spurious[22]), the more difficult it will be to forge a compromise with the other littoral states. Beijing may, of course, simply be counting on the others eventually giving in, one after the other, if it keeps up the pressure and maintains strategic patience. But nationalism, which the government consciously promotes, is an increasingly important factor, in addition to economic issues, in providing CCP rule with legitimacy.[23] The danger with nationalism is, however, that once feelings are aroused, they are difficult to control, as even the CCP has experienced (in 2012, for example, when anti-Japanese demonstrations stirred up by the regime turned violent and had to be suppressed by the security forces).

Taiwan is an even more difficult problem, because 'reunification' has been a prominent goal since the founding of the PRC in 1949, and it has become a symbolic issue. But as since 1949 Taiwan has in practice led an autonomous existence, younger generations on the island now mostly feel Taiwanese rather than Chinese. Furthermore, from 1895 to 1945 Taiwan had been ruled by Japan, the Chinese empire having ceded the island after it lost the 1894–1895 Sino-Japanese war. Except for the few years between the defeat of Japan in 1945 and the creation of the PRC, Taiwan has thus not been part of the development of mainland China for over 125 years. China had nonetheless gained a lot of influence in Taiwan, but that trend was sharply reversed in 2019–2020. China's failure to apply 'one country, two systems' in Hong Kong, whose autonomy increasingly diminished, and the repression of the resulting massive protests, greatly reduced the appetite in Taiwan for a similar solution. Similarly, the Taiwanese contrasted Beijing's belated response to the coronavirus outbreak with their own early reaction, thanks to which Taiwan was almost alone in the world to be able to deal with the virus without requiring a lockdown. Economic ties between Taiwan and the mainland remain very close (China is the island's largest trading partner) and one of the two main Taiwanese political parties continues to seek closer relations with Beijing. But the prospect of China gradually increasing its political and economic influence so that one day Taiwan would fall into its lap has definitely been weakened.

Fears of China forcing the issue by military means instead have increased since Xi came to power and launched China onto a more assertive path. Some suspect that China aims to round off reunification by 2049, the 100th anniversary of the PRC. At the same time, it would be awkward to use force against an island population which Chinese official discourse habitually presents as yearning to return to 'the warm embrace of the motherland'. Use of force would certainly risk triggering a severe international crisis. Only a handful of states recognise the independence of Taiwan. All others recognise only the People's Republic as a state, but they often maintain 'offices' in Taipei that are embassies in all but name, and mostly want to maintain the status quo. The EU and the US certainly want to avoid any changes imposed by force of arms. Perhaps, had Taiwan not been democratised, Americans and Europeans would have long dropped their support, just like they ended cooperation with many authoritarian but anti-communist regimes once the Cold War ended. Today though, Taiwan is a vibrant democracy (and the first in Asia to introduce same-sex marriage, for example). The EU and the US feel a strong moral obligation to support democracy wherever it exists, though it remains to be seen how far they would be willing to go in practice: would they risk their own interests in a confrontation with China in order to defend Taiwan? If Xi or his successors would want to assure their legacy, they could also do so by a grand gesture in the opposite sense: allowing Taiwanese self-determination as a way of demonstrating both the strength of the PRC (which can survive quite without Taiwan) and its magnanimity. As Khan concludes: 'In purely grand strategic terms, the easiest way of gaining a pliable Taiwan is to offer it independence and treat it like the Philippines – incline it to China's will with suitable economic offerings and the occasional threat.'[24] That might be expecting too much pragmatism, however.

★★★

The US undoubtedly thinks of itself as a rational and pragmatic player, but the reality is that this century the US has shown itself to be the most ideological of the great powers. On two occasions, Washington declared a state to be an enemy on ideological rather than rational grounds. In 2003, the US invaded Iraq, basically because the strategic establishment around President George W. Bush wanted to oust Iraqi President Saddam Hussein, whom the President's father, President George H.W. Bush, had left in power even though he defeated him in the first Gulf War in 1991. Taking American exceptionalism to its missionary extreme, these so-called 'Neoconservatives' saw this as a first step in bringing democracy to the Middle East. What they chose to forget, even though many had actually been in leading positions under Bush senior, is that in 1991 the US had consciously decided to keep Saddam in place, in order not to create a power vacuum that would upset the regional balance. That is exactly what happened in 2003, and it created such havoc that in the 2020s the Middle East and the Gulf have still not recovered from it. By focusing on Iraq, the US also allowed its attention to lapse in Afghanistan, where it had intervened in 2001, and probably fatally undermined the war effort there. Moreover, its wilful deception of the international community, pretending that Iraq possessed weapons of mass destruction while its intelligence services knew this not to be the case, increased the general level of suspicion between the great powers, and alienated many of the US' allies and partners.

In another instance of ideological decision making, in 2018 the US withdrew from the Joint Comprehensive Plan of Action (JCPOA), the agreement with Iran to limit its nuclear capacity, which the US, the EU, Russia, China, France, Germany and the UK had reached in 2015. The Trump administration tried to uphold the fiction that Iran was in breach of the agreement, but the EU denied this and saw the undoing of the JCPOA as detrimental to the stability of the Gulf region and to its own security. The real reason behind the US withdrawal was its frustration with Iran's growing influence in the region, including in Syria and Iraq – a development which the US itself had enabled by destroying the Iraqi state – and the wish to support its ally Saudi Arabia against Iran in its quest for regional dominance. But underlying all this was an ideologically motivated, hawkish element in the US strategic establishment that aspired to regime change in Tehran. Hence there was no ear in Washington for the EU's plea in favour of the JCPOA: once it had been decided that Iran was the enemy, reasonable arguments no longer mattered. Once again the US upset many of its own allies and partners, who feared that Washington would launch yet another counterproductive war.

These are but isolated instances, perhaps, but the fact that in the first two decades of the 21st century the US twice based decisions of (potentially) war and peace on ideological grounds, with scant attention for the facts, greatly undermined the rules-based international order that it ostensibly stands for. Inevitably, US allies and partners have ended up less confident that the US will always do 'the right thing'.

Those same American allies, however, have allowed themselves to be carried away and approve ever further expansion of NATO, which has acquired an ideological component too. Some now debate the wisdom of the original decision to offer membership of the alliance to the former adversaries of the Warsaw Pact after the end of the Cold War, and find the reason for rivalry with Russia in NATO's rapid enlargement. One should not forget, though, that the central and Eastern European countries were on the demand side, seeking to guarantee their newly re-established independence. Even with hindsight, the original enlargement was a sound strategy to consolidate Europe's peaceful transition from the Cold War to the new era, paving the way for EU enlargement afterwards. Over time, however, this strategy has turned into a permanent 'open door' policy without any thorough debate about the costs and benefits of admitting new allies; it has become enlargement for the sake of enlargement.[25] As mentioned above, the US pushed to include Georgia and Ukraine without much thought for how Russia would perceive this as a geopolitical challenge. Russia does not hold a veto over NATO expansion, of course, but if the alliance would take steps that might lead to a serious dispute, it should do so in full awareness of the ends that it seeks and the risks it may entail – not unwittingly. After the European allies' rebuttal in 2008, formally the door remains open, but Tbilisi and Kiev know that the presence of Russian troops on their territory precludes NATO membership. But NATO did afterwards welcome Albania and Croatia (2009), Montenegro (2017), and North Macedonia (2020), so that it now counts 30 members. The main thought behind this ongoing enlargement seemed to be not what the new allies could contribute to NATO, or which security challenges demanded their inclusion, but rather a desire to colour in the blanks on the map of Europe.

EU enlargement at some point similarly became an ideological rather than a strategic project. The Union went from 15 members in 1995 to 28 in 2013 without adapting its institutions first. That was only achieved with great difficulty in 2009, when the latest version of the Treaty on European Union (the Lisbon Treaty) entered into force, and that version did not do away with the need for unanimity in foreign and defence policy. The initial enlargement with the core group of central and Eastern European states in 2004 was a major strategic choice, underpinning the security guarantee offered by NATO by including these countries into a political and economic union. But at the same time, and subsequently, certain states were accepted that in terms of political and economic development were not ready for EU membership. Just like in NATO, enlargement became an objective in its own right, until it became counterproductive for the functioning and the public support of the Union. Enlargement has provided the EU with the scale necessary to hold its own in a world of continent-sized great powers. But this only works if the Union manages to pull up the newcomers to the level of its most developed member states, and to stay united.

The irony is that just as enlargement fatigue overcame the earlier drive, in the late 2010s, offering the prospect of membership became strategically important again in order to maintain EU influence in southeast Europe, where Russia and China have gained a strong foothold. It seems logical that one day all the states of the western Balkans will join; they are already surrounded by the EU. But Brussels is struggling to find a balance between this geopolitical imperative, the need to accept only new members with the capacity to effectively implement the Union's complex legal and economic order, and the constraints imposed by its own public opinion. In addition, if one day Norway or Switzerland would apply for EU membership, they would undoubtedly be able to join very quickly. But EU enlargement will probably end there for a long time to come. Membership for Turkey, although it has had candidate status since 1999, is unlikely ever to happen. Further enlargement to the east is bound to increase the rivalry with Russia; and in any case the EU's eastern neighbours will take a long time to reach the level of development that entry requires. The reality is that even if they develop close relations with the EU, like Ukraine, and even if Russia fails in its attempt to create an exclusive sphere of influence, these countries will remain a buffer zone between the EU and Russia.

★★★

Strategy should be rational, but strategy is made by people, and people are emotional as well as rational beings. Emotions can thus never be entirely excluded from the strategic realm. Nor should they, for emotional attachment to the state and to the strategic ends that it pursues is a source of strength. Patriotism, which George Orwell defined as 'devotion to a particular place and a particular way of life, which one believes to be the best in the world but has no wish to force on other people', will inspire people to do their best. Also, patriotism is 'of its nature defensive, both militarily and culturally' – but patriotic citizens will fight and risk their lives for their country. Nationalism, in contrast, 'the habit of identifying oneself with a single nation or other unit, placing it beyond good and evil and recognizing no other duty than that of advancing its interests', is, said Orwell, 'inseparable from the desire for power. The abiding purpose of every nationalist is to secure more power and more prestige, *not* for himself but for the nation or other unit in which he has chosen to sink his own individuality'.[26] On the one hand, therefore, a degree of emotional belief in the ends is a must, as a source of motivation, courage and strength. Based on his experience in the Second World War, Field Marshal William Slim defined four foundations of what he called the spiritual dimension of morale: '(a) There must be a great and noble object. (b) Its achievement must be vital. (c) The method of achievement must be active, aggressive. (d) The man must feel that what he is and what he does matters directly towards the attainment of the object.'[27] Bar the aggressive aspect, this applies to the ends of any grand strategy. But on the other hand, the emotional dimension should always be tempered by reason, in order to prevent emotions from luring the state into the pursuit of unrealistic or even self-destructive ends. The choice of the ways and means should always be the product of a rational analysis of the environment and of the capacity of oneself and the other players.

Thucydides, the historian of the Peloponnesian War, in which he had fought himself, stated the importance of the emotional realm in his famous triad: states make war not only to preserve their interests, but also for the sake of honour, and out of fear.[28] This emotional component is clearly visible in how today's great powers see their place in the world, in particular when it comes to their honour or status.

For Russia, regaining great power status is an end in itself. Putin has described the dissolution of the USSR as the greatest geopolitical catastrophe of the 20th century. It was a self-inflicted catastrophe, for it was Boris Yeltsin who gave the final push that made the Soviet edifice come crashing down, so that he gained supreme power as president of Russia – but all the other constituent republics of the Soviet Union thus won their independence as well. That fact does not diminish from Russia's sense of loss, and from its yearning to be treated as a great power again: 'The basic line of Russian foreign policy ... was not that the European Union and the United States were threats. It was that they should cooperate with Russia as an equal', writes Snyder.[29] I heard a Russian vice-minister of foreign affairs say that what Moscow wants is a return to the Yalta system: a reference to the Crimean conference in February 1945 where Stalin, Roosevelt and Churchill between them settled the fate of post-war Europe. Russia continues to put a lot of emphasis on its indispensable contribution to the defeat of Nazi Germany. According to Gregory Carleton, in these continuous references to the Second World War,

> one hears the echo of the country's ascent from the ruins of the Soviet Union, of its return as a power of consequence on a global scale, and of its success in standing up to the West, crowned by its seizure of Crimea and the jolt sent through its neighbours and all the way to Washington.[30]

But however justified Russian pride in its victory, this is not 1945 anymore. Russia kept many of the trappings of power, such as a permanent seat in the UN Security Council, but economically it is lagging behind. Arguably, in the 1990s the US and the EU did indeed not take Russia sufficiently into account as they remade the European order, though that was also a consequence of Russia's internal disorder. But what would satisfy Russia's quest for status today? Great power status is a vague notion. More substantial involvement in the councils of the other great powers is only possible if their interests and ends can be reconciled. According to Nadezhada Arbatova, however, Russian strategy

> is the result of a reactionary ideology, a superiority-inferiority complex and phantom-imperial pain. It defines

military-political empire as the only form that Russian statehood can take. Russia's equality with other great powers, and the balance of forces between Russia, China and the US, are seen as more important than multilateral cooperation.[31]

As long as Russia persists in its aim of creating an exclusive sphere of influence and continues to use the rhetoric of rivalry as the frame for its foreign policy, a common project with the EU and the US remains impossible, for Brussels and Washington will not support any arrangement that undoes the sovereignty of any other European state. Russia's aim of being treated as an equal, if that means being treated with respect, does not fit altogether well with its other aim of keeping its self-declared rivals off balance by subversion and an assertive foreign policy. It is noticeable, by the way, that publicly Russia always reproaches the US and the EU for their alleged lack of respect; what probably rankles Moscow at least as much, if not more, is that as a great power it has been overtaken by China.

Just like Russia always returns to the Second World War, so China always refers back to 'the century of humiliation', when it suffered at the hands of the great powers, even though China is now without any doubt a great power itself.[32] But the state actively fosters the memory of the 'unequal treaties', through which the empire ceded many concessions and territories. Given the importance of 'face' in Chinese culture overall, the result is that China probably is the most status-conscious country in the world.[33] China easily takes offence, for example, when a state receives the Dalai Lama, even if only in his capacity as a religious leader and without the intention of making any political statement on the status of Tibet. Allowing emotions to dictate diplomacy can be counterproductive, however: Beijing often reacts very aggressively, threatening economic or political consequences – and thus makes a visit by the Dalai Lama into headline news while it would otherwise likely attract very little attention. Similarly, China goes to great lengths to pressure even private companies, such as international airlines, into avoiding any designation that could give the impression that Taiwan is not a part of China. In the end, putting such diplomatic effort in what are but symbolic issues, however important they are to China's self-conception, is counterproductive, for other states logically resent Beijing's interference. They are thus likely to resist or push back, which might in turn reinforce Chinese feelings of loss of face, thus creating a negative spiral. If face is so important, then Beijing could be expected to understand that other states too prefer face-saving solutions to disagreements. Nevertheless, as China perceives itself as being in a competition for status with the US, it is unlikely to relent.[34] And as Slim, who commanded Chinese troops on the Burma front noted: 'Whatever "face" is, and however annoying its repercussions may be to an Occidental, it is well to remember it is a very human thing. The Chinese are not the only people who bother about what the neighbours think.'[35]

The US does not openly avow any concerns about status, but there is an important emotional dimension to its strategic posture too.[36] Graham Allison put it in clear terms:

> For Americans who grew up in a world in which USA meant number one – and that would be every citizen since roughly 1870 – the idea that China could unseat the US as the world's largest economy is unthinkable. Many Americans imagine that economic primacy is an unalienable right, to the point that it has become part of their national identity.[37]

And not just economic primacy, one might add. Because many in the US strategic establishment cling to the illusion of unipolarity, as seen in the previous chapter, the shock of no longer being the undisputed number one is all the greater. This fear of losing status and the irritation at China's rise often translate into a sense of entitlement – as if America's global leadership were a law of nature – and into moral indignation – as if any action by another power that could diminish American leadership is morally reprehensible. This becomes problematic if it stops the US from thinking clearly about strategic ends. The US need not welcome China's great power status, but it must accept it as a fact that it will have to face; undoing the rise of China is not a realistic end, or at least not one that can be achieved peacefully. In the words of Christopher R. Hill, 'Fear and loathing of China is no substitute for self-confidence and unity of purpose in dealing with it. ... Pique is no substitute for policy'.[38] The US must be careful that it does not become as dogmatically anti-Chinese as Russia has become anti-western.

Only the EU has the opposite problem: a lack of emotional attachment. As a composite actor that in its current form has existed for less than three decades, the EU as such does not generate any patriotism. The main attachment of the European strategic establishments is to the national capital of each member state, not to the EU, and that holds even more true for public opinion. Not distinguishing between patriotism and nationalism, the EU has in fact built a narrative of the Union as a post-national project. Aimed against nationalism, this discourse made sense, for nationalism has been a destructive force that enabled two world wars to start in Europe. But by also disparaging patriotism, the EU has created an unnecessary antagonism between national patriotism and belief in the European project. The fact is that EU member states' attachment to national sovereignty is more nostalgic than rational (and for many it is nostalgia for an imaginary past). Many members of the national strategic establishments think they still are leading actors, but in reality they are not even extras – they are no longer performing on the main stage. And yet, instead of rejecting patriotism as an obsolete sentiment, the EU should have encouraged it while pointing out at the same time that it is insufficient, because at the global level the European nation states no longer have the means to safeguard their interests vis-à-vis the great powers. European patriotism should complement national patriotism, therefore. Forging such a European feeling, however, is a long-term undertaking.

The absence of patriotism has advantages: the EU is less easily provoked into overreaction by lack of deference to its status. No president of the European Council or European Commission is ever likely to claim that they have 'a bigger button' than an opponent, as US President Donald Trump boasted of his nuclear arsenal to North Korea's Kim Jong-un in 2018. It gives the EU the opportunity to position itself as a power that is not concerned about status, which could allow it to more easily play a mediating diplomatic role between the other powers – if it wanted to. But it is a weakness as well: without European patriotism, national leaders within the EU can more easily favour short-term national interests and be rewarded for it by their constituents, to the detriment of the common European cause (and their countries' own long-term interests).

Each of the great powers advertises its own 'dream', its way of life, to its citizens and the world. The 'American Dream' is most familiar: liberty and the opportunity to pursue one's own happiness. There is a strong tradition in American strategic culture to see the 'American Dream' as a model for everybody's dreams, and to export it to the world. Many Americans have seen their personal opportunities sharply reduced, however. For them, the 'American Dream' has begun to resemble what one might call the 'Russian Dream' (though Russia itself does not use the term): pride in the power of the country and its status in the world, even though that national greatness does not translate into personal wellbeing and prosperity. Xi Jinping's 'Chinese Dream', which he announced in 2012 shortly after coming into power, combines the promise of individual prosperity with a call for a collective and harmonious effort to achieve national greatness. The 'European Project' or 'Idea' (as it is mostly called) is one of peace: after centuries of internecine European wars, that was a powerful driver of European integration. But today, when war between France and Germany is as unimaginable as war between Texas and Ohio, the idea has lost a lot of its mobilising power, and the EU is left searching for a 'European Dream'. A renewed emphasis on the importance of social security and the welfare state in the wake of the corona crisis could perhaps be the core of a new mobilisation. It is after all the 'European Social Model' that positively distinguishes the EU member states, as Tony Judt so rightly pointed out.[39] When Robert Kagan claims that 'no Western European nation ever became "socialist"',[40] he could not be more wrong: in the sense that they built a welfare state, they all did.

The important thing is not to belittle each other's 'dreams'. How to organise one's own way of life is an ideological choice, which is determined by the outcome of domestic politics. That ideology should not be carried over into international politics and a desire to convince or coerce others into giving up their way of life, however repellent one may find some of its aspects. The 'Chinese Dream' might hold little appeal for an American, for example, but to the extent that this national project is really shared by the Chinese people, external attacks against it can only be counterproductive. Which rules for relations between states one likes to see will be shaped by one's ideology; but ideology's role in international politics ought to end there – it should not extend to seeking to shape other states' domestic politics.

★★★

Harold Nicolson wrote how British Prime Minister Arthur Balfour taught him 'that emotionalism in politics was always wrong: that there was something between emotionalism and cynicism which was difficult of attainment but which, with intelligence, could partially, and only temporarily, be attained'.[41] Perhaps this 'something' could be reason with a touch of irony, the capacity to see the relativity of things that allows one to compromise without jeopardising one's vital interests. Such a mindset allows the great powers to compartmentalise their relations: to disagree on one issue while they cooperate on another, so that not every disagreement leads to a total breach. This is an important mechanism of conflict prevention, but it can only work if reason prevails over ideology, religion and emotion; for these tend to deal in absolutes, whereas reason will look for what is feasible in the context and with the resources of the moment. Reason ought thus to lead the great powers to cooperate when interests coincide, with each other, and with other states. Not even a great power can fully realise all ends of its grand strategy alone – great powers need allies.

4

Allied: One Needs Allies but Cannot Always Choose Them

'There is only one thing worse than fighting with allies, and that is fighting without them', said Winston Churchill near the end of the Second World War.[1] An alliance in the strict meaning of the term is a commitment between states to support each other in war. Europeans and Americans will immediately think of NATO and collective defence: a long-term if not permanent alliance to defend each other in case of aggression against a fellow member. But an alliance can also be concluded for a specific short-term purpose; and that purpose can be to make war. The great powers need allies and partners in all dimensions of international politics though, not only in the military sphere. They seek partners who will work with them to bring their particular view of the world order into practice, for example by voting along with them in existing international organisations, by joining them in creating new multilateral institutions, and by aligning their economic practices.

If one is in an alliance, one must consult one's allies, decide together, and take action together when the purpose of the alliance is at stake. That inevitably takes more time than when one acts alone, and may lead to compromise decisions. After the 1999 NATO air campaign against Serbia, to force an end to the violence in Kosovo, the US complained of the inefficiency of such a 'war by committee'.[2] But allies bring additional resources, and may also add legitimacy to one's actions: the more support a strategy garners from other states, the more acceptable it will appear to the domestic and international audience. When US President Barack Obama created the global coalition against ISIS in 2014, from the start he sought the participation of a number of Arab countries in order to create the perception of a truly international rather than a western initiative, and he consciously avoided the label of the US' standing alliance, NATO. Eventually, the coalition recruited 82 members – not out of military necessity, but for political reasons. In 2018, NATO did deploy to the region (sending a training mission to Iraq), again for political rather than military reasons: Obama's successor, Trump, wanted to see evidence of NATO's contribution to the fight against terrorism, and the European allies chose to appease a president who had loudly vented his scepticism of the alliance.

This example demonstrates that formal allies are not necessarily always effective partners. Allies may indeed be competitors at the same time, certainly in the economic sphere. On a specific issue that is not directly related to the main purpose of the alliance, they can even be rivals and actively work against each other, as when in 2018 Trump instigated punitive sanctions against European companies doing business with Iran in an attempt to force the EU to join the US in withdrawing from the Iran nuclear deal. The EU stuck to its guns, however, and tried to uphold the JCPOA, which in its view had achieved its objective of preventing Iran from acquiring nuclear weapons. Another example is how Pakistan, in spite of being an ally of the US, directly undermined its war effort in Afghanistan, funding and arming the very insurgents that the US was fighting against.[3] On the other hand, 'objective' allies – states that are faced with the same threats and therefore could have an interest in working together, even though they are not formally members of an alliance – do not always do so. ISIS, for example, posed a vital threat to the states of the region, not to Europe or the US: no European state, and certainly not the US, could have been toppled by its terrorist campaign, but it could have brought down states in the Middle East. Yet when ISIS first emerged onto the scene in Syria, Turkey (which is a NATO member) and Saudi Arabia, among others, lent it their support as the most effective fighting force against the Assad regime, which they wanted to see brought down. Only under American pressure did they withdraw their support and join the global coalition.

This also goes to show that one cannot always choose one's allies. Saudi Arabia was an indispensable member of the coalition, because of its prominent role in the Gulf and in the Islamic world in general. But many aspects of the Saudi way of life are nearly as off-putting for the US and the EU as the practices of ISIS. Many in Europe would even argue that Saudi Arabia itself contributed to the terrorist threat against its security, by supporting an archconservative version of Islam on which groups such as ISIS formally thrive. History is not short of other examples of counterintuitive coalitions and alliances. In 1918–1920, the UK and the US, among other foreign powers, intervened in the Russian civil war that followed the October Revolution on the side of the 'Whites' in a vain attempt to bring down the 'Reds' or Bolsheviks. The UK eventually recognised the USSR in 1924, the US only in 1933. During the Second World War, Britain and America found themselves allied with the Soviet Union against Nazi Germany – but only when the German invasion ended the Molotov-Ribbentrop Pact under which since 1939 Moscow and Berlin had been cooperating. Little real trust was lost between 'the big three', however, and at war's end the alliance quickly unfolded, to give way to such strong mutual suspicion that it led to the Cold War. During the Cold War, the West allied with many authoritarian regimes, as long as they were not communist. Even NATO at first was not an alliance of democracies. The authoritarian Portugal of António Salazar was one of the founding members in 1949, because the UK and the US considered the military base on the Azores islands that they had started to use during the war to be essential for the alliance. Ruling out all non-democracies as allies or partners would leave the US and the EU with far too few options; one cannot play chess if 16 of the 64 squares are forbidden, as Otto von Bismarck said.[4] We will see in Chapter 9 that the US and the EU work with non-democratic allies all the time, yet never feel entirely comfortable about it.

Going back further in history, it is worth remembering that prior to the Russian Revolution, Russia was very much a part of the European constellation of power, and a sought-after ally in successive coalitions, from the Seven Years War (1756–1763), to the Wars of the French Revolution and the Napoleonic Wars, the anti-liberal intervention in Austria in 1848 and, of course, the First World War. In those past centuries, Russia and the other European great powers were peer competitors in internecine European wars. Today, the individual European states no longer are great powers; only the EU as such, which has put an end to war between its members, can be considered one. European power politics has been replaced by EU politics. Russia, because of its size, can never be a member of the EU, for it would fatally unbalance the Union. But it does remain a European state, which means that although Russia appears as a rival to the EU and the US today, if it changed its grand strategy it could one day also be their partner in maintaining peace and stability on the European continent.

★★★

Russia today has few if any true allies. Of the former Soviet republics, Belarus has remained closest to Russia. In 1999, Moscow and Minsk even signed the Union State Treaty; on paper this created a supranational state, but in practice the treaty has seen little implementation.[5] Belarus has since been playing a subtle game, from time to time distancing itself just enough from Moscow to convince the EU in particular that it is not always fully aligned with Russia. When in 2020 popular protest erupted against his fraudulent re-election, President Lukashenko did seek Putin's help. But, unlike in the case of Ukraine, Russia did not rush into intervention, knowing full well how unpopular that move would be with the Belarussian public. Other former Soviet republics try to maintain good relations with Russia while deepening bonds with the West and, increasingly, China. In view of the history of the Warsaw Pact, which the Soviet Union forced its Eastern European satellites to join, and of Russia's current grand strategy of recreating a sphere of influence, Russia appears to be feared more than it is trusted. That limits its attractiveness to potential allies in its immediate periphery. Once again, Russia's actual grand strategy is in contradiction with its quest for great power status, which among other things can be measured in terms of the number of allies and partners a power can gather around itself. Further abroad, Russia's military alliance with Syria and its ties with countries like Venezuela and the Central African Republic are very much linked to the individuals in power, just like until 2014 its relations with Ukraine were centred on President Yanukovych. A change of regime would likely result in the end of the partnership, and as the domestic politics of these states are very volatile, they hardly offer a base for a stable alliance, unless Russia is willing to intervene militarily to shore up the president in office, as it did in Syria.

China's closest ally is North Korea, but that country is to China what Israel is to the US: the ally one wishes one never had. For reasons of domestic politics, China cannot abandon the fellow communist regime in Pyongyang, just as no US president could drop Tel Aviv. But Beijing cannot fully control its nuclear-armed ally either, and it often is on the reactive side to North Korea's assertive moves, just like Washington is to Israel, which also has nuclear weapons (the Trump administration, however, actively encouraged Israel). North Korea is China's only ally in the strict sense of the term; relations with its other communist neighbour, Vietnam, are fraught because of territorial disputes (and the countries fought a short but sharp war in 1979). Historically, China did not conclude alliances but relied on the practice of tribute: neighbouring states offered an annual tribute by way of recognition of the empire's supremacy, which was often purely symbolic; in reality most states remained independent. In some instances, the gifts and concessions that the emperor granted in return far outvalued the tribute, meaning that at times China bought peaceful relations from certain neighbours. During the Cold War, the PRC opted for a strategy of non-alignment and non-intervention, and that has remained China's formal position. China has increased its military ties with countries around the world, by exchanging officers between military academies for example. But Beijing has not offered other states security protection, not even in its neighbourhood.[6] Instead, it relies on its economic power to forge influence, in particular through the BRI. China's reluctance to engage in alliances does create a certain limit on the depth of its relationships. States that seek outside military assistance will look elsewhere, notably to Russia or the US.

While many states have deepened their economic relations with China, very few have chosen to align with China politically, though some have been brought under its influence. Countries like Cambodia and Laos are often seen as clients of China, doing its bidding in international organisations such as the Association of Southeast Asian Nations (ASEAN) in return for economic favours. Most states in Asia as well as on other continents try to maintain good relations with different great powers at once, however. Indeed, as seen in Chapter 2, the fact that China has no allies in the strict sense of the term does not mean that if its rivalry with the US escalated into a new cold war, everybody would side with the US. If a choice were forced upon them, several states might just opt for China, in view of their proximity and economic dependence. For the majority of states, however, the preferred option is to sit on the fence. In the intensifying Sino-American competition, most capitals strenuously avoid choosing sides.

★★★

A key question for the course of international politics in the 21st century is: are Russia and China allies? In the strict sense of the term they are not. Beijing and Moscow have tightened their military relationship since 2018, when China (together with Mongolia) was the first country, except for the former Soviet republics, to take part in Russia's quadrennial Vostok ('East') military manoeuvres.[7] But China and Russia have not concluded a mutual defence arrangement, nor are they likely to do so.

China is wary of Russia's use of military force to pursue its grand strategy of recreating a sphere of influence in the former Soviet republics: it goes against its own principle of non-intervention. The 2014 Russian invasion of Ukraine, for example, put a halt to the increase in China's economic presence in the country. That was temporary, however, and China has since become one of Ukraine's most important trade and investment partners. Ukraine furthermore occupies an important geopolitical position in the context of the BRI, which it joined in 2017. China has not openly condemned the invasion, but neither has it expressed its support for Russia.[8] Beijing might have seen some positive side effects in that the EU, and to a lesser extent the US, while they were preoccupied with Russia and Ukraine had less attention to devote to China's activities – but that was a passing effect at most. On the whole, China would rather not see further Moscow-initiated military adventures in Eurasia in pursuit of Russia's quest for status and influence, for that would have a destabilising effect on China's own strategy as put into practice through the BRI.

China's position is somewhat ambivalent, though: if a security issue would emerge in one of its partners in the former Soviet sphere and the state in question could not itself cope with it, then it would probably look to Russia for assistance, in view of China's own reticence, until now, to intervene militarily. China has stepped up arms exports to the region, and has created military facilities in Tajikistan, but Russia remains the region's main security guarantor.[9] Its intervention in the war between Armenia and Azerbaijan in 2020 was a case in point. Whether Russia itself is entirely satisfied with such a division of labour – Russia acting as the policeman, China as the entrepreneur – is another question. Perhaps after it 'lost' Ukraine, Russia preferred a Chinese over a western economic presence in that country,[10] but Moscow could hardly see this as a model for Eurasia as a whole (where thanks to the BRI China's economic and political influence has been growing fast). Yet things did in fact largely play out in this way in another country where Russia intervened: Syria. China was more welcoming of the Russian intervention there, voting along with Russia in the UN Security Council, because Russia's action forestalled a western intervention against President Assad. Beijing itself kept a very low profile, however, but could expect big economic gains: as Assad stayed in power, western companies were excluded from the post-war reconstruction of Syria.[11] This dynamic pleads against a traditional alliance, which would limit China's margin of manoeuvre and make it more difficult for Beijing to stay out of the fray.

Russia moved closer to China after it invaded Ukraine, in part to compensate for the loss of political and economic opportunities with the US and the EU, in part to signal to the latter that Russia did not need them as much as they thought, and that the sanctions that they imposed would not be very effective. But China did not really need Russia either: Beijing welcomed closer relations with Moscow, but at the same time made it clear that Russia was on the demand side.

Negotiations on a gas deal that had been blocked for years were quickly concluded in late 2014, for example, but only because Russia accepted to significantly drop the price. However, if Sino-American tensions would mean that China could not import energy from the US, Russia would gain in importance as a supplier in the eyes of Beijing, also because China fears for the security of its maritime lines of communications to the Middle East. Both Russia and China have a strong intensive to maintain their energy relationship, therefore.

Many in the Russian strategic establishment nevertheless feel that closer relations with China cannot compensate for the loss of relations with the EU. Some see the creation of a partnership with China and other countries in Eurasia as a way of gaining a more favourable position from which to negotiate a return to normal with Europe. For Andrey Kortunov,

> Paradoxically, the only realistic path for a Russian return to Europe today is via Asia. In other words, if Russia cannot effectuate a return to Europe – on acceptable terms – on its own, then it may only be through the creation, jointly with China, India and other Asia partners, of a 'Greater Eurasia' that Russia can acquire the expanded negotiating positions and potential it would need for its eventual dialogue with Brussels.[12]

But uniting Russia and 'all of non-Western Eurasia' in a 'non-Western pole', as Sergey Karaganov advocates,[13] is largely wishful thinking. Acting together, China and Russia certainly are better positioned to block specific US and/or EU initiatives that they deem harmful to their interests. But Beijing has absolutely no interest in complicating its own vital economic relations with the EU by making them dependent on a package deal with Moscow. Russia will have to find its own way back to Europe.

Indeed, other Russian scholars warn that Russia's foreign policy has become unbalanced, relying too much on China to the detriment of its ties with Europe. Russia 'needs to be more careful', says Dmitri Trenin: 'For Russia, developing further cooperation with China only makes sense if it does not lead to one-sided dependence on it. Becoming part of a *Pax Sinica*, China's sphere of influence, is absolutely unacceptable to Russia.'[14] 'Moscow has no more desire for a China-dominated Asia than it has for a US-dominated world', adds Bobo Lo.[15] Aligning itself too closely with China also jeopardises Russia's relations with other Asian states that are economically important yet have fractious relations with China, such as Japan, South Korea and the members of ASEAN;[16] that is another reason why some sort of 'Eurasian bloc' is not a realistic proposition. Many prominent Russian scholars plead for a 'rebalancing' of Russian foreign policy, therefore, by restoring good relations with the EU while continuing the partnership with China. But that avenue is closed, as we saw in the previous chapter, as long as the Russian government cannot consider a compromise on Ukraine. The very interventionism that serves Russia's quest for great power status renders a rebalancing between Brussels and Beijing impossible.

As a result, Russia does run a certain risk of ending up as a junior partner to China, just like the EU is in many ways incapable of emerging from under the shadow of the US. And this rankles, because the Russian strategic establishment has been reared in a strategic culture that postulates Russian leadership, yet China has overtaken Russia by far in terms of economic and political power. Vice versa, it rankles in Beijing that in spite of this, Moscow often still behaves as if it were the leading partner, as in the early days of the PRC – another example in addition to those seen in Chapter 3 of how emotions are never fully absent from international politics. One must remember the historical background: during the Cold War, a different ideological and strategic outlook had led to a Sino-Soviet split, culminating in armed border clashes in 1969. The two communist powers refrained from all-out war, but in an American strategic masterstroke, President Richard Nixon and his national security advisor Henry Kissinger used the split to drive a wedge between Moscow and Beijing. Teaming up with the PRC against the Soviet Union, Nixon and Kissinger managed to divide the communist camp. Another historical element that remains potentially divisive is the fact that during 'the century of humiliation' the Russian empire too acquired large swaths of Chinese territory – important parts of which have never been returned.[17]

These strategic concerns and lingering emotions explain why the relationship between Russia and China has been based, in Trenin's words, on the principle: 'never against each other, not always with each other'.[18] A real alliance, involving much more systematic coordination and alignment of foreign and defence policy, would limit freedom of action much more than either Russia or China are willing to contemplate. At the same time, they are unlikely to loosen their 'wary embrace', as Lo has called it,[19] for both also feel the need to cooperate in the face of a world order shaped, and in their perception still dominated, by the US.

***

The other two great powers are in an alliance, be it indirectly. The US is not allied with the EU as such, but through NATO it is allied with 27 European states, plus Turkey (3 per cent of its territory, with over 10 per cent of the population, is in Europe, the remainder in Asia), and Canada. All EU member states are either full members or institutional partners of NATO, except for Cyprus (because of the dispute with the northern half of the island, which Turkey has recognised as a state). The EU and the US do have close bilateral relations too, of course, although Washington has always insisted that NATO is the primary forum for consultation on strategic issues. Twice this century this deep transatlantic relationship has been severely shaken, and a transformation may be in the offing.

The first shock happened in 2003, when the US invaded Iraq. This confronted its European allies with a difficult choice. How best to defend their interests: by supporting the US even though they felt war against Iraq was illegal and unnecessary, or by risking Washington's ire and condemning the invasion? The Europeans were deeply divided, so NATO, which operates by consensus, could not play a role in the operation. In the EU, the US actively widened the rift by playing on differences between what it called 'old' and 'new Europe': the established western member states versus the Eastern European states set to join in 2004. The EU drew an important conclusion from this: divided, it had no chance at all of influencing US decision making. The EU had already learned in the 1990s that the US could not be counted upon to come and solve all of Europe's security problems, when the US initially declined to intervene in the civil war in former Yugoslavia. Rightly so: the EU ought to have been capable of managing this crisis in its own backyard. In 2003, the EU began to appreciate that even when the US does act, it does not necessarily do the right thing – the invasion of Iraq destabilised the entire Middle East for decades and greatly harmed the EU's security interests. This was the driver behind the adoption of the European Security Strategy later in 2003, in order to re-forge a consensus on the EU's strategic role.

The second time the transatlantic alliance was shaken was not because of a single US decision, but because of the entirely new approach to international politics of the 2017–2020 Trump administration. Donald Trump came into office feeling that the US had been taken advantage of, not just by its adversaries but by its allies as well, in particular by the EU and Germany. The president withdrew or nuanced many of his more outlandish statements, but the underlying attitude of his administration remained: suspicion of the real intentions of the EU, scepticism of the added value of NATO, rejection of multilateral organisations as an instrument to manage international relations, and upholding competition as the main principle of the National Security Strategy. For the first time, the EU was confronted with a US president who seemed opposed to the idea of European integration, who publicly supported EU governments that had violated EU legislation, and who openly encouraged other member states to follow the example of Brexit. Moreover, Trump consistently used the threat or actual imposition of economic sanctions on the EU as a way of resolving differences on specific policies. For the first time too, Europeans began to fear that the US might withdraw from NATO. When Trump met Putin in Helsinki in 2018, Europeans actually were afraid that the president of the US would make a deal with the president of Russia behind their backs, at the expense of the European interest. On top of all this, Trump's aggressive style, the rapid turnover of secretaries of state and defence and other senior personnel, and the fact that many positions in the State Department and the Pentagon simply remained vacant, deprived the Europeans of obvious interlocutors. Since it became a great power, the US has been a partner of (Western) Europe; naturally, it always was and will be an economic competitor too. Policy differences were always settled through diplomacy, however. At times US diplomacy could be heavy-handed, but never before Trump had the US behaved as a rival that actively worked against specific EU policies.

One assumes that in terms of style and personality Trump will remain a unique case; every other president will be a lot more easier for the Europeans to communicate with. But the thrust of US grand strategy had already changed substantially before Trump entered the White House. It was his predecessor, Obama, who in 2012 announced the so-called 'pivot' to Asia: the refocusing of US grand strategy on China. 'If I can epitomise in one word the lesson I learned in the United States, it was "China"': this Churchill cabled, somewhat surprisingly, to General Wavell after visiting Washington in 1942; it certainly applies to every European visitor today.[20] A stable and prosperous Europe obviously remains an important American interest. But the order of priority has changed. As seen in Chapter 1, in the Second World War the European theatre came first. So it did during the Cold War: through their allies, the US and the USSR fought proxy wars in Asia, Africa and Latin America, but the point of their confrontation was the control over Europe. It was always clear that if push came to shove, Berlin had priority over Saigon; and indeed, while one is now Ho Chi Minh City, the other did not become 'Khrushchevstadt'. Since the 'pivot', competition and rivalry with China have priority, and that rivalry plays out first and foremost in Asia. Europe has become a secondary theatre, therefore, and the US has come to see the European states in a more instrumental way. They are still allies worthy of protection, but many in the US strategic establishment, Democrats and Republicans alike, also see the Europeans as free-riders who do not spend sufficiently on their own defence, and who should be mobilised to actively support the US and adopt a more confrontational stance against Beijing instead of putting their economic interests with China first.

Strategy towards China may become a major divergence between the US and the EU. The Trump administration saw other policy differences emerge too, such as over the Gulf, where the US supported Saudi Arabia against Iran in its quest for regional dominance, while the EU preferred not to take sides, and over the Iran nuclear deal, which the US left, while the EU hoped to salvage it. International organisations such as the WTO and the WHO became a bone of contention too: Washington and Brussels often agreed on the problems, but while the latter sought to negotiate solutions, the former opted to block bodies or leave them altogether. Different US administrations may have different policies on these and other issues. In his presidential campaign, Joe Biden announced a return to both the JCPOA and the WHO, for example. But on China there is a strong bipartisan consensus that the US is engaged in a long-term strategic rivalry. This is the most important divergence, therefore, not only because it is unlikely to diminish, but because it concerns the world order as a whole and China's place in it, and the role that the US, the EU and NATO should play.

The EU is increasingly aware of the need to safeguard its own sovereignty in the face of China's growing influence, but it does not perceive China as an overall rival in the same way as the US. For Washington, the emergence of China as a challenger to its position as the leading great power amounts to an identity crisis, as explored in the previous chapter. The European powers, in contrast, experienced the loss of their dominant role at the end of the Second World War. For the majority of the European strategic establishment, therefore, the re-emergence of China as a great power is, obviously, of major importance, but it is not in itself a threat to Europe's position in the world. It all depends on how China behaves in international politics, hence the EU's formal stance, as mentioned in the introduction, that China is a partner, a competitor and a rival at the same time. If China were to use its power aggressively, the Europeans would undoubtedly move closer to the US approach. But if China pursues its interests more or less within the rules of the world order, refraining from the aggressive use of force and from creating an exclusive sphere of influence, and demonstrating sufficient reciprocity in respecting the rules and opening its markets, then the mainstream European view is that one can live with China as a great power. That it is a great power is indeed natural, given its size and economic weight. Towards the US, therefore, the EU will remain allied, but not necessarily aligned, as the EU's Brexit negotiator, Michel Barnier, put it.[21]

Unless China turns into an aggressor, the EU is not inclined to join the US in Sino-American rivalry, therefore, but seeks to maintain constructive relations with both while looking after its own interests. This is not an equidistant position: the European way of life is much closer to the American than to the Chinese one, and the US is an ally – but that does not mean that China is ipso facto an adversary. While the EU certainly prefers to pursue its interests together with the US, it does not intend to subordinate them to the US interest.[22] Brussels judges its relations with the other great powers on their own merit rather than on the American appreciation of them, and it reserves the right to cooperate with the other powers too when interests coincide. If Sino-American tensions gradually escalated into a new cold war even if China did not turn aggressive, EU and US interests would risk diverging further and further. The EU would probably never side with China, of course, but Brussels would want to keep its economic relations with China open, and would continue to seek to involve China in multilateral cooperation. Brussels and Washington have a strong interest, therefore, in building a substantial dialogue on how to deal with China, in order to manage the divergences between them. At the end of 2019, the US succeeded in convincing its European allies to put China on the agenda of NATO, but that is not sufficient. For the Europeans, NATO's raison d'être remains deterring Russia, and they do not see the alliance as the main forum to make strategy on China. Russian sabre-rattling reinforces unity in NATO about the need to deter Russia, but the effect does not extend to other issues. Any US administration has to directly engage the EU on China, also because on many of the political and economic issues at stake, the EU has decision-making power rather than the individual member states. The EU itself finally took the initiative to launch such a dialogue with the US in June 2020; a first brief meeting between the EU High Representative and the US Secretary of State took place just before the November presidential election, so no substantial dialogue took place during the Trump presidency. The real start of the dialogue was finally announced in March 2021, when Biden's Secretary of State, Antony Blinken, first visited Brussels.

★★★

The initial US reluctance to discuss strategy on China with the EU is explained by the fact that, as a rule, Washington still prefers to work through NATO, of which it is the leading member, while it can never be a member of the EU. But NATO, a purely intergovernmental organisation, can only ever be an instrument of its members, whereas in many policy areas the EU is a player in its own right. This tangle has confused transatlantic relations ever since the creation of the EU in 1993.

NATO was, of course, created a long time before the EU, and the EU's predecessor, the EEC, played little or no role in foreign policy and defence. As a consequence, many in both the American and European strategic establishment still perceive a hierarchy in which NATO comes first and the EU second, as if the EU can only make decisions within a prior strategic framework set by NATO. In reality, things work the other way around: NATO's role is to provide a military instrument that is put to use within the framework of a grand strategy that is defined elsewhere. In Washington, as far as the US is concerned; in Brussels, as far as the EU member states are concerned. The transatlantic response to the Russian invasion of Ukraine illustrates the actual strategic 'line of command'. The European response depended on which relationship Europeans wanted to offer Ukraine, on the price that they were willing to pay for that, and on how they saw long-term relations with Russia itself. Of course, the Europeans took into account Washington's position, but they could only take these political and economic decisions collectively, through the EU. Within this broadly defined EU understanding, the European allies contributed military forces to Enhanced Forward Presence in the Baltics and Poland, under the NATO flag, while applying sanctions against Russia through the EU. Diplomatic initiatives at the highest level to end the conflict have mostly been undertaken by Germany and France. But their leverage also derives to a large extent from their membership of the EU: only the EU can apply or end economic and diplomatic sanctions; no individual European state will adopt sanctions unilaterally and confront Russia on its own.

In practice, the EU member states are often too divided to arrive at a common EU position. But in such cases, if they concern issues of grand strategy, the Europeans will not have much impact. Alone, even the largest European states cannot do much about the war in Ukraine, the war in Syria, or the rise of China. If the EU does adopt a strategy and it coincides with US strategy, then Europeans and Americans can have recourse to NATO if implementation requires military action. In those instances when the EU does not set strategy, NATO cannot fill the void, for it has neither the competence nor the authority to step in and decide on issues of foreign policy, trade and investment, or energy.

But even in its own area of defence NATO will find it difficult to act if the EU is divided. Absent an EU strategy, the majority of EU member states will have at most a token policy, for lack of leverage, or they may simply follow the US. If the lack of EU strategy is mostly the result of inertia, the US may still be capable of convincing many or most Europeans to follow its lead and to act jointly, either through NATO or through a broad coalition of the willing. If, however, the EU member states are actively divided on an issue, the US will find that it will then also be very difficult to mobilise NATO, or to have more than a handful of European states sign up for an ad hoc coalition. If the Europeans are divided when they meet in the EU, logically they will be no less divided when they meet in NATO or with the US. The example of the invasion of Iraq has already been mentioned: as the EU was split right down the middle, the US had to forego the active support of all but a few European allies. The 2011 air campaign during the civil war in Libya is another example: formally presented as a NATO operation, in reality it was a British-French-US led coalition that made use of the NATO command structure. Very few European allies participated, and the EU initially abstained, in the face of German disagreement with the intervention. In such cases, the EU's political and economic instruments and resources, many of which are controlled by the supranational European Commission, cannot be made available, or at least not from the start.

If the US and the EU want their partnership, and the NATO alliance, to run smoothly, they would be well advised to achieve a common understanding of the exact role that each should play. Unfortunately, many on both sides of the Atlantic see this as a zero-sum game – what the EU gains, NATO loses, and vice versa – and have dug in their heels. This never-ending debate within the 'Brussels bubble' and the 'Washington Beltway' is not set to come to a conclusion any time soon.

★★★

Instead, the changed focus of US grand strategy further complicates transatlantic defence arrangements. The EU is unique among the great powers in that it does not assume sole responsibility for its own defence. The Treaty on European Union does contain a collective defence guarantee, but most member states interpret that as just a symbolic expression of EU solidarity. The EU institutions do not plan for collective territorial defence, therefore, but leave this to NATO, even though this does not include all EU member states. NATO provides the defence planning to set force goals for its members; the contingency planning for actual operations to defend alliance territory; and the headquarters to command such operations. The backbone of the alliance is the US military, with the US nuclear umbrella as the ultimate guarantee of European security. Indeed, the credibility of NATO's ability to deter, and if necessary, to defend against aggression has come to rely mostly on the fact that the US is a member. That perception is not entirely wrong; as seen in Chapter 2, the Europeans can boast impressive troop numbers, but their readiness is limited. Most importantly, the Europeans are seen to lack the decisiveness of the other great powers. In an emergency, many feel that only the US could cajole NATO allies into resolute action. Fortunately, NATO has never had to face the test of an attack: its collective defence guarantee, embedded in Article 5 of the Washington Treaty, has only been invoked once, after the terrorist attacks on the US on 11 September 2001 – and the US politely declined NATO assistance. That does mean that the effectiveness of NATO deterrence rests even more on the perception that potential aggressors have of the resolve of the alliance as a whole and of the US in particular.

The US has adapted its national defence strategy, however, in the wake of the changes in its grand strategy, and that potentially has a great impact on NATO. After the Cold War, the US maintained a 'two-war standard': it aimed to be capable of fighting two regional wars, against regional powers, simultaneously. Now it has moved to a 'one-war standard' aimed at defeating another great power; it does not have the resources to fight two great powers at once.[23] For the US Department of Defense, the priority theatre is the Indo-Pacific – in other words, it no longer is Europe, and the great power to be defeated, if necessary, is China.[24] Hal Brands and Evan Montgomery fear that 'If American troops were involved in a major contingency but the United States lacked sufficient reserves to fight other rivals, then revisionist actors might see a window of opportunity to alter the status quo in their favour and jump through it while they had the chance'.[25] In other words, if the US were engaged in a major crisis in Asia, that might provoke aggressive moves on the part of Russia in Europe. Russia would be taking a serious gamble, though: it might score an early military success against hesitant Europeans, but it does not have the resources to win a great power war against the combination of Europe and the US, which would eventually come in. Moreover, nuclear deterrence still applies. Nevertheless, the Europeans had better taken into account that in future scenarios US reinforcements may arrive later and in smaller numbers than they had envisaged up until now. NATO's first line of defence will mainly consist of European conventional forces. How long should they be able to hold out, and where, until American (and Canadian) reinforcements land? Even during the Cold War, doubts existed, as expressed by Field Marshal Montgomery: 'In two world wars Europe has seen the United States watching from the touchline during the first two years of the war; the European nations do not want this to happen again.'[26] Replaying the Second World War would indeed not be an enticing prospect: if the opening battles are lost, all is lost, and one has to wait four years for the allies to land in Normandy.

The US have been demanding for a long time that the European allies increase their military capabilities. But the Europeans are stuck in a paradoxical vicious circle. They feel weak, so they rely on NATO and the US. Consequently, they are afraid of taking any initiative that might be construed as undermining NATO or loosening the bonds with the US. For European governments, therefore, thinking of a stronger European first line of defence is a taboo subject even within NATO, let alone in the EU. But as a result, the Europeans have stayed weak. Some in the European strategic establishment have fallen into an attitude of subservience towards the US – although the caprices of the Trump administration must have made even the staunchest Atlanticist doubt his convictions. A true alliance is in any case based on mutual respect rather than subservience. Or will Americans and Europeans come to see each other as is sometimes said of the Dutch and the Flemish? The Dutch like the Flemish, but they don't respect them; the Flemish respect the Dutch, but they don't like them. Arguably, unless the Europeans become confident that they can provide at least for their own conventional defence, while continuing to rely on the US nuclear umbrella, the EU can never be a fully sovereign great power. That does not mean that the Europeans would have to rebuild the massive armed forces that they maintained during the Cold War; they would need sufficient forces to make it clear to Russia that even against a European-only first line of defence, it could not win a short war.[27] It ought not to be anathema, for this was the original intention of NATO's founding in 1949: to help put the Europeans on their feet, so that the US need not maintain large forces in Europe.[28] Until the Europeans achieve such strength, the US is in a strong position to put pressure on them to align with its China strategy, or threaten consequences for NATO, even though Europeans may feel that focusing more on China would also detract from NATO's strength – another paradox.

Will the US forever accept the current state of affairs? Presumably not, yet Washington is partially to blame for the situation, as it perennially asks for more European defence spending but without accepting a greater European say in defence policy – that is the opposite of how politics works. The US has been facing this dilemma since the end of the Cold War. Should it continue to prioritise working with individual European allies, through NATO? That would make it easier to maintain American leadership – but of less capable allies. Or should it support defence integration, including through the EU, in the hope that this would render the Europeans militarily stronger and more capable of relieving the burden of the US, which could thus focus more on Asia, even if that would mean accepting a greater European role in decision making? Some in the US go even further: under the heading of 'restraint', Barry Posen has advocated the dissolution of NATO, in order to force the EU to mount its own defence structures, after which a new US–EU bilateral alliance could be concluded.[29] Others have called for a 'minimal exposure strategy' that would prioritise the need to push allies to defend themselves.[30] This remains an unlikely scenario, but since Trump no longer an inconceivable one; Europeans had better beware that this school of thought is gaining adherents in the American strategic establishment. Posen has similarly urged the US to force its Asian allies to assume more responsibility for their own defence.

Unlike Russia and China, the US is indeed at the centre of a worldwide network of alliances. As Sir Lawrence Freedman notes: 'No other country is so important to the security of so many others, and for that reason its performance is continually monitored by allies.'[31] Because of the rise of China, America's Asian allies find themselves in the forefront of US strategy. Arguably though, the US pivot to Asia hinges on a more capable Europe. One could even see US strategy focusing on the Indo-Pacific and EU strategy focusing on the Eurasian landmass as two arms of one grand strategy – if the US and the EU were to really concert their grand strategies, which has not been the case. NATO's main concern remains Russia. Security crises in Europe's southern periphery that do not directly threaten EU or NATO territory are increasingly dealt with by European coalitions of the willing – some with, some without US participation – rather than by NATO as a whole. In Asia, the trend goes in the opposite direction: states that each have a bilateral alliance with the US have started to concert more in the face of China's growing power.[32] Yet just like America's European allies, its Asian allies are seeking to maintain a fine balance: while hedging against China by deepening their military ties with the US, they also seek to maintain constructive relations with China. In order to maintain its alliances, the US must thus at the same time inspire confidence in its military might and its will to use it when necessary, and reassure its allies that it will not revert to the use of force unless absolutely necessary.

★★★

The words of Lord Palmerston, spoken in the House of Commons in 1848 when he was Britain's foreign secretary, are as valid as ever: 'We have no eternal allies, and we have no perpetual enemies. Our interests are eternal and perpetual, and those interests it is our duty to follow.' That is not a call to give up on alliances or to exchange current allies for new ones. Rather it is a warning: even within an alliance, each must continue to look after its own interests, for interests never overlap completely, and in the end the national interest will always come first. A state that no longer has the capacity to defend its own interests and relies entirely on its allies, is at risk of losing its independence. It also means that there may be an interest in diversifying one's alliances and partnerships, and that is exactly what the great powers have been doing.

Russia and China invested in the BRICS format, joining up with Brazil, India and South Africa for an annual summit since 2010. Although certainly the first two of these partners might one day become great powers, for now they are regional powers. More importantly, the interests of the BRICS countries are very diverse, and relations at times very tense. From May to July 2020, for example, in the midst of the corona crisis, clashes at the Chinese–Indian border left dozens of dead, bringing back memories of the 1962 border war in which thousands of troops fell. At the same time, reports came in of Russia delaying delivery of S400 anti-aircraft missiles to China, and speeding up delivery of the same to India. Consequently, the BRICS have not mustered sufficient unity to systematically forge a common ambition in international politics. Russia and China are also members of the Shanghai Cooperation Organisation (SCO), launched in 2001, together with four of the five Central Asian states, India and Pakistan. In the wake of the US and NATO interventions in Afghanistan, the SCO served to curb a further expansion of American influence in Central Asia. Its members focus on cooperation against security threats, in particular terrorism, but the SCO has also moved into the economic field. The SCO plays little or no role outside its own region, however, and even there the dynamic has shifted to China's BRI and Russia's Eurasian Economic Union.

Americans and Europeans set out to build new partnerships only more recently. The US was driven by the rise of China, and invested, for example, in the Quadrilateral Security Dialogue, better known as the Quad, with Australia, India and Japan. The Quad briefly existed from 2007 to 2008, but was revived in 2017, and is solidifying through combined military exercises. In July 2020, Japan's defence minister launched the idea of Japan joining the 'Five Eyes', the intelligence community of the US, the UK, Canada, Australia and New Zealand, strengthening its focus on China. In the same month, the US called for a broad 'alliance of democracies' aimed at curbing China's influence. This idea was not new: it was already on the table in 2003, when the US, having failed to secure UN Security Council authorisation for its planned invasion of Iraq, sought other frameworks that could legitimise the intervention. The Trump administration similarly seemed driven by its dislike of the EU and the less than enthusiastic reaction in NATO; a 'coalition of democracies' might bring America's European and Asian allies together and create more scope for stronger US leadership over their China strategies. Europeans, however, quietly ignored the 'alliance of democracies'. They had already reacted to both China's and the US' disregard for the rules-based order by announcing the creation of the Alliance for Multilateralism at the 2019 UN General Assembly. A Franco-German (rather than an EU) initiative, it is a network rather than an organisation, which seeks to build ad hoc coalitions on specific issues, with the overall aim of preserving international rules. The first meeting was attended by Canada, Chile, Ghana, Mexico and Singapore. Finally, both the US and the EU (as a 'non-enumerated' member) are in the G7, with Canada, France, Germany, Italy, Japan and the UK. Previously the G8, Russia's membership was ended after its invasion of Ukraine, thus making the G7 into a 'western' grouping again.

So far, these various new formats have not led to the emergence of two 'blocs', a Chinese-Russian and an American-European one. Most other states want to maintain cordial relations with all great powers, and the great powers have too many divergences among themselves. Arguably, the new partnerships that have the most concrete impact on international politics are those that creatively bring states together in new constellations that cut across great power competition. A good example of how such flexible diplomacy can work was the creation of a temporary mechanism to replace the WTO appellate body, which was blocked by the US, with a group comprising the EU, China and 14 other WTO members, on 27 March 2020. In this sense, the Alliance for Multilateralism holds more potential than an 'alliance of democracies'.

Another way of cutting across existing divides would be for the US to seek alignment with Russia against China – Nixon and Kissinger in reverse, as it were – a notion entertained by some in the US strategic establishment, including, in 2020, Trump's Secretary of State Mike Pompeo.[33] Trump actually proposed to invite Russia back into the G8, but the European members blocked that idea. A US–Russia alignment seems unrealistic in any case: Chinese and Russian interests are too far apart for those two great powers to turn their existing partnership into an alliance in the strict meaning of the term, but neither will they easily abandon it. Moreover, China has already built a massive presence in Russia's near-abroad; there is little that the US can offer Russia now that would better safeguard Russia's interests than cooperation with China itself. Much more pertinent is the risk of pushing China closer into Russia's arms, if Sino-American relations would become so confrontational as to make any form of cooperation impossible and leave only rivalry. In such a scenario, which limits its margin for manoeuvre anyway, China might yet opt for a much deeper partnership with Russia. That awareness should not stop the US, and the EU, from reacting adequately if their red lines are crossed. And, while recruiting Russia against China is asking too much, Washington and Brussels should remain aware of the opportunity to play into the differences that do exist between Moscow and Beijing, and to work with Russia and China separately on specific issues of common interest.

Vice versa, while the Trump administration was launching a trade war against China and adopting tariffs against the EU at the same time, there arguably was an opportunity for China to move closer to the EU, for example by quickly finalising the bilateral investment treaty that they had been negotiating for years, and thus increase the distance between Brussels and Washington. If Europeans had felt vindicated in their less confrontational strategy towards China, this approach might have had some success, though, of course, nobody in the European strategic establishment would trade in the alliance with the US for closer relations with China – Beijing could have gone only so far. The Chinese leadership, in any case, was too focused on the US or too intransigent even towards the EU to consider such a move. At the time when Trump lost the elections in November 2020, negotiations on the investment treaty were still dragging on. Only on 29 December 2020 did Brussels and Beijing announce agreement in principle on a new *Comprehensive Agreement on Investment* (CAI).

Nevertheless, the US and the Europeans will have to carefully manage their relations. After 70 years of existence, NATO is more likely to endure than to suddenly fall apart. Europeans and Americans are and will most likely remain each other's closest allies – in a world of increased great power competition, abandoning their alliance would not make sense. But how to run an alliance if the Europeans see Russia as the threat, and the Americans China? Divergence can be managed – but the trend is indeed that interests will diverge, so managing this will require more proactive commitment on both sides of the Atlantic. Europeans and Americans probably will also have to manage the balance of forces within the alliance. Europe should not become the Austria–Hungary of the 21st century: not a bad place to live, all things considered, but with the trappings of power rather than real military power and a complex decision-making system that in the end leaves it in a subordinate position to its main ally – imperial Germany for Vienna, the US for Brussels. The European strategic establishment ought to realise that NATO alone will not guarantee the European interest. Only the EU can stand up for the European interest in all dimensions of international politics. Just like the other great powers, therefore, the EU needs military as well as economic and political power – grand strategy is comprehensive.

5

Comprehensive: There Is No Hard, Soft or Smart Power – Just Power

Every state has political, economic and security interests, just like every issue in international politics has a political, economic and security dimension. Grand strategy has to be comprehensive, therefore, and tackle all three dimensions at once. A strategy that defines ends in only one dimension while ignoring the others is unlikely to achieve durable results. A state that does not develop instruments and muster resources in all three dimensions will soon run into situations in which it has no way of acting. A great power must thus surely be a power in political, economic and military terms in order to sustain its ambition to have global impact. Political power, that is the attractiveness of one's way of life as well as one's influence in another state or in an organisation (which can acquired by legal or illegal means), allows one to convince others to act in accordance with one's interests. Economic power can be a carrot as well as a stick, to entice another state or to coerce it, by offering or withholding trade, investment and development cooperation, or access to one's domestic market. Military power too can entice as well as coerce, offering assistance or threatening war.

Convincing, enticing and coercing, or hard and soft power, go hand in hand. The best strategists manage to convince the other so that they do not have to revert to coercion. but it is easier to convince or entice when the opposite party knows that you have the power to coerce it (through economic or military ways) if you decided to, even if the option is not openly put on the table. Diplomacy does not always need to be directly underpinned by economic and military power to be successful; a small state that acts as an honest broker can achieve remarkable success – but the actual parties to the negotiations will be aware of the balance of power and how they will fare if they do not find agreement. 'Diplomacy, underneath the conventions of form, recognises only realities', concluded De Gaulle.[1] Vice versa, the result of coercion will probably be more durable if afterwards the opposite party can be enticed into accepting it by the offer of political and economic benefits. Joseph Nye has coined the term 'smart power' for the integrated use of soft and hard power,[2] but one could also simply call it power, for power is indivisible. A state cannot just be a soft power. A power *has* power, in all dimensions, or it *is* not a power.

★★★

When a state intervenes in another state, the need for a comprehensive strategy, or the resulting problems if one does not have one, become most obvious. The US invasion of Iraq in 2003 has become a classic example of a strategy that was everything but comprehensive. After the resounding military defeat of the Iraqi armed forces, President George W. Bush, speaking on the aircraft carrier USS Abraham Lincoln, proclaimed the end of the war. But although the US never doubted its military success, it was not prepared for victory: it had no clearly defined political and economic ends, except the vague notion of bringing democracy to the country and the region. That had become the avowed objective only after Washington had had to admit that the Iraqi weapons of mass destruction that purportedly motivated the invasion were nowhere to be found. Absent a political and economic strategy to win over the Iraqi people, the conditions for real peace could not be created, the apparatus of the state was destroyed, and Iraq sank into a brutal civil war. In the severe judgement of Thomas Ricks, 'the US effort resembled a banana republic coup d'état more than a full-scale war plan that reflected the ambition of a great power to alter the politics of a crucial region of the world'.[3] At the beginning of the 2020s, Iraq remained a very weak state. The lesson must be that a state that does not manage to provide its citizens with the core public goods (security, prosperity and a say in decision making) will not have their full support; citizens that have joined (or have been pressed into) its armed forces will not risk their lives for it; and external powers will find it easy to gain influence among a population that is already disaffected.

Many in the European strategic establishment, including those who supported the invasion, heavily criticised the way the US handled it. But in Libya in 2011 the Europeans made exactly the same mistake. France and the UK convinced the US (not the other way around, as usual) to create a coalition and intervene in the civil war that had broken out in the wake of the 'Arab Spring' that had brought down the presidents of Tunisia and Egypt. With a mandate from the UN Security Council, the coalition launched an air campaign, thanks to which the opposition against President Muammar Qadhafi won the war – and then the Europeans and Americans left. Some blame must be put on the Libyan opposition which, unlike the Iraqi people, had asked for intervention. The opposition was very fragmented, agreeing on two things only: to get rid of Qadhafi, and to avoid any western boots on the ground afterwards. The Europeans yielded only too willingly, and delegated a half-hearted attempt to stabilise the country politically and economically to the UN. The result was that Libya entered the 2020s still in a state of civil war.

Lessons were learned, though. The victory of the Libyan opposition pushed many of the mercenaries who made up Qadhafi's armed forces into Mali. The ongoing civil war there subsequently escalated; when in 2012 armed rebels threatened to conquer the capital, Bamako, and to take over the state, the Europeans saw themselves forced to intervene again in order to avoid Mali following the fate of Libya – permanent fighting between ever-changing factions in a state in Europe's periphery. Since then, France (which undertook the initial intervention) and the EU and the UN (which followed up with a training and a peacekeeping operation respectively) have maintained a military presence in Mali, now as part of an overall strategy for the country and the region.[4] A comprehensive strategy is not a guarantee for success: Mali's problems have been contained rather than solved, and after initial progress the political and security situation deteriorated again, culminating on 18 August 2020 in a military coup by the army that the EU had been training. Brussels tacitly accepted the new government that the coup installed. Nevertheless, a comprehensive approach (or, as the EU calls it, an integrated approach) creates a chance of success that military action alone can never achieve.

★★★

Americans and Europeans have learned, through trial and error, that a comprehensive strategy is vital for success – though whether they will consistently apply that lesson in future interventions remains to be seen. Yet they were very much taken by surprise by the comprehensive nature of Russia's strategy against Ukraine. Russia's approach started with propaganda, promises of economic benefits and threats of economic reprisals, and propping up Russia-friendly political leaders, before moving to fomenting armed rebellion by covert arms deliveries and troop contributions (which quickly became known), and culminating in the invasion and annexation of the Crimea. This caused great alarm in the US, the EU and NATO over what has become known as 'hybrid warfare' or 'grey zone warfare'.[5] A hybrid approach and a comprehensive approach are the same thing, though: the integrated use of instruments in all dimensions of power in order to achieve one's ends – which is inherent to strategy since time immemorial. Many American and European observers would argue that the difference lies in the objectives: that Russia's ends were illegal under international law – that its hybrid approach is the comprehensive approach gone over to the dark side of the force. But the American invasion of Iraq was as illegal. The real reason why Americans and Europeans were so shaken is more likely that they were no longer used to them or their partners being the target of another power's strategy. Many feared that Ukraine was but the prelude to a wider 'hybrid war' against NATO and EU members, forgetting that prior to the Russian invasion a good part of the Ukrainian population was disaffected already, that after the invasion the large majority turned against Russia, however, and that similar actions against a NATO or EU member state would trigger their collective defence guarantees. This American and European alarmism led to a 'hybrid hysteria' that produced confusion rather than good strategy in response.

The indiscriminate use of the terms 'hybrid' or 'grey zone' warfare does not distinguish between situations of war and peace. Yet the difference is crucial: war means that a state has opted to use armed force to pursue its ends, and the targeted state will use force in self-defence. Force can be used legally, with a mandate from the UN Security Council or at the invitation of a state that requests assistance, or illegally. The point is that in both cases violence will be used and people will die, and the other party will retaliate in kind, until one way or another the conflict is settled. In peacetime, many states do at times pursue their ends by illegal ways, but short of using armed force, and the targeted state will limit its response as well. A 'grey zone' between the two does exist, because instruments other than the use of force can kill too. A cyber-attack on an air traffic control system, for example, could result in many casualties. So could, in previous days, a naval blockade of a country – killing without using force is nothing new. The targeted state could decide to interpret such action as an act of war and revert to the use of force in response – at which point the two states would ipso facto be at war. The 'grey zone' is but a transitory phase between peace and war, therefore; states are either at war or at peace. Pretending that there no longer is a distinction between war and peace is faulty, and can only result in confusion about which ends one is actually pursuing, and which ways are permissible under the circumstances. In war, the end is to militarily defeat the enemy, in order to force them to surrender or agree a ceasefire and make serious concessions on vital interests, or to create regime change. Such ends cannot be realistically pursued in peacetime – or if one attempts to, they can provoke war.

Since international politics is inherently comprehensive, and since every state with a modicum of strategic sense acts comprehensively all the time, in war and in peace, calling any specific set of actions 'hybrid' is a mere tautology. The term could therefore be dropped altogether. As confusing as the term 'hybrid' is the notion of 'weaponising' trade and investment.[6] This falsely suggests an unprecedented use of economic instruments, while in reality they have always served grand strategy. Moreover, 'weaponising' has connotations of aggression, but states evidently use economic instruments on a permanent basis, in war and in peace. It is more sensible to speak of 'geo-economics', analogous to geopolitics, although the term 'strategic economics' would be more accurate: the use of economic instruments to pursue the overall ends of grand strategy in addition to specific economic objectives. Geography is one but not the only factor shaping such use. Every academic dreams of coining a term that will enter into common usage, because one's original article will then be quoted forever more (though often without it being read). But if a new concept such as 'hybrid warfare' could, as Sir Lawrence Freedman points out, 'mean almost anything',[7] and blunts one's faculty to distinguish between war and peace, it is distinctly counterproductive. Instead, one should modulate one's strategy according to whether another state is pursuing its ends through war, coercion, or illegal or legal ways of enticing and convincing.

Every war sees the joint application of military, economic and political instruments, in new combinations – throughout history, many statesmen and generals have reverted to ruses to achieve surprise.[8] One only has to read about the Trojan horse in the Ilias to realise that Russia's war against Ukraine was not a display of dark new powers but a novel use of time honed tactics. Russia and China have also used some of the same tactics against states which with they are at peace. Both have used coercion, through economic and military ways, such as incursions into national airspace and territorial waters by the armed forces or paramilitary units, and the threat of cutting off energy supplies, imposing tariffs or reducing tourism. They have also engaged in subversion: illegal ways of enticing and convincing, in order to reduce the target state's capacity to exercise its sovereignty, such as spreading 'fake news', cyber-attacks (to collect data or to cause disruption), espionage, and corrupting politicians and other members of the strategic establishment. They also attempt, of course, to gain influence in perfectly legal ways, through propaganda, lobbying, sponsorship, market access, investment, and, specifically in the EU, by playing one member state off against another. And, one should not forget, by inviting academics for lunch. A state is not obliged to welcome even these legal activities on its territory and may take measures to curb them. The important thing is not to throw these various uses of power on one heap under the blurry heading of 'hybrid' but to design a specific response to each.

Yet the US, the EU and NATO have all created departments and adopted strategies to address 'hybrid threats'. These 'threats' are but instruments of strategy, however, and one cannot make strategy aimed at an instrument. A strategy against 'hybrid threats' is as meaningless as a war on terrorism; one cannot defeat a tactic – strategy should address the state (or non-state actor) that employs the tactic. Specific defensive measures must obviously be taken. If one fears aerial bombardment, one invests in air defence and shelters; if cyber-attacks are a likely threat, one builds up one's cyber defence. These and other measures are often grouped together under the heading of 'resilience'. They are really about safeguarding sovereignty: ensuring that no external power gains undue influence, so that the state can continue to make its own decisions. Some of these measures are in the province of the security services and the armed forces, but as grand strategy itself is comprehensive, 'resilience' too demands a state-wide approach at the grand strategic level, involving all departments of the government. States limit foreign investment in critical infrastructure, for example, have rules against foreign subsidies in specific sectors, diversify supply of critical resources, and support an indigenous production capacity in sensitive sectors. The aim is to prevent any foreign entity from gaining leverage to undermine state sovereignty. The corona crisis demonstrated that under certain circumstances, almost any sector of the economy can be leveraged, including the supply of face masks, for example. In the end, a 'resilient' state is a state that provides effective government and has the capacity to provide its citizens with all of the public goods that they legitimately expect, without interruption. The state must also communicate that effectively, in order for citizens to feel committed to the state.

Building up 'resilience' and defence is but the passive component of the response to coercion, subversion and influencing. Another issue is whether states can be deterred from employing such tactics by the threat of retaliation, or which types of retaliation are advisable if deterrence fails. A high-profile case of attempted murder on the territory of an EU member state provoked sharp condemnation and diplomatic countermeasures: in 2018, dozens of Russian diplomats were expelled from the EU after the failed poisoning by the Russian intelligence services of former Russian spy Sergei Skripal and his daughter Yulia in the UK (then still in the EU). In a similar case, in June 2020 Germany formally accused Russia of ordering the murder of a former Chechen rebel commander in Berlin's Tiergarten Park in 2019. More difficult is the question of how to sanction forms of coercion and subversion that do not result in the loss of life without provoking a further escalation. One option would be to apply 'cross-domain deterrence': deterring coercion or subversion in one area by threatening reprisals in another.[9] For example, an actual cyber-attack could be met with a cyber-attack in return, or with economic sanctions. On 30 July 2020, the EU for the first time adopted sanctions (a travel ban and freezing of assets) against two Russian and four Chinese individuals involved in subversion in the cyber sphere. The key issue always remains which states, with which interests, might use coercion or subversion against one, for which purposes. If one perceives Russian attempts at subversion, one does not just need an anti-subversion strategy – one needs a Russia strategy.

Americans and Europeans have been shocked into remembering that they too can be targeted by other states, but many appear to have forgotten that they have targeted others in the past, and still do. During the Cold War, Americans and Europeans regularly engaged in subversion. Various regimes in Latin America, Africa and Asia were brought down and replaced by a leader judged to be more amenable to the West.[10] In the 21st century, the US and the EU first of all seek to gain influence in other states through legal ways. In particular, they fund dissidents, human rights activists, trade unions and political parties in many countries, and sometimes leverage their economic power to promote respect for human rights and democratisation. Washington and Brussels stress that they pursue benign ends and only use legal ways, but the states on the receiving end may nevertheless perceive their actions as a form of subversion or coercion, and respond accordingly. What is democratisation for one is regime change for another. In addition to these overt attempts at influencing, the US and individual EU member states do also engage in covert activities, just like China and Russia. An illegal act by one power does not justify another to do likewise. But one must be aware that all great powers venture into illegality, and even though some do so more often than others, when Americans and Europeans put on too strong a show of moral outrage that rather detracts from their credibility. Before one can lead by example, one must actually set an example.

★★★

Not all great powers are equally powerful in all dimensions of power. Although their approach to a specific intervention might be very comprehensive at the tactical level, at the level of grand strategy comprehensiveness may be lacking, and that does have consequences.

The Russian invasion of Ukraine could be construed as a military victory and a great example of the tactical application of the comprehensive approach. But did it serve Russia's interests in the long term, at the grand strategic level? The Soviet military interventions in Hungary in 1956 and in Czechoslovakia in 1968 crushed any hope these countries had of an independent course, and scared the other satellite states of the Warsaw Pact into submission. Russian interventionism in the 21st century alienated the majority of Ukrainian public opinion, and caused concern even in the states most closely aligned with Russia, none of which wanted to see Russian troops on their territory. Moscow did prevent future EU or NATO membership for Ukraine, but, arguably, the EU benefited more, for it gained a western-oriented buffer state on its eastern border. The EU never describes Ukraine as such but, in reality, that is what its geopolitical position amounts to. At the same time, the EU acquired an interest in building Ukraine into an effective state, which remains a tall order – it did not take too long for a degree of Ukraine-fatigue to set in in Brussels.

Russia's grand strategic objective of creating an exclusive sphere of influence seems difficult to realise if the main instrument used to pursue it is military force. Moscow does have a political and economic project, the Eurasian Economic Union, but it does not possess sufficient political and economic power to render it attractive to the target states. In the political sphere, Russia positions itself as standing up for the rights of Russian speakers in other countries. But by linking this linguistic, cultural and religious bond to military posturing and hinting at the possibility of intervention, Russia hardens resistance against it in the states concerned. In the assessment of Dmitri Trenin, 'This is the core of Russia's soft power, but thinking of it in hard-power terms only destroys it.'[11] The Russian communities' desire for interference from Moscow is limited, certainly in the Baltic states but even elsewhere, as long as the Russian way of life offers little or no improvement over their current situation. Russian popular culture does not have any traction beyond the Russian-speaking communities. To the extent that Russia has political influence, it is based on subversion more than attraction. Russia does have economic power, but often uses it as a way of coercion, for example by threatening to reduce energy supplies. That does not serve to increase its attractiveness either. Apart from energy (which accounts for over half of Russian exports), other natural resources and arms, Russia exports preciously little beyond its immediate neighbours. No Russian products are to be found in the world's shopping malls.

The contrast with China is huge: Chinese smartphones and computers are sold the world over, and other consumer goods, such as cars, are bound to follow. China uses its economic power to pursue its interests in a most creative way, as the next chapter will analyse, and has thus gained enormous political influence. It does not hesitate to use its economic power coercively as well, threatening to reduce trade and investment to deter states from certain courses of action, such as banning Chinese telecom firm Huawei from bidding for the 5G network. Chinese diplomats everywhere have become very assertive, at times using quite undiplomatic language to condemn policies in the host country that China disagrees with. That is a double-edged sword, however: using economic power to 'punish' other states creates distrust and provokes calls for economic decoupling. Furthermore, China's political power per se, its attractiveness, is, like Russia's, much more limited than its economic power. There is a large Chinese diaspora, but it is a safe haven for critics of the regime as much as a source of influence in the countries concerned. People buy Chinese products, not the Chinese way of life. Beijing may serve as a model to authoritarian leaders, but citizens even in less prosperous countries find little to attract them. For now, Chinese popular culture also has but limited appeal beyond the Chinese-speaking world. Nevertheless, thanks to its smart use of its economic power, China has enticed many members of the strategic establishment in many states.

Under the leadership of Xi Jinping, however, China began to deploy its military power much more assertively as well, although, arguably, it was being very effective in achieving its ends relying mostly on political and economic power. The construction of military bases on islands and artificial features in the South China Sea and the unilateral announcement of an air defence identification zone amount to a de facto annexation of what the other great powers and the other littoral states consider to be partly international waters and partly other countries' exclusive economic zones. The results have been mixed. On the one hand, China has created a fait accompli that will be difficult to undo, short of military action. On the other hand, the assertive use of the military instrument has cast grave doubts over China's discourse of peaceful rise and harmonious development, and has created great suspicion of China's true intentions. Several neighbouring states have intensified their military cooperation with the US; a regional arms race has well and truly started. Even several EU member states, notably France and from 2021 also Germany, participate in 'freedom of navigation operations' (FONOPS) in the South China Sea. For Beijing, that might be a price worth paying, however, for greatly enhancing the protection of its sea lines of communication against the threat of interruption by the US in case of a confrontation. Moreover, China can use its economic power to mitigate the consequences of its military actions, through a mix of coercion and incentives. Under President Rodrigo Duterte, the Philippines, for example, have vacillated back and forth between China and the US. Once again, one notices that even China's provocative actions in the South China Sea are not sufficient to change most states' preferred strategy of maintaining working relations with both Beijing and Washington.

There is a limit to how far China can go, however, in such assertive or even aggressive use of the military. The Chinese saying *wu ji bi fan* means that things go into reverse when pushed to the extreme: if China pushes too hard, it risks provoking more active push-back or even retaliation, including with military means. Even now, there is a great risk of incidents between American and European forces engaged in FONOPS and Chinese coastguard and military units assertively defending China's claims. Warning shots could hit a target, scrambling fighter aircraft could crash into each other – and the resulting crisis would undoubtedly lead to high tension. There is an internal limit to the use of military force too: will public opinion support it? In the case of China, the public would likely support a war to maintain China's territorial integrity as presented by the CCP – including Taiwan and the South China Sea. Increasingly nationalist propaganda has prepared the public for such eventuality. It is more doubtful whether the Chinese public would be supportive of the use of force for other reasons, unless it felt provoked by another state. Even in the case of Russia, which has a strategic culture more prone to the use of force, public support for military intervention is limited. The government felt obliged to obfuscate and hide the number of casualties in Ukraine, for example. But the more China and Russia stir up nationalist feelings, and the more the US does the same in response, the more the constraints on the use of force will be loosened.

★★★

The US is the most powerful of the great powers in all dimensions of power. It enjoys enormous influence, thanks to its economic power, but also thanks to the spread of American culture, and the attractiveness to many people of the American way of life. And yet the US often has recourse to military posturing or the actual use of force, including in the 21st century. In Richard Betts' analysis, American military interventions after the Cold War have been driven more by what the US strategic establishment saw as opportunities than by actual threats: 'Instead of countering immediate dangers, American policy aimed to stabilise the world in order to prevent dangers from arising.'[12] Rather than preventing dangers, however, American interventionism has created new risks. A lack of attention for the political and economic dimension led to failure in Iraq, as related above, and in Afghanistan: the US ousted the Taliban government in 2001, but on 29 February 2020 concluded a peace agreement with the same Taliban movement providing for the withdrawal of foreign troops. Even President Obama, who sought to end the 'forever wars' as they had been dubbed, ordered a surge in the number of troops first, in a repetition of the US engagement in Vietnam, where the war was intensified before it could be ended.

American interventionism often undermines rather than strengthens the confidence of its allies and partners. In the course of the heated exchange between President Trump and North Korean President Kim Jong-Un in 2019, for example, allies around the world began to worry more about the US escalating the crisis than about Pyongyang's nuclear weapons programme that actually caused the crisis in the first place. Similarly, America's European allies were rattled by the threat of war against Iran, and were pushed into defending the regime in Tehran for not breaking the nuclear deal, even though the EU had little sympathy for the Iranian government per se. The willingness to make active use of its powerful military is a tenet of American strategic culture, however; in combination with American exceptionalism, it can lead to a very activist strategy, which can usually count on strong public support. And vis-à-vis real or potential adversaries, it remains a very powerful deterrent. This explains why former US Defence Secretary Robert Gates, in an article condemning the 'over-militarisation' of American foreign policy, also stated that a 'strong military underpins every other instrument of American power, and so every president must ensure that the US military is the strongest and most technologically advanced in the world, capable of dealing with threats from both nonstate actors and great powers'.[13]

The US has also never hesitated to use its economic power to coerce, rather than to entice, other states. Notorious was the case of Japan: when in the 1980s the Japanese economy boomed and Americans who felt threatened began to talk of an 'economic Pearl Harbour', the US launched, and won, a trade war, which directly led to Japan's 'lost decade' from the mid-1980s to the mid-1990s. Using tariffs against an ally was not a new thing, therefore, yet when under President Trump the US also imposed trade restrictions on the EU, Canada, Mexico and other allies and partners, their surprise at being targeted was still great. Washington sought to force allies and partners to align with it on specific issues, such as Iran, or the role of Huawei in 5G. More purely economic reasons clearly played a role in the latter example, as it did in Washington's quest to prevent Europeans from building the Nordstream 2 pipeline to Russia. Ostensibly this was out of security concerns, but the US was also eying its own energy exports to Europe – a clear example of how allies are competitors at the same time. Some in the US even suggested to link diversification of Europe's energy supply as well as adherence to US sanctions regimes to America's contribution to NATO.[14] US sanctions greatly undermined the European trust in America: once Washington had used sanctions to stop Europeans from trading with one country, the fear arose that it could forbid trade with others as well.

Surprise and concern were even greater, notably in the EU, when in 2018 the Trump administration started a trade war against its perceived rival: China. Europeans and Americans had identified many of the same problems with barriers to market access and discrimination of foreign companies in China, but the EU was wary of a confrontational approach. To some extent the EU benefited from the clash between the US and China: as China was unwilling to enter into a dispute with the world's other largest economy at the same time, Beijing adopted a somewhat more conciliatory approach to Europe. Fundamentally, however, the trade war served mostly to harden attitudes in both Washington and Beijing. The US measures could in any case never have met the avowed objective of restoring jobs in American industry; production simply moved from China to other low-cost producing countries.[15] Tariffs are a blunt tool.[16] Both the US and China suffered, in fact, with American consumers facing higher prices and Chinese companies losing exports,[17] while the rest of the world entered the 2020s fearing further escalation and a disastrous ripple effect throughout the global economy. American (and European) complaints about China's lack of reciprocity in its economic relations were justified, but moving from competition to rivalry in response did not prove immediately beneficial for anybody. One American observer called it 'mutually assured economic destruction'.[18]

★★★

The EU not only does not assume sole responsibility for its own territorial defence, as seen in the previous chapter; it also has limited power projection capacity. Of more than 1.3 million men and women in uniform, at most 10 per cent are estimated to be available for expeditionary operations. Given that forces on operations rotate every four months, this means that only one third of these or some 40 to 50,000 troops can be deployed at any one time. This is a sizeable number – only the US can do better – and as they deploy regularly, the armed forces of many EU member states have a core of very well experienced troops, but they are obviously not very cost-effective. In comparison, the US was able to deploy some 250,000 troops on operations in Afghanistan and Iraq out of similar overall troop numbers, while maintaining hundreds of thousands more in permanent overseas bases.

More important, however, is the perception that Europeans lack the will to use force. European strategic culture has indeed become markedly reticent to go to war, as a result of Europe's own bloody historical experience, in particular the mass slaughter in the trench warfare of the First World War and the genocidal Second World War. 'It is not the horrors of war that will deter any virile young man from welcoming it, but the plain truth that, instead of a gallant adventure, he is setting out on a farcical futility': the sentiment expressed by Sir Basil Liddell Hart, who had been gassed during the 1916 Battle of the Somme, remains very strong.[19] That acts as a useful brake on military adventurism: interventionists are always better at starting wars than at ending them with any measure of success. For a long time, many in the European strategic community celebrated this lack of power projection capacity and presented Europe as a 'civilian power' that had consciously abjured the use of force. But the same states who made up the EEC and then the EU were always members or partners of a military alliance, NATO, so they obviously never abandoned military power as an instrument of statecraft. They just organised themselves militarily in one organisation, and economically in another; with the creation of the EU and its foreign and defence policies, all strands of European cooperation, in all dimensions of power, came together under one roof.

Acquiring military power did not undermine the EU's political and economic power, as some pretended;[20] rather its absence had weakened its impact. The EU should take care, as Sir Hew Strachan warns, not to 'to see itself in insular terms, cocooned from the great power rivalries emerging in the Pacific, and clothed in a regional bubble of atypical but seemingly eternal security'.[21] If other states come to believe that the Europeans will almost never use force, not even when important interests are directly at stake, they will not take Europe's red lines into account. As a result, they may undertake actions that effectively threaten European security and will actually necessitate a military response. The paradox is that if the EU had a more credible power projection capacity, it would probably have to intervene less often, for it would have a deterrent effect. If other players knew that Europeans would act, with military means if necessary, if their red lines were crossed, that would affect their calculations, and they would likely be more amenable to European diplomatic and economic approaches. In the EU, just like in the other great powers, all dimensions of power reinforce each other.[22]

The above-mentioned case of Libya is a clear illustration of what happens when the EU's neighbours ignore Brussels. After the 2011 air campaign, European military involvement in the ongoing civil war was limited to an ineffective naval operation – it proved incapable either of stemming the flow of migration to Europe or of enforcing the arms embargo, but at least it contributed to saving people from drowning when attempting to cross the Mediterranean. The EU formally supported the UN-recognised Government of National Accord (GNA) in Tripoli, but Brussels did little in practice either to forge a deal to end the civil war with the forces of Benghazi-based Field Marshal Khalifa Haftar or to provide military assistance. Where the EU left a void, others moved in: Turkey on the side of the GNA, Russia and Egypt on the side of Haftar. In fact, the EU itself became divided, as even France at one point began to support Haftar.[23] The country on Europe's doorstep thus became the theatre of another proxy war. Turkey and Egypt were both eying Libya's energy resources, while Russia could entertain hopes of establishing a second Mediterranean military base in addition to Tartus in Syria.

The EU does have great economic power. Introducing yet another label, Ian Manners dubbed the influence that the EU wields thanks to the size of its market its 'normative power'.[24] As Brussels often imposes the most advanced rules, for example in the areas of food safety, environmental impact and data protection, foreign producers adopt EU standards so their products can then be exported to other markets with less stringent standards too. This so-called 'Brussels effect' should not be exaggerated.[25] The EU exercises its 'normative power' in many technical fields – it does not wield similar influence in the political realm. Like the American way of life, the European way of life is attractive to many people across the world; hence, both attract many people aspiring to become citizens. But this attractiveness to people does not mean that other states necessarily recognise the European democracy as the norm; nor can economic power easily be put to use to promote it. The EU tried to, by way of conditionality: linking partnership and support to political change, but the target states mostly introduced but token reforms, and the EU in the end usually did not insist and disbursed its funds anyway. 'Normative power' as such cannot be the basis of a comprehensive grand strategy, therefore. Setting technical norms and standards is a major source of influence in itself, however. The EU cannot take it for granted: as China's market size grows, and as in some high-technological areas it has advanced further than the EU, the struggle for 'normative power' will intensify, for example in the Eurasian countries targeted by China's BRI.

In crisis situations, the EU is not always able to leverage its economic power. When the US withdrew from the Iran nuclear deal and installed sanctions against any companies doing business with Iran, the EU in January 2019 created a special purpose vehicle, the Instrument in Support of Trade Exchanges (INSTEX). This was meant to allow trade to continue by avoiding the US dollar and the Society for Worldwide Interbank Financial Telecommunication (SWIFT), the network for communications between financial institutions from which Iran had been excluded. European companies did not trust the mechanism to effectively shield them from US sanctions, however. Determined to preserve their access to the US market above anything else, they were not prepared to take any risks and refrained from using INSTEX, and trade with Iran collapsed. Only in March 2020 was INSTEX used for the first time, and then only to send medical supplies to Iran in the face of the corona pandemic. The EU did maintain its position in favour of the JCPOA, and EU member states refused, for example, to join the naval operation that the US deployed in the Persian Gulf in 2019 in order to deter Iran. Instead, a number of EU member states joined the French-led operation, European Maritime Awareness in the Strait of Hormuz (EMASOH). But the EU alone could not normalise relations with Iran and remove the regime's fear of military intervention, the two objectives that Tehran had sought to achieve through the nuclear deal.[26] The result was that Iran was driven to seek closer relations with Russia and China. Russia and Iran were already acting alongside each other in the war in Syria. China and Iran in 2020 negotiated a 25-year partnership agreement, including military exchanges – not the outcome that the Trump administration had foreseen.

★★★

The EU's inability to translate its power into effect has to do with its weak strategic culture and its composite nature, which results in hesitant decision making and a lack of resolve. In the military field, it is also a result of the fragmentation of its capabilities, and of European states thinking small.

During the Cold War, when America's European allies focused on territorial defence, the building block of NATO's combined force structure was the army corps, typically of 50 to 60,000 troops. Even the smaller allies, such as my own country Belgium, contributed a self-sufficient corps. That corps was pre-positioned in Germany: each national corps took its place in the line along the Iron Curtain, and was supported by the multinational NATO command structure and a few specific multinational assets, such as the radar aircraft of the Airborne Warning and Control System (AWACS). After the Cold War, the focus of the European strategic establishment shifted to expeditionary operations around Europe, until in 2014 the Russian invasion of Ukraine put territorial defence, now of a much expanded NATO, firmly back on the agenda. At the start of the 2020s, expeditionary operations still continued unabated, however, in particular in Europe's southern periphery. Several European states also deployed the armed forces at home to support the security services in the fight against terrorism, in the wake of a wave of attacks from ISIS in 2014–2016, and some had recourse to the military to assist in the fight against COVID-19.

As they enter the 2020s, many European states find themselves struggling to reconcile all of these commitments. Most have abolished conscription, all have reduced the size of the professional armies, and all went through a long period of reducing the defence budget. As a result, Europe sees a plethora of small-scale armed forces, almost none of which represent by themselves a comprehensive force package with the required capabilities in army, navy and air force to undertake all types of operations, including combat. When necessary, most or all units are employable for 'homeland security' tasks. Even those not usually carrying a rifle, such as signals or logistics, can patrol the streets. For expeditionary operations though, most European states already count a mere infantry battalion (5 to 600 troops) as a major deployment – if they do not think in terms of just companies or half-companies (1 to 200). Only the largest European states can deploy as much as a brigade (some 5,000 troops) abroad, and even then only if other Europeans or, in most cases, the US provide support. Europe lacks 'strategic enablers': the capabilities that make power projection possible, such as sea and air transport, intelligence (based on satellites, aircraft and others), command and control structures and so on, without which no significant operations in terms of size and intensity can be undertaken. More European forces are supposed to be employable for the defence of the national territory, of course. But for most European states the forward deployment of forces, such as NATO's Enhanced Forward Presence (EFP) in the Baltic states and Poland, in practice amounts to an expeditionary operation, and thus the same constraints apply.

Since 1999, when the EU created what is now called the Common Security and Defence Policy (CSDP), its member states have been paying lip service to the idea of increasing military cooperation as the logical answer to the fragmentation of the European defence effort. More than 20 years later, however, limited progress has been achieved, although promising new instruments have been created: Permanent Structured Cooperation (PESCO) between 25 of the 27 member states who in 2017 signed up to binding commitments, and a European Defence Fund (EDF) of €1 billion per year as from 2021, the first time that defence entered on the budget of the European Commission. If the member states of the EU decide that they need to be able to undertake expeditionary operations autonomously – without support from non-EU countries – and perhaps also assume more responsibility for their own territorial defence, the only way forward seems military integration. Instead of focusing on interoperability, that is the ability for units from different countries to operate alongside each other, they could be integrated in permanent multinational formations.

Taking the army as the example for how European military integration could operate, the building blocks could be national brigades, the largest army unit that with a few exceptions every EU member state is still able to field. But just a very few member states still possess the full range of combat support and combat service support units that should frame a brigade's manoeuvre units (the infantry battalions), hence in many operational scenarios many brigades cannot be used. A brigade without an air defence unit, for example, can be deployed in hardly any expeditionary scenario, as even irregular opponents such as ISIS now have access to commercial drones that are easily weaponised. By combining national brigades into multinational divisions and corps, member states, first, could pool their support units, thus ensuring that the division or corps as a whole would have the full range of required support capabilities. Second, they could maximally harmonise all future equipment between the brigades; today, European states waste heaps of money by continuing to use a multitude of different weapons and equipment. Third, the states that make up the multinational division or corps could acquire the strategic enablers needed to deploy it together, so that they can project it without having recourse to assets of others. Similar schemes could easily be applied to naval and air forces, using frigates and squadrons as the building block. The EU member states that would create such integrated capabilities could still use them under any flag: NATO, the UN, the EU itself, or an ad hoc coalition of the willing.

Whether all or some EU member states are really willing to abandon the illusion of military sovereignty in favour of actual collective sovereignty (as they have done in many domestic policy areas) remains an open question.

★★★

The most absolute instrument of power that the great powers (and a few others) possess are nuclear weapons. Unfortunately, they cannot be un-invented, which means that the five nuclear weapon states that are recognised by the Treaty on the Non-Proliferation of Nuclear Weapons – China, France, Russia, the UK and the US – will likely maintain their arsenal until a reliable way is found to mutually disarm.

For the EU, however, nuclear weapons are a taboo topic, although one of its members, France, is a nuclear weapon state. Some plead for nuclear disarmament, but one should heed Field Marshal Montgomery's warning from the Cold War that this would risk leaving the entire EU as a buffer zone between the other great powers: 'On no account can we allow [Europe] to become a sort of "hedgehog" between two great giants who alone have the latest weapons.'[27] Every few years a predictably inconclusive debate re-emerges about whether France ought to 'Europeanise' its *Force de frappe* and create a European deterrent. Paris has stated in the past that its vital interests are not limited to French territory. The 2019 Treaty of Aachen between France and Germany also states that they will use all means at their disposal to assist each other in case of an armed attack.[28] But this is short of a formal nuclear umbrella for Germany, let alone for the EU. The 21 EU member states who are members of NATO thus continue to rely on the US nuclear guarantee. Arguably, the EU could only achieve full strategic autonomy if it provided its own nuclear deterrent but, as we have seen, it is already a challenge for the Europeans to provide for their own conventional defence. 'Extended nuclear deterrence' – the US accepting the risk of nuclear war on behalf of its allies in Europe as well as in Asia – thus remains the order of the day. As Sir Lawrence Freedman and Jeffrey Michaels note, however: 'The fact that these guarantees have stayed in place for over 60 years is impressive, but it is a long time since they have been tested, and their foundations are becoming more fragile.'[29] President Trump repeatedly hinted that European and Asian allies who in his estimation had not contributed enough towards their own defence might not be able to count on

America's full support – a grave undermining of deterrence, which is all about perception and trust. Europeans certainly feared the impact on Russia's strategic calculus. China, though, might actually prefer the US nuclear umbrella if the alternative is that some of its neighbours, such as Japan, would be tempted to develop their own nuclear arsenal.[30]

The US does continue to modernise its nuclear arsenal, partly in reaction to Russia putting more emphasis on nuclear weapons again in its defence strategy. In a worrying evolution, both Russia and the US have returned to considering tactical nuclear weapons: low-yield weapons that, supposedly, can be used on the battlefield without escalating into a full-scale nuclear war in which the opponent's entire territory would be targeted. In reality, it seems crucial to maintain an absolute nuclear threshold, for once it is crossed, it is difficult to see how escalation can be avoided. Another negative development is that the fabric of arms control and disarmament treaties has been greatly weakened. In 2019, for example, the Trump administration withdrew from the Intermediate-Range Nuclear Forces Treaty (INF), in response to Russia's violation of its prohibition to develop missiles with a range of 500 to 5,500 kilometres. The US also voiced its position that given the changing power constellation, the major arms control treaties, all dating back to the US–USSR confrontation, would become meaningless if not joined by China. Beijing immediately responded that it did not feel concerned, however. Possessing a much smaller arsenal than the US and Russia, China fears for the viability of its second-strike capability: the guaranteed capacity to retaliate with nuclear weapons against any nuclear attack, no matter how severe.[31] The trend for the future of arms control and disarmament looks negative, therefore. Probably only a joint initiative by all four great powers could reverse it.

★★★

At the other extreme from nuclear weapons is the power of attraction. In the wake of the 2020 coronavirus outbreak, all four great powers have lost a lot of soft power and credibility, both internally and externally.[32] In China, authorities at different levels initially reacted very slowly and attempted to cover up the situation, until it exploded in their faces. It is doubtful whether the spread to other countries could have been prevented even had China acted earlier; there were already signs of the virus' presence in Europe at the end of 2019, for example. Furthermore, even as the severity of the outbreak in China became clear, governments and the public outside Asia continued to see it as just another 'alien' virus that would pass them by, just like the 2003 SARS outbreak had had little impact beyond Asia. In the

EU, Russia and the US, governments all took resolute measures only when the reality of the pandemic hit them in the face. Nevertheless, China's initial mismanagement showed a callous disregard for human life, which brought back memories of the worst excesses of Mao's days, and greatly damaged the legitimacy of the CCP with the public. The regime then used all its power to organise an effective 'lockdown' to bring the pandemic under control, while donating or (more often) selling face masks and other medical supplies to other countries, in particular in Europe, in order to demonstrate to Chinese citizens that it was on top of things – what better proof than images of grateful Europeans? Within the EU at least, people were unlikely to forget China's original failure though, so the impact of its 'mask diplomacy' was limited.

The first Russian reaction to the pandemic that anyone noticed was a widespread disinformation campaign, alternatively blaming the US, Europe and China for the outbreak. Early on, President Putin also sent aid to Italy, in military aircraft marked 'from Russia with love' – one assumes that Russian forces in Syria and Ukraine use other markings. Within Russia, measures were but grudgingly adopted until the nature of the problem could no longer be denied. In the US, Trump started by pretending that the coronavirus was just a Democrat hoax, before shifting gear and blaming everything on China. It took months for Trump to recognise the severity of the crisis and even then the measures taken were chaotic and incomplete. Not until late July 2020 did Trump finally accept the value of face masks. The image presented to the world was unprecedented and greatly dented the credibility of the US. Furthermore, the US remained strikingly absent from the international scene. Instead of taking the lead in international solidarity and coordination, Trump withdrew the US from the WHO, leaving the field wide open to China's diplomacy. The EU as such could not act on the health crisis, because member states never gave it authority in that area; the EU is better placed to deal with swine flu than with any human flu. Many national governments acted selfishly at first, refusing export of medical supplies to fellow member states and closing borders without any coordination. Even when deciding on the EU strategy for recovery, some of the wealthiest member states showed their narrow-mindedness rather than their solidarity. Much later than China, but before agreement on its own recovery strategy was reached, the EU also started providing foreign aid, reorienting more than €15 billion of existing funds for external action to support partner countries across the globe.

All of the great powers thus came out of the corona crisis with their reputation damaged. In dealing with the pandemic, none of them proved to be much of a power at all, in fact, in spite of their resources. Clearly, their approach to the threats and challenges confronting them was not comprehensive enough.

★★★

Hard power works best for those who have soft power. The use of economic or military coercion does achieve results, but rendering them acceptable to the strategic establishment and the public in the target state, as well as in other states and powers, requires convincing and enticing. Results that are not accepted, will not be durable: local players will attempt to undo them, and other powers with interests there may be tempted to intervene. Paradoxically, it is much easier therefore to coerce one's friends than one's enemies, as both the US and China have discovered. Allies and partners will want to preserve good relations and economic benefits, and will, therefore, often be more amenable to pressure. Once states have become rivals, however, coercion will often just provoke retaliation, certainly among (near) peer competitors, as the indecisive US–China trade war shows. Moreover, as tensions between the great powers intensify, they are increasingly inclined to support states that are targeted by another power, like Russia and China support Iran against the US. This also means that one should be careful how much pressure one puts on a partner before pushing it into the other camp. Clearly, the blunt use of power can be counterproductive – power must be put to use in a creative way.

6

Creative: An Art as Well as a Science

Grand strategy is more than planning. Planning is necessary: the strategist needs to plan how to mobilise the resources that the strategy requires. He must also plan for the implementation, simultaneously or successively, of the various instruments that he has chosen to achieve his desired ends. The force of habit and the weight of procedure often reduce this to a linear process: budgets are allocated, the means are acquired within that framework, and then put to use in the same way as before, without exploring alternative ways or reassessing the ends. This creates the false impression that whenever the ends are not met, the answer simply is to increase the means or, in military terms, to put more boots on the ground. Such a mechanistic approach leads to unimaginative and hence sub-optimal strategy: 'ends + ways + means = (bad) strategy', as Jeffrey Meiser puts in an appropriately formulaic manner.[1] What is missing is creativity: the stroke of the imagination, and occasionally of genius, that will lead the strategist to combine instruments in new ways, or to design entirely new instruments, and to settle on novel ends in order to safeguard the interests of the state. Even a genius has to take into account the available resources, of course; that is why Field Marshal Slim wrote that 'Imagination is a necessity for a general, but it must be a controlled imagination'.[2] Nevertheless, creativity makes all the difference; that is why strategy is an art as much as a science. In Churchill's words:

> We often hear military experts inculcate the doctrine of giving priority to the decisive theatre. There is a lot in this. But in war this principle, like all others, is governed by facts and circumstances; otherwise strategy would be too

easy. It would become a drill-book and not an art; it would depend upon rules and not on an instructed and fortunate judgement of the proportions of an ever-changing scene.[3]

'Instructed judgement', Churchill says: strategy can be taught – or I would not have written this book – but only up to a point. Since strategy is based on reason, everyone can learn its principles and the method of making strategy, just like everyone can learn how to play a musical instrument. But not everybody will have the talent to become a star musician or a leading strategist. Becoming a leading armchair strategist is an aspiration that it is easier to fulfil; but the role of the academic study of strategy should not be derided. Unless they themselves have served in government, no academic student of strategy will indeed know whether, given the chance to occupy a position of responsibility, they would make good strategic decisions. Yet that does not mean that an academic cannot give sound advice or help educate those who will be strategists. A naturally talented musician will still have to learn how to read a music sheet; the music teacher need not be a world-famous composer. Similarly, a talented politician, diplomat or military officer will perform even better when equipped with the theory and history of strategy; the professor who lectures on it need not have won a battle or concluded a treaty himself.

Strategic studies is an applied science: its principles are developed not for the satisfaction that can be derived from the beauty of a theory, but to be put to use in practice. If the expectations of theory obscure the view of what is actually happening, cloud judgement and stifle creativity, theory becomes counterproductive or even, as Sir Hew Strachan puts it, 'positively pernicious'.[4] Clausewitz explained the purpose of strategic studies thus:

> Theory exists so that one need not start fresh each time sorting out the material and ploughing through it, but will find it ready to hand and in good order. It is meant to educate the mind of the future commander, or, more accurately, to guide him in his self-education, not to accompany him to the battlefield.[5]

The same holds true for the diplomat at the negotiating table and the politician in a cabinet meeting. Historically, many leading politicians, diplomats and military officers not only did their job, therefore, but studied it as well. Field Marshal Montgomery recounted how he came to study strategy:

I had read somewhere the remarks of Frederick the Great when speaking about officers who relied only on their practical experience and who neglected to study; he is supposed to have said that he had in his Army two mules who had been through 40 campaigns, but they were still mules.[6]

The armed forces were usually first to establish defence colleges and institutionalise study. After the Second World War, comprehensive colleges and courses were set up that brought together the military, diplomacy and politics, such as the National War College in Washington, created in 1946. The EU, as a new entity, was the last to launch an analogous body, in 2005: the European Security and Defence College (ESDC). The ESDC launched its first course at the level of grand strategy, the Advanced Strategic Course, in 2020, at the initiative of Belgium's Egmont Institute, together with the Institut d'Hautes Études de Défense Nationale (IHEDN) from Paris and the Bundesakademie für Sicherheitspolitik (BAKS) from Berlin.

Education in strategic studies, in combination with merit-based promotion, is necessary also to identify promising strategists. No state can rely for its grand strategy solely on the presence of a genius, for not every generation will produce one, and even if it does, genius is not always recognised or appreciated. German Chancellor Otto von Bismarck certainly was a strategic genius, managing not only to unite the various German principalities into an empire, but also to consolidate its position in Europe through a network of alliances with the other great powers. Yet in 1890, two years after assuming the throne of the German empire, Wilhelm II had enough of the 'iron chancellor' and dismissed Bismarck, and his sound strategy with him. Subsequent German grand strategy, improvised by a capricious emperor, weak chancellors, and political generals and admirals, would become a study in failure. If that constellation seems familiar: François Heisbourg has in effect compared Wilhelm II to Donald Trump.[7]

★★★

Late Wilhelmine Germany allowed Bismarck's alliance system to unravel and made many enemies. A most successful example of creative grand strategy from antiquity shows how a power can co-opt its enemies instead. Luttwak exposes how the 'genius of Byzantine grand strategy was to turn the very multiplicity of enemies to its advantage, by employing diplomacy, deception, payoffs and religious conversion to induce them to fight one another instead of fighting the empire'.[8]

Defeating but not destroying each successive invader from the east in turn, the empire then settled them on its lands and incorporated them into the imperial army, which thus reinforced stood ready to confront the next threat. Thanks to its imaginative grand strategy, Byzantium or the East Roman Empire ruled for a thousand years more after the fall of the Roman Empire in the west.

A more recent grand strategy that is often derided for being static and entirely lacking in imagination, that of France in the interbellum, actually started out as a creative approach. The initial idea of building the Maginot Line, the fortifications and bunkers on France's eastern border, between Switzerland and Belgium (but not along the Belgian border to the Channel coast), was not to cower behind it waiting for the next German onslaught. Rather it was to serve as a secure base for offensive operations. Belgian cooperation was assured through the conclusion of a military agreement in 1920, while the 'petite entente' (after the 'entente cordiale' with the UK before the First World War) with Czechoslovakia, Romania and Yugoslavia gave France partners on Germany's eastern borders. The strategy began to unravel, however, when France and the UK refrained from undoing Nazi Germany's successive breaches of the Treaty of Versailles, culminating in their acquiescence, at Munich in 1938, in the dismemberment of Czechoslovakia. The other east European states were gradually pulled into the German orbit; Belgium for its part returned to neutrality in 1936. Britain and France declared war after Hitler invaded Poland on 1 September 1939, but even then left the initiative on the continent to Germany.[9] Thanks to a daring military-operational plan, in May–June 1940 Germany utterly defeated the allied armed forces in the battle for France. Fortunately, German creativity at the operational level could not compensate for an unrealistic grand strategy, and Germany lost the war.

The end of the Second World War saw an example of a brilliantly creative grand strategy, the results of which shape the world to this day: the US, together with the UK, and bringing on board De Gaulle's France and Chiang Kai-Shek's China, convinced the USSR to create new global institutions and a rules-based order. In return for their commitment, these five powers received a permanent seat and the veto right in the new UN Security Council. The US further used its enormous economic power to help restart the economies of the west European states and to stimulate European integration, by making its support under the 1948 Marshall Plan conditional on cooperation between the Europeans.[10] Thus Washington stabilised the region while tying it into the US economy and, in the event, into US grand strategy, as Stalin forbade the east European states under his control from accepting Marshall aid. Thus the divide that would become the Cold War began to rule relations between east and west. From 1949, NATO guaranteed the security of America's European allies against the fear of further expansionist moves from Moscow. Similarly, at the global level, the multilateral economic and financial institutions, backed up by the dollar as the world's reserve currency, cemented US influence, while under the Truman Doctrine the US made it its policy 'to support free peoples who are resisting attempted subjugation by armed minorities or by outside pressures', as President Harry Truman put it in a speech to Congress on 12 March 1947. The US thus created an international economic order that guaranteed American interests while being so beneficial to the rest of the non-communist world that it eagerly embraced the notion that if it was good for America, it was good for them.

When President Roosevelt explained his project for the UN to De Gaulle in 1944, the latter in his acerbic perspicacity concluded: 'As is only human, idealism cloaks the will to power.'[11] But precisely because there was an element of sincere idealism and altruism, American grand strategy was so incredibly successful. Unlike the USSR, the US did not have to coerce its European allies into aligning with it.

★★★

When the Cold War ended, there was talk of a 'new world order', but it would be more precise to say that the former communist states, and even some who formally remained communist such as China and Vietnam, integrated into the western economic order, and embraced capitalism. They had always been a part of the political and security order, as embodied by the Security Council, but the bipolar confrontation had often paralysed this crucial body. From the 1990s onward, thanks to more constructive relations between the permanent five, the Security Council was able to play a much more proactive role. At the same time, America's Cold War allies continued to align closely with the US, for they looked to Washington for continued leadership in proving global public goods, such as guaranteeing security and an open economic order.[12] Contrary to the expectations of some, alliances such as NATO were not dissolved, therefore. The existing rules of the world order, and the predominant position of the US in that order, thus seemed set to be consolidated. In the 21st century, however, US leadership gradually eroded, because at several instances the US proved unwilling to lead when the order was shaken, or even violated the rules itself. As a result, the order as such began to erode.

The US invasion of Iraq in 2003 was a turning point: it was clearly illegal under international law, but it was also widely seen as illegitimate – absent undisputed and acceptable grounds for the intervention, there was little willingness outside the US to excuse what might otherwise have been condoned as a 'creative' interpretation of the rules for the greater good. The contrast with the global reaction to NATO's air campaign against Serbia in 1999 was great. That intervention too lacked a mandate under international law, but its stated purpose of ending massacres in Kosovo was widely accepted, and, in the end, there was little protest outside Europe against a European and American intervention to restore peace in Europe. In 2003, however, the US (and the UK, which supported it) lost a lot of the credit and sympathy that it had gained after the '9/11' terrorist attacks. As the war in Afghanistan dragged on, partly because the US shifted its focus to Iraq, other states began to see that campaign too in a more critical light, whereas when the US launched it in 2001 nobody doubted that it was a legitimate exercise of the right of self-defence under Article 51 of the UN Charter. The US, like all great powers, had regularly flaunted the rules to the benefit of its national interest, but never so blatantly and never so obviously to the detriment of the security of many of its allies and partners. From 2003 onwards, Hanns Maull perceives a cumulative momentum in the erosion of the international order.[13]

The system certainly took another hit in 2008, when an American financial crisis turned into a global crisis, which the US proved both unable and unwilling to manage. In the Iraq crisis, no alternative leader to the US emerged: the EU was divided, with the UK supporting the US and France and Germany rejecting the invasion; Russia and China at that time had neither the military nor the diplomatic clout. The response to the financial crisis, however, marked the definite arrival upon the scene of China as a great power and an alternative pole to the US. As the EU was hard hit by the crisis too, many states, including in Europe, turned to Beijing instead. Having escaped relatively unscathed, China was able to inject huge amounts into the global economy. That further diminished the leadership status of the US. It also made it much more difficult, for those who had benefited from China's role, to criticise Beijing when it subsequently put its economic power to less benign uses or continued to disrespect core rules of the WTO – many were reluctant to bite the hand that had fed them.

When Trump entered the White House, the erosion of American leadership of the rules-based order definitely accelerated. The Trump administration actually took the lead in weakening the multilateral architecture. First, the US put in question regional trade agreements.

The US withdrew from the negotiations to create a Trans-Pacific Partnership, which it had launched itself, under Obama. Then Trump pressurised Canada and Mexico into renegotiating the 1994 North American Free Trade Agreement (NAFTA), which in 2020 was replaced by the United States–Mexico–Canada Agreement (USMCA). Next, in 2019, the US started the process to exit the 2015 Paris Climate Agreement; Washington also pulled out of several arms control treaties, and, in July 2020, at the height of the corona crisis, from the WHO. Thus the US, to the great surprise of its allies and partners who saw the rules-based order as a safeguard for their interests, began to tear down the superb edifice that it had itself constructed. The stated motivation was the assessment that the US had been treated unfairly: that other states benefited more from the system than the US, although the US contributed more, and that this explained many of its internal woes. China was often singled out as having subverted the purpose of international organisations, though the same argument was used even against the US' European allies.

How differently the UK reacted when towards the end of the 19th century Germany and the US overtook it as an industrial power. Thanks to its early industrialisation, colonial expansion and the power of the Royal Navy, Britain had become the primus inter pares of the great powers. It was a multipolar world, but to the extent that the Royal Navy patrolled the seas in order to maintain the freedom of navigation so that British trade could thrive, the UK underwrote the stability of everyone's trade. Moreover, Britain carefully guarded its reputation: wherever a British trader, political agent or missionary was injured or even only insulted, a fleet and a landing party were sure to appear. The expense was great, but it was considered both an investment and Britain's mission. Even when this Pax Britannica began to facilitate the expansion of other powers, therefore, Britain continued to invest in the world order, because that was still much more in its interest than giving up on it.[14]

America's disengagement from the multilateral architecture not only surprised but also dismayed its allies and partners, because the avowed reasons were so patently untrue. At the start of the 2020s, the US remained at the centre of the international financial and economic order; its policy decisions continued to reverberate throughout the world economy, and the US benefited from it more than anyone else.[15] The potential consequences of disengagement are great, therefore. Most directly, when the US retreats from an international organisation, it actually makes it more easy for China and others to fill the void and shape the organisation's rules and purposes. The

EU and like-minded states who are in favour of the existing rules do not always have sufficient power to act as a counterweight. Given China's growing power and its justified claim for a commensurate position in the multilateral architecture (which does not mean that the substance of its proposed policies is always justified or agreeable to the other member states), maintaining the existing rules-based order was bound to be a challenge. The preferred European response was to invest in multilateralism and reform it in such a way that China can be accommodated and continues to operate within the order, while maintaining the core rules. The isolationist policies of the Trump administration have only made the challenge more difficult. In the long term, such policies might undermine the very core of America's economic power. Trump's unilateral approach, forcing states to review existing treaties and punishing foreign firms for doing business with third states against which the US had sanctions even when that was legal under their own national legislation, has opened Pandora's box. It has already led many states, and even the EU, to question the position of the dollar as the world's reserve currency, and to explore ways of bypassing the US. The European Central Bank, for example, has so far prioritised management of the Eurozone itself, but were it to start offering swap lines to central banks in the EU's partner countries, one might see a substantial shift from the dollar to the Euro.

Restoring trust in the equitable use of America's power will not be easy. Some feel that Trump needed to shake up things in order for America's allies and partners to start paying attention to its demands, but that is putting a very positive spin on things.[16] The Trump administration has squandered America's image as a benevolent hegemon. America's allies and partners understood, of course, that the US would look after its own interests first, but in the past they safely assumed that Washington would duly take into account their interests as well, and the interest of maintaining a rules-based order as such. Nobody who is in an alliance with the US is thinking of abandoning it: the fear of potential security threats that are too big to be managed alone remains a powerful binding force, notably for the European states that share a border with Russia. As seen in the previous chapter, the Trump administration has started to reorient existing alliances towards China. This has been very successful with Australia and Japan, and others who regard China as a potential military threat in their immediate vicinity. But the European allies and Canada have been less than eager to make China the focal point of their alliance with the US or to fully subscribe to Washington's China strategy. America's alliances are not just founded on the need to jointly deter and defend against threats; they are also grounded in the allies' confidence in the US as a sound leader and a stable provider of global public goods. In the words of John Ikenberry: 'The United States may no longer be the world's sole superpower, but its influence has never been premised on power alone. It also depends on an ability to offer others a set of ideas and institutional frameworks for mutual gain.'[17] That applies even more to America's partners, who are not in a formal alliance with the US. The Trump administration, having undermined that confidence, failed to come up with a convincing alternative project. Democracy and human rights definitely resonate forcefully in America's democratic allies and partners, who join the US in condemning China's human rights violations. But an anti-Chinese agenda, or even a pro-democracy and human rights agenda, may be insufficient to forge a joint grand strategy if the US and its allies and partners no longer share a view of the desirable world order.

Arguably, even before Trump, the US position in the world was resting too much on past laurels. The US view of the world order and the global economy, based on an untrammelled belief in the free market, had already lost much of its appeal in many parts of the world.[18] The worst case scenario for those of America's allies and partners who still adhere to the rules-based order that American might has created, would be that they could no longer feel convinced of America's project for the world, but would instead begin to feel coerced to remain in an alliance and a partnership in which they no longer fully believed. Under Trump, US foreign policy began to resemble that of the great khan of the Mongols as defined by Steven Runciman: 'His foreign policy was fundamentally simple. His friends were already his vassals; his enemies were to be eliminated or reduced to vassaldom.'[19] As we concluded at the end of Chapter 5, the US and the EU, and the other allies and partners, will need to coordinate much more proactively if they want to maintain a common project. On the US side, this would demand not only a reinvestment in the multilateral architecture, but also the definition of a new substantial project with worldwide appeal. Even for a Democratic US administration, that is a tall order, since in their ranks too scepticism towards multilateralism has gained a lot of ground.

★★★

The project that the whole word talks about since its launch in 2013 is China's Belt and Road Initiative (BRI). Nobody is talking about Russia's Eurasian Economic Union, the EU's EU–Asia Connectivity Strategy, or the US' Blue Dot Network. The latter two were indeed reactions to BRI – China has been setting the agenda. That in itself is a measure of its success: like the Marshall Plan, BRI must be assessed not just on its economic achievements per se, but on its political consequences – for like the Marshall Plan, BRI is a grand strategic project.

Perhaps it did not start out that way. First came the plan to spur development in China's own land-locked western provinces, so that they could catch up with its eastern seaboard. Beijing then reached out to Central Asia and launched the notion of a new 'Silk Road' to Europe and the Middle East. As ambitions grew, what was first known as One Belt, One Road (OBOR) and then as BRI came to encompass six major overland 'corridors': the New Eurasian Land Bridge, linking China through Russia and Belarus with the EU, with terminals in the ports of Hamburg, Rotterdam and Antwerp; the China-Mongolia-Russia Economic Corridor; the China-Pakistan Economic Corridor, terminating in the Arabian Sea port of Gwadar; the China-Central and Western Asia Economic Corridor, through Central Asia and Iran to Turkey and the Arabian peninsula; the China-Indochina Peninsula Economic Corridor; and the Bangladesh-China-India-Myanmar Economic Corridor. In addition, the Maritime Silk Road connects China via South East Asia with Africa, and an Arctic Silk Road is projected to make full use of the opening up of the seas north of Russia. The core of BRI is investment in the infrastructure of connectivity (roads, rail, ports, pipelines and cyber), mostly through loans, to an estimated accumulated amount of some $200 billion in 2020.[20]

BRI is a grand project, and some in the Chinese strategic community proposed grandiose ambitions for it, envisaging a new form of international politics with BRI as the model. By 2020, nearly 140 countries had effectively signed a memorandum of understanding with BRI, including in regions beyond the major corridors. At the same time, BRI remains difficult to pinpoint. It does often feel as if anything that China achieves with any country is labelled a success for BRI. Jasper Roctus demonstrates, however, that China deliberately opted for an 'adjusting by doing' approach that left the concrete direction that BRI would take open. When Deng Xiaoping launched the 'reform and opening up' campaign in 1978, a flurry of local experiments followed, some of which were expanded while others were terminated; the narrative of what were the ends and what constituted success was constructed along the way.[21] So for BRI: one advertises what works, and quietly shelves what does not. This approach is another example of Chinese pragmatism; it offers great flexibility within the long-term orientation and continuity that BRI does provide.[22] And, as Khan rightly states, a bold and ambitious label creates excitement: 'Since

Beijing is committed to economic relations with these countries anyway, it does not hurt to have an appealing slogan.'[23] Some of the grandiose rhetoric has, in fact, been toned down, and at the 2017 World Economic Forum in Davos, Xi Jinping, instead of talking of BRI as an alternative form of governance, positioned himself as the defender of free trade and sustainable development.

This was a response to the many critiques of BRI: that China's state-owned or state-controlled companies and banks had an unfair advantage and pursued projects without regard for their financial, economic, social and ecological sustainability; that China would thus saddle countries with unviable investment projects and debts they would not be able to repay; that these countries would lose their sovereignty and end up as clients of China; so that, finally, a Chinese sphere of influence would result. At the same time, many argued that BRI could not work, that many projects were doomed to fail, that China would not be able to sustain the funding, and that in many less stable countries it would get embroiled in political tangles and security problems. This combination of fear and wishful thinking betrayed the nervousness that BRI caused in many quarters. The criticisms are at least partially true, though, and BRI has so far been only partially successful.

Before China could launch a project like BRI, it had to build up its own economy. Once it had created strong national champions in its still very protected domestic market, these big companies were ready to venture abroad. Many criticisms of China focus on the fact that many Chinese firms are state-owned enterprises (SOEs), and that even privately-owned firms are ultimately controlled by the state and the party. That is largely beside the point, however: how to organise its economy is for China to decide. In many EU member states, the state plays a far lesser role in the economy than in China, but still a substantially bigger one than in the US (notably in the utilities sector, but also in the defence industry). If Belgium, for example, decides that the state has to maintain a majority share in the country's primary telecom firm, that is a political choice that the kingdom is fully entitled to make, and which from a moral or legal point of view is neither good nor bad. Besides, many American critics tend to forget that when the US government puts its weight behind a defence company, in order to promote the export of the F35 combat aircraft, for example, for the state on the receiving end it does not make much of a difference that Lockheed Martin is a private company and not state-owned. What matters, therefore, is how China's SOEs and other firms obtained their market share: when they receive government subsidies that enable dumping practices and otherwise distort the market; violate intellectual property rights (IPR) and steal data and technology; and benefit from market access abroad while China refuses to reciprocate and upholds barriers to foreign firms operating in China – then criticism and action are more than justified. When foreign firms first entered the Chinese market, profit margins were so huge that they took the lack of reciprocity into the bargain. When Chinese firms became competitive and profit margins grew smaller, they belatedly, but justifiably, demanded action. In the US, the Trump administration reacted by launching a trade war, while the EU started negotiations for a bilateral investment treaty. China will have to accept that if it does not show real reciprocity, both the US and the EU will have no choice, reluctantly or otherwise, but to reassess Chinese access to their markets.

The advantage of a state-controlled economy for BRI is that China can order SOEs to invest in projects that are unprofitable, and in which therefore no American or European company would invest, if that serves China's national interest. BRI projects must not only be judged against their economic results, therefore, but against the broader strategic ends that China is pursuing. Nevertheless, even China's resources are not unlimited; a sufficient number of projects must be economically viable for BRI to be sustainable – although the cost of BRI until 2020 pales in comparison to the $6 trillion that the US had by then spent on its 'global war on terror'.[24] The economic recession caused by the corona pandemic may reduce the available means, both for China and for the target states. Sustainability must, of course, also be assessed from the point of view of the latter, who have to repay the loans. Sri Lanka, for example, is widely perceived to have fallen into a debt trap, after borrowing $1.5 billion (among other loans) to construct an unprofitable port in Hambantota.[25] In order to relieve the burden of debt, the country then leased the port to China, which holds an estimated 9 to 15 per cent of the country's total external debt, for 99 years, in return for $1.1 billion.[26] As a result, however, other BRI partners have become more careful, and that has an impact on China's strategic ends. With regard to other standards (trade union rights, the environment, transparency, anti-corruption, and so on), China indeed aims as low as the government of the target state allows it to, in spite of signing up, as a member of the G20 group of countries, to the 2019 Principles for Quality Infrastructure Investment. But when it comes to their sovereignty, with a very few exceptions, no state is looking to become a vassal of China.

Through BRI, Beijing needs to achieve a fine balance, therefore: make an offer that is sufficiently large to generate political influence (or even to create the capacity to coerce the target state), but not so large as to provoke resistance and possible rejection. Overall, China's relations with the BRI countries are far removed from those of the USSR with its satellites: a state that joins BRI does not disappear behind an iron curtain, but remains accessible to other powers as well. The US and the EU, besides, still own far more debt of the developing countries than China, although the latter's share has been rising quickly in the last decade. From the point of view of the target countries, the rise of China has presented them with more options: in addition to the US, the EU, and in some regions Russia, there now is a Chinese offer to be sampled – and played off against the others, as most states seek to maintain good relations with various powers. As long as China does not force a state to join BRI, nor forces it to sever relations with other powers if it does, BRI is a legitimate use of its power.

China has experienced that its power is not always sufficient, though, to overcome internal political and security problems in its partners. Authoritarian, weak or kleptocratic rulers may play to its advantage, but just as often they raise obstacles that are impervious to China's might. Pakistan, for example, is proving a difficult partner – as the US could have told China – and the China-Pakistan Economic Corridor is plagued by bureaucratic obstacles and local politics. Moreover, as BRI is so encompassing, it includes countries that have disputes among each other, such as Pakistan and India. Success with one country may be to the detriment of relations with another. The more its presence grows, the more China becomes involved in the security situation of the target states as well, if only from the point of view of the security of its own citizens and assets. China has started to develop closer military ties with the BRI countries, as well as to increase arms exports.[27] But, as seen in Chapter 4, its non-interventionist strategic culture means that in practice it relies on other powers to act in case of many likely security crises – Russia in Central Asia and the Caucasus, and, actually, the US in Europe, the Arabian peninsula, and (to some extent) South East Asia. If in the future China would be willing to engage more in the security and defence dimension, that might change the equation, both to its advantage and disadvantage: some states might opt for closer military relations with China; others would undoubtedly see it as a reason to counterbalance China by moving closer to the US.

Since 2017, China invites the leaders of the states that have signed memoranda with the BRI to a Belt and Road Forum. The participation of dozens of heads of state and government, including from EU member states, is a demonstration of China's convening power. The core of BRI remains each country's bilateral relationship with China, however. Creating a BRI 'community' is difficult, given the number and diversity of participating states. Moreover, Beijing usually prefers to deal with individual countries, seeking to avoid third countries from coordinating their positions. In 2014, China did launch an important multilateral initiative and created the Asian Infrastructure Investment Bank (AIIB). This new multilateral development bank started operations in 2016. By 2020, it counted 82 members and had invested some $20 billion in 87 projects. The US reacted strongly and advised its allies and partners not to join, but most did not heed its warnings. The UK was one of the first to join; meanwhile Australia has signed up too, as have 19 EU member states; only Japan and South Korea have abided by the US. Washington misread the sentiment among its allies. The EU, for example, took a very positive view of the AIIB. Was this not exactly what Brussels and Washington wanted: China opting for a multilateral, instead of a unilateral mechanism, and inviting western states to join? They would thus be able to guarantee standards of transparency and sustainability from the inside. The AIIB has not become the bank of the BRI, though, as many initially thought it would, so it does not provide its members with an avenue to exert influence over China's bilateral initiatives. Compared to BRI, the AIIB remains a much smaller player, but the infrastructure needs in Asia are so enormous – $1.7 trillion per year until 2030, according to the Asian Development Bank – that there is ample space for all players in the field. That was one of the reasons, along with the fact that the US did not put an alternative proposal on the table, that so many American allies ignored Washington's injunctions.[28]

Has China achieved its grand strategic purpose for BRI? One of the aims, according to the academic Jisi Wang, who is seen as the intellectual architect of BRI, is to ensure that supply lines to the west remain open if the sea lines of communication were interrupted.[29] In that sense, BRI and the annexation of the South China Sea are two halves of the same strategy. For now, the overland corridors represent only a fraction of China's trade, however. Trade by rail to Europe, for example, amounted to less than 90 million tons in 2020, while the EU's sea ports handle nearly 900 million tons every quarter. While BRI is still developing, in particular the Pakistan corridor, it is hard to imagine that it could ever compensate for a blockade of China's eastern seaboard. BRI has achieved another grand strategic objective, though: China has tied in many states into its economy, and has greatly augmented and in many ways consolidated its political influence.

★★★

BRI is all about connectivity. Just like hybrid warfare, this is but a new buzzword for an age-old practice – though a less confusing one. States and empires have always sought to obtain guaranteed access to markets and resources, and to secure their lines of communication with them; connectivity always had both an economic and a political dimension. In the past, connectivity was very competitive: the great powers aimed to conquer states that offered enticing markets or resources, and make them into colonies or protectorates; exclusive spheres of influence emerged. In the 19th century, the combination of great power rivalry and new technologies led to a frenzy of activity. 'Cape to Cairo' and 'Berlin to Baghdad' were the slogans of the day, as the great powers built roads and railroads to connect their ever-expanding colonial empires. Britain eventually managed to create one contiguous 'red zone' of British-controlled territory on the map from north to south Africa. The railway to Baghdad underpinned imperial Germany's influence in the Ottoman Empire. Competitive connectivity led to many incidents: in 1898 Britain and France nearly went to war over the control of the upper Nile after Anglo-Egyptian and French expeditions met at Fashoda in the Sudan. Asia was no exception. Navies needed coaling stations and states acquired bases along the sea lines of communication. In Manchuria, control of the railroads became the focal point for the geopolitical competition between the Russian and Japanese empires. The battle for the railroad hub of Mukden (present-day Shenyang), during the 1904–05 Russo-Japanese War, was the greatest land battle ever fought until the First World War. Afterwards, Japanese-controlled Manchuria could be best described as a railroad company with an army (the Kwantung Army), until in 1932 Japan created the satellite state of Manchukuo (and installed Puyi, the last emperor of China, as emperor there in 1934).

In the 21st century, connectivity usually is created in consensual ways: the powers seek the consent of the target states in order to trade and invest – though at times consent is given under strong pressure. Economic connectivity is consolidated politically by concluding partnerships and alliances rather than by conquest. Coercion of the target state has indeed become counterproductive. The Russian conquest of the Crimea, for example, has decreased connectivity, both for the peninsula, which is cut off from all states but Russia, and for Russia itself, which is suffering from economic sanctions. In economic terms, the annexation of the Crimea is a failure: rather than an asset, it is a drag on the Russian economy. The case of Ukraine illustrates, however, that the question remains whether connectivity can also be created in a consensus between the great powers themselves, by adopting connectivity schemes that are not mutually exclusive, and that hence do not force other states to choose between one or the other power. This is exactly what happened in Ukraine, artificially forced to choose between the EU and Russia, and thus torn apart. All powers that engage in connectivity schemes must be aware of this risk.

The coronavirus outbreak has demonstrated how vital but also how vulnerable connectivity still is in the 21st century, even for the great powers. As production sites were shut down and borders closed, complicated supply chains crossing multiple countries broke down. Fortunately, most states were able to keep up supplies of food and other essentials; had the shelves in the supermarkets gone empty, the public would not have been so docile in obeying the rules of the 'lockdown' and a serious threat to public order might have arisen, even in the wealthiest countries. As a consequence, the pandemic accelerated the pre-existing trend to reorganise globalisation to a certain extent: all too fragmented supply chains will likely be rationalised, and in certain sectors, such as medical supplies, states will in the future seek to have an autonomous capacity for production. At heart, the great powers will remain deeply economically interdependent, though, and dependent on exports, and on imports of natural resources. Globalisation will be reorganised, not undone, and so connectivity will remain as crucial today as at any time in the past.

★★★

Russia launched its own scheme in 2014: the Eurasian Economic Union (EAEU). Unlike BRI, this is a multilateral scheme, with permanent institutions, creating a single market and a customs union. Aiming at the former Soviet republics, the EAEU now counts five members: Armenia, Belarus, Kazakhstan, Kyrgyzstan and Russia – the others have been reluctant to join. Having its roots in earlier treaties in the 1990s, the EAEU was first and foremost a reaction to the EU reaching out to these states. Timothy Snyder even sees it as primarily a spoiler mechanism, aimed to prevent states from building close relations with the EU.[30] And, of course, once a country is in a customs union with Russia, it can no longer conclude a free trade agreement with the EU. By its nature, therefore, the EAEU is a much more exclusive scheme than China's BRI or the EU initiatives – which explains its limited attractiveness to many states. Even those who have joined the EAEU continue to emphasise their sovereignty, contrary to initial Russian plans for deeper political integration.[31] At the start of the 2020s, it is China's influence that is rising fast in the post-Soviet space, not the EU's, thanks to the scale of investment on offer, with which Russia cannot compete. Formally, Putin and Xi agreed on cooperation between the EAEU and BRI (in 2015), but in practice the two schemes exist alongside each other.[32] Where cooperation exists, it is rather like a 'forced marriage'.[33] The reality, which Moscow prefers not to openly acknowledge, is that it is competing for influence as much with Beijing as with Brussels. Indeed, Russia probably worries more about the growing presence of China nowadays, but as long as Russia's relations with the EU remain fraught, it has no choice but to keep up the pretence of cooperation with BRI.

The US came late to this particular geo-economic area: its focus was on the instrument of free trade rather than government-initiated investment schemes, and when Trump came to power, he halted US engagement even in that field. In reaction to China's growing influence, the US in 2019 launched the Blue Dot Network, with the participation of Australia and Japan, which seeks to certify infrastructure projects that adhere to certain standards, in order to help them attract private capital. White House national security adviser Robert O'Brien called it 'a Michelin Guide' for investment projects.[34] The main aim is to mobilise private capital, including from major institutional players such as American pension funds. But without a core of government funding, leveraging sufficient private investment to have significant political impact will be a challenge.

★★★

The EU has itself been a 'target' of China's BRI. Eighteen EU member states have signed a memorandum of understanding with BRI, including Italy in 2019 – the first G7 country to do so. Moreover, twelve EU member states together with five other central and east European states have joined the '17+1', a regional framework established by China in 2012. One of its key objectives now is to promote BRI. The EU has always deplored that its member states joined the 17+1, for it obviously makes it very easy for China to divide member states and undermine the EU's negotiating position. This is an example of how a creative Chinese strategy has divided the EU, whereas a more aggressive Russian strategy has mostly served to unite it against Moscow. Undoing the 17+1 would be very difficult without provoking a diplomatic crisis – although the Europeans perhaps overestimate China's appetite for such, and underestimate its dread of losing face by seeing the end of a major initiative. But it is unlikely that all EU member states would withdraw; another option would be for all remaining EU member states to join in, in which case the format would lose its main interest to China, but it might be seen as an implicit validation of the scheme too. Meanwhile, China has very effectively created the impression that it is a major investor in central and eastern Europe, by selecting prominent projects and organising high-level bilateral visits.[35] In fact, the bulk of Chinese investment in the EU goes to Germany, France and Italy, and to northern Europe, while the large majority of investment in the EU's eastern member states comes from within the EU itself. Another reality is that the big member states, and Germany in particular, often prioritise their own economic interests with China to the detriment of the common EU interest.

At the same time, Germany and France constitute the powerhouse of the EU economy: as long as they, together with Belgium, the Netherlands and the Scandinavian member states, decline from signing a BRI memorandum, China cannot hope to gain a determining influence over the EU's economic policies. The 'adjusting by doing' approach to BRI described by Roctus thus did not work vis-à-vis the EU: instead of inspiring the Western European states, China's cooperation with the 17+1 countries has alerted them to the risks. Urged on by France and Germany, the EU has actually become more sceptical of the Chinese presence in Europe. Initially economic concerns drove Paris and Berlin: the fear that Chinese investment was aimed at acquiring technologies more than anything else, and would rob Europe of its competitive edge without making a productive contribution to its economy in return. Security concerns then were added on top of that, as a result of China's (and other's) use of illicit methods to obtain data and technology, and of the increasingly assertive tone that Chinese diplomats began to use, using China's economic weight to put pressure on governments and companies to adhere by Chinese policy. The sovereignty of the EU and its member states was seen to be at stake. The EU reacted by introducing an investment screening mechanism in 2019, which obliges member states to have the EU advise on foreign investments that could threaten the security or public order of the EU. It was launched as a voluntary mechanism – the final decision rests with the member state – but it does give member states who want to decline an investment from China or another non-EU country a lot more leverage to do so. In 2020, the EU followed up by addressing subsidies to companies in the EU from non-EU countries, in order to prevent market distortions, notably with regard to acquisition of companies in the EU and public procurement procedures.

The EU's single market remains one of the most open markets on the globe, but increasing competition and rivalry between the great powers have forced Brussels to reassess its policies and shield off its market from those who seek only to abuse its openness. While the EU remains strongly committed to free trade, it has started to attach more and more importance to reciprocity, in particular from China.

The EU will not resort to tariffs and sanctions and undo some of the existing economic bonds as readily as the US. But as stated above, if China remains unwilling to offer European players the same facilities that Chinese players have in the EU, Brussels at the very least will be more restrictive with regard to any future initiatives.

In 2018 the EU also launched an initiative of its own aimed at third countries: the EU–Asia Connectivity Strategy. This strategy is aimed at Eurasia, which is also the core of BRI, to which it was largely a reaction. Actually though, the EU has much more experience than China with creative initiatives to forge multidimensional relations – and generate influence. Upon the end of the Cold War, from 1991 onwards, the EU concluded a series of 'Europe Agreements' with its central and Eastern European neighbours, which set them on a path to full membership. In 1995, the EU offered a new generation of association agreements (without the prospect of membership) to its southern neighbours as well, in the framework of a new multilateral format, the Euro-Mediterranean Partnership (EMP). In 2004, after the accession of ten new member states, the European Neighbourhood Policy (ENP) became the encompassing framework for bilateral relations for the EU's immediate neighbours to both the east and the south, for whom membership is not on offer (except for the countries of the Balkans, with whom pre-accession talks are ongoing outside the ENP). Within the ENP, the Union for the Mediterranean (formerly the EMP) and the Eastern Partnership (EaP) offer two multilateral platforms: the former covering the Mediterranean littoral states, the latter Belarus, Moldova and Ukraine, and the three Caucasus countries of Georgia, Armenia and Azerbaijan. The multilateral formats hold but limited appeal for the neighbouring countries, however: a regional affinity cannot be created by an external power. The neighbours prioritise their bilateral relations with the EU, the operating principle of which is 'positive conditionality': in return for the implementation of mutually agreed upon economic and political reforms, the EU awards aid, investment, market access, visa liberalisation and other support.

The ENP has generated the most political influence in EaP countries that aspire to the European way of life, including democracy, the rule of law and respect for human rights: countries such as Georgia and Ukraine and, to a lesser extent, Moldova. It has been less successful in countries that organise their society and politics on a very different basis than the EU member states: a way of life cannot be re-engineered from the outside. In practice, therefore, even as the EU maintains its rhetoric on democracy and human rights, Brussels has come to mostly disregard the lack of political change and has maintained its influence through pragmatic political, economic, and security cooperation wherever interests coincide. The EU's influence has nonetheless been diminished where the partner countries face security issues in which the Union has been unwilling to intervene (as in Libya) or where new players on the scene have put more attractive offers on the table, with fewer conditions attached, as China has done in the EaP countries.

The EU–Asia Connectivity Strategy was a new departure for the EU. Geographically, it goes far beyond the EaP and covers all of Eurasia; previously, the Union's Asia policies focused mostly on China and on relations with ASEAN. More importantly, from the start the aim of the new strategy was not so much to engender political change in the target countries as to maintain a level playing field in their economies, and thus to safeguard their sovereignty in the light of China's mounting presence – and to maintain the EU's standard-setting power. As with most sound strategies, the basic idea is simple: if the EU feels that China, through BRI (or in some places Russia, through the EAEU), is gaining too much influence in a country where the European interest is at stake, the EU has to put a better offer on the table. Thus the EU seeks to convince states that it is in their interest to maintain an open economy and engage with various powers simultaneously rather than putting all their eggs in a Chinese or Russian basket. The EU clearly aims to establish 'connectivity with consent': Brussels does not seek exclusivity itself; it only seeks to prevent the other great powers from fencing off an exclusive sphere of interest.

The EU plans to invest public means in order to attract private investment. The EU–Japan Partnership on Sustainable Connectivity and Quality Infrastructure, established in 2019, may create synergies and effects of scale. Nonetheless, mobilising sufficient means to make a difference and generate influence will be a huge challenge, even more so as the need to fund Europe's own recovery after the pandemic affects the means available for external action. Without sufficient means, the EU's connectivity strategy will come to nothing, but Brussels does have an interesting offer to make: it is a chance for states in Eurasia to diversify their relations with the great powers; the EU seeks partners, not clients, which is not so clearly the case for China and Russia; there is a promise of access to the EU's huge domestic market and to innovative strategies such as the Green Deal. As the strategy is implemented, the EU could broaden its offer and explore opportunities for political and security cooperation with the target states as well. Shared foreign policy objectives, military exchanges, combined military exercises and so on could give more depth to the connectivity strategy. Connectivity is not only created in the physical world, by building roads, ports and cyber infrastructure; it is also a matter of partners feeling connected. That requires political investment, including high-level bilateral visits, as China's approach to the 17+1 has expertly demonstrated.

As the EU tentatively set out on a Eurasian strategy, it also announced, in 2020, a review of its strategy for its neighbouring continent to the south: Africa. China has become a major presence in Africa, to the concern of the EU and the US, which have seen themselves crowded out by large-scale Chinese investments, often with scant regard for democracy and human rights and for sustainability. In many ways, China is just treating Africa the way Europe and America did until at least the end of the Cold War, including the emphasis on the extraction of natural resources. The major difference is that China brings in a large Chinese labour force rather than relying on local labour, and, until now, focuses less on military cooperation (though its military presence has been on the increase). The EU and its member states together remain the biggest donor of development aid to Africa. But many Europeans have come to see Africa in an exclusively negative light, as a source of threats to be contained, and of migration to be stemmed. If the EU wants to recoup its lost influence in Africa, it will have to overturn this defensive approach.

★★★

In the past, the EU was the pioneer of creative 'partnership diplomacy', building comprehensive political, economic and security relations with a variety of countries. In countries that saw the EU way of life as an attractive model or that had a big interest in linking their economies to the EU's single market, Brussels gained great influence. EU influence remained limited, however, when its political ambitions ran too high, as authoritarian states resisted democratisation, or when its security role was too limited, as states at war looked for military support above all else. After 2003, the EU also established strategic partnerships with key powers. From the 1990s, China too had embarked on a frenzy of 'partnership diplomacy', establishing dozens of strategic partnerships across the continents. Very often, however, both Europe's and China's strategic partnerships, in spite of the summitry involved, remained highly declaratory, except in the economic sphere.

The focus on connectivity represents the latest creative approach to international politics. Economy remains at the heart, but with a new focus on investment in infrastructure as a way of connecting states to one's own market and promoting one's norms and standards. In the political sphere, the aim is not to export one's own model, but to ensure access and cement influence. This approach fits well with the strengths of China and the EU, with their strong tradition of public investment in infrastructure. The EU might indeed wish to consider whether it ought not to step up public involvement and strengthen EU agencies such as the European Investment Bank, so that it can invest more resources directly in the target state, instead of donating to multilateral and local partners and losing visibility and impact as is now often the case. Instead of always criticising the heavy weight of the state in the Chinese way of doing things, Europeans and others could to some extent step up the role of the state themselves. The connectivity approach is less well geared to Russia, however, for lack of means, and to the US, where the state traditionally plays a much smaller role in investment. The fact remains, though, that connectivity cannot be developed with a country involved in conflict. States seeking an alliance will not be satisfied with a connectivity partnership. The military dimension, in which American power is unsurpassed, will always be vital.

Creativity is essential for the success of grand strategy – but innovative ideas still have to be implemented. Turning established policies and practices around can be cumbersome. Strategic players, therefore, also need agility to make and implement decisions as fast as the situation requires.

Agile: Taking Decisions, Acting, and Taking New Decisions

'No operational plan extends with any certainty beyond the first clash with the main enemy forces', taught Field Marshal Helmuth von Moltke, architect of military victory in the wars of German unification that Bismarck triggered between 1864 and 1871.[1] Or, as Field Marshal Slim put it more laconically: 'I should have remembered that battles, at least the ones I had been engaged in, very rarely went quite according to plan.'[2] It is another military adagio that applies to grand strategy as a whole. The other players have a strategy too, hence implementing one's own strategy requires agility: the willingness and the decision-making structures to rapidly and flexibly adapt strategy to changing circumstances. Deciding on grand strategy usually requires long debates and complex procedures, however, involving many entities within the state: different parties or factions, different ministries, the armed forces. Once the decision is taken, those players usually are reluctant to make great changes, for fear of upsetting the equilibrium between them, or of domestic political consequences. It is only human that the people who have signed off on the strategy become attached to their 'beautiful' strategic concept and their 'perfect' plans – but that is a decidedly unstrategic attitude. The principles of grand strategy may be summarised in ten words and carved into stone (or so I pretend), but actual strategy should be subject to constant assessment and review. 'A little more time, a little more help, a little more confidence, a few more honest men, the blessing of Providence and a rather better telephone service – all would have been well!': every scheme can be a close run thing, as Churchill indicated. And if it does go wrong, one needs to adapt fast.[3]

One way of ensuring a regular review is to institutionalise it, and to enshrine in law that a new grand strategy must be adopted at fixed intervals. As seen in Chapter 1, every US president has a legal obligation to present a National Security Strategy. In China, the five-yearly congress of the CCP provides a regular framework. No equivalent obligation exists in Russia, but Moscow issues new strategies regularly. Only the EU stands out among the great powers for not yet having adopted a system of producing grand strategy; hence much time elapsed between its first grand strategic document, the 2003 European Security Strategy, and the second iteration, the 2016 Global Strategy. Installing a procedure alone is not enough, though: there is always a risk that it becomes an exercise in 'ticking the box', going through the motions because one has to but without actually questioning the underlying assumptions of the strategy. As Hal Brands and his colleagues write: 'Too often, the historical pattern has been one of policy proceeding along a familiar and comfortable course as the assumptions underlying that policy become steadily more outdated until some unforeseen and unwelcome strategic shock exposes the weakness of those assumptions and perhaps shatters them altogether.'[4]

However, it is even more difficult to revisit grand strategy in between such fixed moments for review, when procedures may have to be improvised, and one may not have the luxury of exploring all the various options and consult all stakeholders in a lengthy debate. An institutionalised review mechanism provides crucial anchor points, therefore. If the grand strategy itself is systematically reviewed every four or five years, it become easier to create agility at the level below. The specific thematic or geographic strategies that translate grand strategy into more detailed and actionable plans may indeed require more change, more often, in reaction to crises or to actions by the other powers. A state must have the agility to alter its specific strategies, or to adopt new strategies, in a flexible manner, as the situation demands. If the changes at this level affect grand strategy as well, then the next fixed review will provide the opportunity to incorporate these into the next iteration of one's grand strategy. Systematically reviewing grand strategy does not imply an obligation to change, of course: the conclusion of a review can be that a grand strategy remains valid – but in that case a state does not introduce changes because it has thought about it, not because of inertia, as was the case for the EU between 2003 and 2016.

Agility is not the same as improvisation, as shown in Chapter 1. Agility is to act within an existing strategic framework and to adapt it when necessary. One thus has a clear a priori idea of one's interests, and of the ends, ways and means chosen to pursue them. Using that framework as a grid to analyse the evolving situation, one can more easily decide whether ends, ways or means must be changed in order to continue to safeguard one's interests. Improvisation is what one is forced to resort to in the absence of a strategic framework. Without predefined ends, ways and means, and often with just a vague idea of one's interests, reacting to a new situation means starting from scratch, and one will inevitably lose time. Instead of quickly assessing whether a crisis affects one's interests, one still has to establish what one's interests are in the first place. Instead of analysing whether existing strategy can deal with the new situation, an entirely new strategy must be imagined. In a dire crisis, the capacity to improvise will be an asset; but sound strategy precisely aims to prevent a state from ending up in such a crisis.

Agility requires unity of command. As Lloyd George said to Churchill: 'It is not a question of one general being better than another, but of one general being better than two.'[5] Changes in strategy cannot be made if it is not clear who has both the authority and the responsibility to undertake them. Given the comprehensive nature of any strategy, a multitude of departments will always be involved, but ultimately only the supreme political leadership of a state can make decisions on grand strategy. Even more specific thematic or geographic strategies will require approval at the political level – the bureaucracy and the military cannot make strategy on their own authority. But the procedures must be in place to allow the apparatus to review and propose changes rapidly, and to put them on the political agenda fast, in order for the state to achieve the agility that effective strategy requires.

No creative genius can obviously undertake strategy on his own. Strategic decisions require an organisation for their preparation, and then for their systematic and methodical implementation. 'The basic principles of strategy are so simple that a child may understand them', said General Eisenhower, 'but to determine their proper application to a given situation requires the hardest kind of work from the finest available staff officers.'[6] Once again, a British field marshal put it even more laconically: 'The making of plans is just child's play as compared to putting them into execution', Alanbrooke wrote in his diary.[7] Staff work, by diplomats, officials and the military, must not become an impediment to agility, however. International administrations in particular, such as NATO and the EU, have grown into large and complex entities, which demand a lot of internal coordination before anything can be decided, let alone implemented. Already in the early days of NATO, Montgomery judged that

> Simplicity and decision, two absolute essentials in war, have disappeared from the NATO military organisation. We are producing commanders trained in the art of compromise.

The staffs of the major headquarters have grown beyond
all possible peace-time needs; they should be ruthlessly
pruned. The output of paper is tremendous; so much time
is taken with reading it, that few officers have enough time
to think; all work suffers accordingly.[8]

But any state apparatus too is a complex machinery that might as well
obstruct as conduct agile strategic decision making.

Just like the other characteristics of grand strategy, agility demands a
balancing exercise. Eisenhower also wrote that 'History has proved that
nothing is more difficult in war than to adhere to a single strategic plan.
Unforeseen and glittering promise on the one hand and unexpected
difficulty or risk upon the other present constant temptation to desert
the chosen line of action in favour of another'.[9] Strategy is to provide a
sense of direction; if the direction is changed too often, disorientation
will result. Agility must be balanced against patience, therefore. Strategy
needs time to generate effect: strategists must show patience and not
alter a strategy before the chosen instruments have had a reasonable
chance to prove their effectiveness. Occasionally, a lightning campaign
can produce early results, but many have become so accustomed to
see immediate effect that they even fail to recognise early results when
they see them. The NATO air campaign against Serbia, with the
aim of ending violence in Kosovo, lasted from 24 March to 10 June
1999: less than three months, yet at the time many despaired that the
intervention would yield results. The Libya air campaign started on
19 March 2011 and was concluded on 31 October, after the death
of Qadhafi. By that time, the intervening Europeans and Americans
were already so impatient to see results that afterwards they readily
abandoned any major role in post-conflict Libya.

★★★

Agility may appear unprincipled and ruthless. A supreme example is
the grand strategy of the Soviet Union during the interbellum. Initially,
Moscow ordered the European communist parties to focus on the
struggle against the non-communist left. Gaining absolute control
over the left often overrode all other priorities; the resulting divide of
the left undoubtedly was a key factor in the rise to power of Nazism
and fascism. Belatedly, the Soviet Union changed its strategy to one
of allying with the socialist parties against the extreme right. Then,
in a volte-face that left many sincere communists bewildered, Stalin
agreed a non-aggression pact with Hitler. In the Molotov-Ribbentrop
Pact (named after the two foreign ministers) of 23 August 1939, Nazi

Germany and the Soviet Union agreed on the partition of Poland: the German invasion of Poland on 1 September was followed by the Soviet invasion on the 17th. The Molotov-Ribbentrop Pact also assigned the Baltic states to the Soviet sphere of influence, as well as Finland and the Romanian region of Bessarabia. The USSR duly launched the Winter War against Finland in November 1939 and, in spite of severe initial defeats, in March 1940 forced Finland to cede 11 per cent of its territory. The Baltic states were occupied in June 1940 and formally annexed two months later; Bessarabia was annexed in July. Soviet-German cooperation came to an end only on 22 June 1941, when Germany launched Operation Barbarossa and invaded the Soviet Union. Moscow then immediately turned to London and on 12 July 1941 concluded a military alliance, the Anglo-Soviet Agreement.

The western allies were relieved that the USSR finally entered the war on their side, for they were desperate for support. Even though in December 1941 the US joined the war as well, it is doubtful whether Nazi Germany, after its initial stunning victories in the west, could have been defeated without the Soviet Union. What could easily be seen as Moscow's treacherous and immoral behaviour, therefore, was brushed aside during the common struggle against Hitler. Once the war ended, however, the UK and the US had to face a Soviet strategy that took off where the Molotov-Ribbentrop Pact had ended: the wartime annexations were not undone, and all the central and Eastern European countries that the Red Army had liberated from Nazi Germany became Soviet satellites. From the Soviet point of view, its strategic agility was perfectly rational. As Stalin had told Churchill during their August 1942 meeting in Moscow: 'he knew Germany was certain ultimately to attack Russia. He was not ready to withstand that attack; by attacking Poland with Germany he could make more ground, ground was equal to time, and he would consequently have a longer period of time to get ready.'[10] Even so, the Soviet Union was only able to halt the German onslaught after first incurring staggering losses of territory, matériel and human life. The massive purges of the officers corps in the years leading up to the invasion had greatly contributed to the initial disaster. Fortunately, when it invaded the Soviet Union Nazi Germany seriously overreached.[11]

From the perspective of the Soviet regime, its grand strategy had nonetheless been successful: its rule had been legitimised by victory, the sovereignty of the USSR preserved, and its power hugely extended. The effect of the strategic shifts on the comrades in the west was irrelevant: their role always had been to serve the mother party in Moscow, regardless of local circumstances. Ideological motivations were found to justify the treatment of Poland, while the creation of a single vast buffer zone was no more than a reiteration of Russian grand strategy since the early days of the Romanovs – only infinitely more successful. Soviet grand strategy, in other words, stayed true to Soviet interests and values.

The Soviet example shows that agility not only differs from improvisation, but also from mere fickleness and from tactical opportunism. Fickleness is agility taken too far: if every change in the environment leads to a change in strategy, or if a strategic community alters the definition of its interests too often, a state will ultimately be left without any sound strategic footing. Opportunism is agility that takes insufficient account of predefined interests and ends: if every opportunity that presents itself at the tactical level is grasped without due consideration of the implications for grand strategy, the short-term benefits risk being offset by longer-term losses. Fickleness and opportunism are weaknesses; agility is a strength, because it starts from the state's own values (from who the state is) and its interests. Violating one's own values is indeed a red line in conducting strategy; we shall return to this in Chapter 9.

★★★

It is often pretended that authoritarian states achieve agility more easily than democracies; the issue came to the fore early on in the corona crisis.[12] In authoritarian states there certainly is a concentration of power at the top, which allows for decisions to be made quickly and, if necessary, ruthlessly, and their implementation can be enforced by the entire repressive apparatus of the state. But authoritarianism also suffers from a serious disadvantage: the reluctance to speak truth to power when power is absolute. In every authoritarian state, officials on the lower rungs of the system, fearing for their careers or even for their physical security, tend to paint a more positive picture of the situation than it really warrants. And without sufficient and correct information, sound decision making is impossible. Moreover, the more authoritarian a system, the more important it is to maintain the image of infallibility, for if the state if omnipotent, the state bears full responsibility for failure. The temptation is always great, therefore, even when the leadership is fully informed of a problem, to simply pretend that it does not exist, or, if that fails, to pin the blame on an easily identifiable internal or external enemy. The same applies to populist leaders who have come to power in democracies. Thus Trump's somewhat contradictory pronouncement on the coronavirus (in his second television debate with Biden in October 2020): 'I take full responsibility. It's not my fault that it came here. It's China's fault.' Leaders who base their power on a direct appeal to 'the people', whose true concerns they pretend to voice, while they seek to bypass the actual pillars of democracy (parliament, the political parties, the media, the justice system, the bureaucracy, and so on), cannot permit themselves to be seen to fail the people. Rather than risk failure, authoritarian or populist leaders sometimes even temporarily disappear from sight until they are sure they can stay in control. In 1941, after the German invasion, Stalin had briefly disappeared from the public eye, leaving Molotov to address the people of the USSR on the radio. When he got a grip on the situation again, he reappeared and assumed command of the war. Similarly, in China, Xi momentarily took a step back after the coronavirus outbreak, leaving Prime Minister Li Keqiang in the spotlight. The latter would certainly have been blamed had the lockdown measures failed; when that turned out not to be the case, Xi resumed his visible leadership role. In August 2020, the first museum exhibitions opened in Beijing and Wuhan, celebrating China's alleged speed in dealing with the pandemic under Xi's leadership.

All of these mechanisms could be clearly observed from the beginning of the pandemic in 2020. Authoritarian China, where the outbreak started, obfuscated at first: initially the local administration in Wuhan did not want to report a problem it could not solve to Beijing; when the issue did reach Beijing, the national leadership did not want to admit the extent of the crisis either, until the outbreak could no longer be denied. Then China belatedly put in place very effective lockdown measures, and mobilised the full apparatus of the state for the surveillance and repression of its citizens, which was, of course, already in place, to strictly enforce the lockdown. At the same time, the rather preposterous rumour was created that the virus originated in the US. There, a populist president did everything he could to put the blame on China, in order to divert attention from his own failure to recognise the seriousness of the threat until it was too late to prevent a massive outbreak in the US as well; even then, measures were taken only half-heartedly. In Brazil, President Jair Bolsonaro acted in a similar vein; just like Trump, even after testing positive for the coronavirus himself, he continued to downplay the depth of the crisis. The methods of authoritarianism and populism are not necessarily very sophisticated: 'CHINA!', Trump simply tweeted on 29 May 2020. The democracies in the EU were slow to act too. Once the gravity of the situation was clear, however, successive European governments took effective lockdown measures in response to the first wave of infection. Thanks to the existence of a strong state-organised public health system, healthcare was able to cope with the crisis, while the extensive social security system and economic compensation measures provided a buffer against total impoverishment. But in spite of all this, the supposedly well-organised European states were not able to avoid being swamped by a second wave in the autumn of 2020, and in many places a third wave in the spring of 2021, before vaccination got well underway, in sharp contrast to the various countries in Asia.

What the corona crisis demonstrated is that agility is not determined by the form of the state – democratic or authoritarian – but by the strength of the state: of its leadership, of its apparatus, and of the lines of command that link them. States remain the key players in domestic as well as international politics. The top of the strategic community, and the political leadership in particular, must develop a mindset that favours agility, and muster the willpower to take far-reaching decisions when the interests of the state necessitate it, based on the best information available. The better established the state apparatus is in terms of its expertise and resources relevant to the issue at hand, the more it will be able to advise the political leadership, and to act quickly and effectively upon its decisions. Agility cannot be achieved if the machinery of the state is too weak to effectively implement the decisions of the leadership, even in an authoritarian state where on paper it has absolute power. Vice versa, a strong bureaucracy may to some extent compensate for weak leadership in a democratic or authoritarian state, but without explicit political decisions it can only go so far. One could observe, for example, how the career diplomats and civil servants pushed back against some of the impulses of the Trump White House, on the domestic as well as the international front; but on many issues the president ultimately decides. Simple lines of command greatly facilitate the whole process. Confused lines of command and competing centres of authority may render even states with strong leaders and expert bureaucracies ineffective. It is a myth, for example, that Nazi Germany was a smoothly organised, efficient state: in reality, overlapping competences between various ministries and special assignment holders produced permanent infighting and waste of resources. Even in the armed forces, Nazi Germany never achieved joint unity of command between army, navy and air force, as the UK and the US established thanks to their institutionalised joint chiefs of staff meetings. Only Hitler himself had the full picture of the war, and he could obviously not run the war by himself, even had he really been a military genius.[13]

Another factor that explains strategic agility and success is the degree to which society accepts the role of the state in the policy areas concerned. As we have seen, the tendency in the US and the EU to mostly rely on the private sector of the economy may have gone too far: more public money, spent through government agencies, may be required to give substance to their respective connectivity strategies. When competition in a given policy area intensifies, the state in the end steps in – as when in the 1980s the US government intervened to help its companies maintain their primacy vis-à-vis their Japanese competitors. In a crisis that affects the totality of society, the involvement of the state will become total as well. The Second World War was a total war: all combatants eventually became planned economies, in order to mobilise each country's full war potential. In the corona crisis, all states, including the US, eventually opted for massive intervention in the economy. If the state declines to act in policy areas that are indispensable to defend its interests, it will lose out.

★★★

The EU is the only one of the great powers that is systemically handicapped, because it has no centralised decision-making system in foreign and defence policy. As these remain intergovernmental areas, in which decisions are taken by unanimity between the member states, the EU leadership and apparatus act alongside the 27 capitals and their national leadership and bureaucracy. There is no formal hierarchy; if anything, the EU institutions act within the confines of what the member states allow rather than the other way around. Such a set-up does not lend itself to agile decision making. The system can be made to work fast when the interests of all member states are obviously and directly at stake. The naval operation Atalanta, securing commercial shipping from Somali piracy since 2008, is a case in point: as everybody's commercial fleets pass there, blocking the shipping lanes would hurt all, hence the EU launched its first ever naval operation relatively quickly and has maintained it ever since. Though that can be seen as a failure as much as a success: success in deterring pirates, but that is but a symptom of the instability of war-torn Somalia, where all efforts at stabilisation have so far failed. The moment the EU (and the other states present with ships in the region) withdraws, piracy will immediately surge again. But if Atalanta is an example of fast and resolute action in response to an external problem, in general the EU system, more than anything else, tends to be a consensus-building exercise between the member states themselves.

> There was a copious flow of polite conversation, at the end of which a tactful report was drawn up ... Thus we had

arrived at those broad, happy uplands where everything is settled for the greatest good of the greatest number by the common sense of most after the consultation of all.

It reads as if Churchill witnessed a meeting of the EU's Foreign Affairs Council.[14] The 27 foreign ministers meet in the Foreign Affairs Council on a monthly basis, with the EU high representative in the chair – the EU foreign minister in all but name, because the UK when it was still a member vetoed that title (just like it vetoed any formal mention of an EU flag; officially, the EU only has a logo – though when that logo is printed on cloth and flying from a flagpole, it looks very much like a flag). Every month, the system works itself into a frenzy, with last-minute negotiations often lasting well into the night, in order to produce lengthy Council conclusions – and then, very often, it ends there. Council conclusions often end up longer than is good for clarity and readability because member states all want to see their national points of view reflected; and if one insists on mentioning EU autonomy, then another will not yield until a sentence is devoted to the importance of EU–NATO relations; and, of course, any conclusions on security must refer to Security Council resolution 1325 on women, peace and security. By this point in the negotiations, the diplomats around the table just want to close the text; whatever happens to it afterwards is business for later. Reaching consensus within the EU thus too often is an end in itself. It is considered a success if the 27 can agree on a common position, which then becomes legally binding upon them – but adopting a common position as such has no impact on the world. That is just declaratory diplomacy; real diplomacy, in the sense of convincing states outside the EU, only starts once the EU position is clear.

This is not to belittle EU actorness: the EU and its member states have mediated key international agreements, deployed election observers, adopted sanctions, and launched military operations and civilian missions. But as the EU is not (yet) a state, not every issue of international politics automatically enters onto its agenda: the EU can only discuss what the member states agree to discuss. Hence the EU does not deliberate on every issue that, from the perspective of its interests, it ought to concern itself with. The Middle East and the Gulf is an obvious blind spot: the EU and its member states have sought to maintain the Iran nuclear deal, and have contributed to the defeat of ISIS in Syria and Iraq – but there is no strategic view on the desired regional order or even the desired end-state in Syria. Moreover, even when member states do agree, their record of implementing what they have decided is sketchy at best. In defence in particular, member states commit time and time again to cooperate more closely – and then do not. This is why the CSDP has yet to yield a substantial increase in military capability.

A proactive high representative makes a difference. An incumbent who waits for the member states to reach consensus risks waiting for ever, and ending his term with little to show for it. A high representative who wants to achieve something must push the member states into action and occasionally create a fait accompli, knowing how far he can go too far. Of course, a high representative can only make policy with the member states, never against the member states. Besides the high representative – the de facto foreign minister – the president of the European Council and the president of the European Commission play a role in international politics as well. This is often presented as an overly complicated structure, but in fact it duplicates the functions that most states have: the European Council is the meeting of the 27 heads of state and governments – its president can be seen as the EU head of state; the Commission is best understood as the EU government and its president as the EU prime minister. The Commission president in particular can play a crucial role, because other than classic diplomacy and defence, all other dimensions of international relations fall within the Commission's remit, and are decided upon by qualified majority: aid, trade, investment, climate, migration, connectivity and so on. Furthermore, the EU to a large extent achieves leverage in international politics thanks to its single market, which the Commission administers: its size gives the EU the power to set standards; modulating access to it, in particular in the light of the degree of reciprocity offered by another state, is a key instrument of a comprehensive grand strategy.

The fact remains though that the institutional set-up of the EU makes the exercise of leadership difficult, even when the top positions are held by far-sighted and resolute leaders. As a result, concludes Jolyon Howorth, 'European security policy – unlike traditional 'heroic' notions of defence and security policy – is in a very real way leaderless'.[15] This is indeed the case in security and defence policy in particular. The EU, a French diplomat once told me, has no 'chef de guerre': it is still the national head of state or government who will send a letter of condolence to the next of kin of those killed in action, even when deployed on EU operations. In fact in recent years, most combat operations have not been undertaken by the EU or even NATO, but by ad hoc coalitions of European states. One way of overcoming this lack of agility and leadership would be to introduce majority voting in all policy areas. But even if that were possible, the main challenge remains to forge a true political consensus based on mutual trust between member states. In the long term, a more federal EU with a directly elected president of the Commission could strengthen the agility of the Union. That is a commendable long-term goal, but not more than that: it does not solve any of the EU's problems today.

★★★

Unfortunately for the EU, since the 2010s a number of member states regularly attempt to block EU decision making – and such a complex system is easy to block, especially where unanimity is required. The EU has traitors in its midst: certain governments willingly act as agents of China or Russia or both and consciously slow down, water down or block EU decisions to suit their master's interest. Some governments, notably that of Hungarian Prime Minister Viktor Orbán, even appear to be returning to authoritarianism, thus flaunting the basic values themselves on which the EU was founded. Such behaviour may buy the governments in question some short-term benefits, but in the long term they cut into their own flesh as they weaken the negotiating position of the EU as a whole, their own states included. Indirectly these governments also weaken NATO, but paradoxically they feel they can safely go against the EU institutions and the large majority of their fellow members because they judge that whatever happens, the US will always support them.

After the Second World War, the US strongly encouraged European integration. The success of the EU's predecessor, the EEC, was intertwined with the success of NATO, which cemented the American security guarantee to Europe. This has now come to work both ways, however. Before, the EEC and then the EU could not do without NATO. But because the EU has become indispensable to the political and economic stability of Europe, NATO can no longer do without the EU either. Without the EU, there would be political instability and economic crisis, which could only result in rivalry between European states. And if the states of Europe once again became rivals, Europe would no longer be a source of allies for the US, but a source of risks. In sum: if the EU were to flounder, that would be the end of NATO as well. In such a scenario, the US might seek to replace a defunct NATO with a set of bilateral alliances – but not necessarily with all current European allies. Europeans would do well to understand that if another power were to seek to exploit the floundering of the EU and NATO to gain control of significant parts of the European continent, the US might intervene, but not necessarily in defence of all European states. Where the US would draw the line would depend on which parts of Europe it would judge to be essential to the *American* interest, and on how many resources it would be willing to spend on Europe in the context of its strategic competition with China.

The Trump administration openly sided with the Polish and Hungarian governments in their disputes with the EU institutions. But undermining the EU might precisely provoke other powers to take advantage while the Europeans cannot be sure of the future strategy of a US that is focused on China. The conservative Polish government may feel that inviting the US to build a 'Fort Trump' on its territory, as it did in 2018, is a sufficient guarantee against any eventuality. But when push comes to shove, the cavalry manning the fort may decide that those living around it are expendable. That is why the populist European political parties and governments that are actively undermining the cohesion of the EU are playing with fire, as are those Americans who support them. Orbán may espouse the fiction of what he has called 'illiberal democracy', but he forgets that today the purpose of NATO is not just to defend the territory of its members, but also the democratic model that they have created in their countries. That was not the case when NATO was founded, when for strategic reasons more than one dictatorship was invited to join. But today, any democratic government in a NATO ally would be hard put to convince its public to put its armed forces in harm's way in order to defend a dictatorship in another NATO country. It is first and foremost the EU's responsibility to uphold democracy in all of its members, yet it is surprising how little NATO, and the US, have to say about the democratic backsliding in several allies. The primary responsibility, of course, lies with the EU member states themselves. They are behaving like the crusader kingdoms: quarrelling among themselves while Saladin is poised to take Jerusalem.

★★★

The EU and the US demonstrated great strategic agility at the end of the Cold War. The creation of the EU was in itself a most agile response to a quickly evolving international situation. Originally the EEC was set to take further steps towards economic and monetary union at an intergovernmental conference of its members. Sensing that bipolarity was coming to an end and that international politics was entering a new paradigm, the member states decided to add political union to the agenda. In 1991 they signed the Treaty of Maastricht, creating the EU, and equipping it with a foreign and security policy so that the Union could chart its own course in the new strategic context. Maastricht was a major leap in European integration. As seen in the previous chapter, the EU then launched an impressive series of initiatives, culminating in its enlargement, and in the creation of the ENP. Added to this was the reorientation of NATO: the US and its European allies agreed to open the alliance to new members from the other side of the Iron Curtain, and gradually focused NATO on new tasks. From the collective defence of alliance territory, NATO shifted its priority to expeditionary operations around the globe. Instead of dissolving the alliance, as some advocated in light of the dissolution of the Soviet Union, the US was thus able to maintain it as a key source of power. Working closely together, Americans and Europeans made full use of the opportunities that the end of superpower confrontation offered to revitalise the UN Security Council, to expand and deepen the multilateral architecture, and to consolidate democracy and capitalism on the European continent.

Faced with the arrival of full-fledged multipolarity and the intensification of competition between the great powers in the 21st century, the EU started to further reorient its grand strategy, more gradually this time, because its path now tended to diverge from that of the US. Over time, the EU started to establish itself as an independent power in international relations. But the habit of looking to Washington for strategic guidance, and the desire to avoid too brusque changes in order not to undermine cordial relations with the US and the strength of NATO, in combination with divergences of opinion within the EU about future relations with the US and China, meant that the EU could not show the same agility as during the 1990s. The attitude of the Trump administration to Europe and China did push the EU to try and define its own strategy more precisely. At the same time, the margin of manoeuvre for the EU to act as a mediating power also depended to a very large extent on China's strategy. By the start of the 2020s, the EU had thus only begun to explore its potential role in a multipolar context. To the extent that Brussels was keeping its options open, this could be understood as a form of agility; but it could also be a symptom of indecision or internal dissent.

Early in the 21st century, the US itself allowed its grand strategy to be hijacked by terrorism. The 9/11 terrorist attacks in 2001 understandably shocked the US strategic community and the nation at large, and were met with a justified response in the invasion of Afghanistan and the destruction of al-Qaeda as an organisation. But the US went much further than necessary and declared a 'global war on terror'. That did not make strategic sense in the first place: as we have seen, one cannot focus strategy on an instrument that various players with widely different interests and ends are using. Moreover, it led to a very unidimensional view of international politics and of the American interest, which suffered as the Bush Junior administration dogmatically looked at every issue through the prism of terrorism. Only under President Obama did the US regain its strategic agility. Obama did not quite succeed in ending the wars in Afghanistan and Iraq as he had promised, but he did reorient US strategy towards the key question of the century: how to deal with multipolarity and the re-emergence of a peer competitor to the US.

Agility turned into absolute fickleness under the Trump administration, however. Both the US' allies and its adversaries had to adjust to constant changes in US policy – and to policy being made live on Twitter, following the president's whims, rather than through officials channels. This fickleness extended to strategy towards the other great powers. We have already seen how US and NATO deterrence measures after the Russian invasion of Ukraine risked being undermined by Trump's seemingly trusting approach of Putin. Even Trump's constantly hawkish stance on China appeared to be offset by confidential meetings with Xi in which Trump privately offered to abandon support for Taiwan and other mainstays of US policy in return for Chinese actions that would benefit his re-election, as former National Security Advisor John Bolton revealed.[16] President Trump was not just fickle; he did also demonstrate enormous agility – but the constant behind it was always his personal and not the American interest. The standing of the US reached a low ebb as both allies and adversaries realised that as long as Trump occupied the White House they could not count on US policy being the same in the afternoon as it was in the morning. On the domestic front, the fact that the Republican Party continued to support President Trump meant that foreign policy too became increasingly partisan.[17] The US strategic establishment is coming to be as polarised as American society as a whole, which does not bode well for the quality of the American strategic debate. The Biden administration that came after Trump had to start with a lot of re-building.

★★★

China, by comparison, has since the turn of the century more consistently shown agility, adapting its grand strategy to the new possibilities opened up by the changing international environment and the shifting balance of power. Leveraging its economic power to gain influence, including in the EU, when Americans and Europeans were momentarily out of action after the 2008 financial crisis, is a good example. Under Xi Jinping, China adopted a more assertive, confrontational stance, however, which risks reducing its agility. On the one hand, Beijing's assertiveness reduces other states' openness to cooperation with China as often as it increases it; in many cases, it pushes states into coalescing against China. Arguably, a confrontational approach thus limits the opportunities that a more agile strategy might exploit. On the other hand, once a state is stuck in a confrontational mode, it often is difficult to change back to a more constructive approach. Domestically, a strong nationalism has been called forth and cannot be simply wished away again. Factions within the party and state apparatus, including in the armed forces, that have a stake in a confrontational strategy will actively labour to maintain it. In international politics, once suspicion of one's motives has been provoked, it takes a long time to rebuild sufficient trust to enable renewed constructive relations.

China's more collective leadership that ruled before Xi's centralisation was naturally more pragmatic and cautious, argues Minxin Pei.[18] Xi has indeed greatly increased the centralisation of power, building himself up as the 'core' of the party regime. Internally, his rule has seen increased repression, whereas until then there had been a modest and gradual loosening of controls. Centralisation has left less space for debate within the CCP. The disastrous management of the coronavirus outbreak led to a resurgence of criticism within the party, but whether this may lead to an evolution of China's strategy over time is difficult to assess. An important test will be whether Xi steps down as president of China in 2023, after two terms, or stays on, making use of the abolition of the two-term limit introduced by Deng Xiaoping that Xi engineered in 2018. In doing so, Xi has inserted a significant element of instability in a system that Deng created precisely to consolidate stability after the upheaval of the end of Mao's rule. First comes the uncertainty about whether Xi will effectively seek to remain president for a third term or even for life. If he does, then comes the question of how the succession will be arranged afterwards, having abandoned the system that ensured a peaceful and organised handover of power since the 1980s. If the factions in the party that are hostile to Xi would manage to force a return to more collective leadership in 2023, that should not be mistaken for abandoning China's great power aspirations, but it might just mean a softening of its approach, both at home and abroad, that leaves more room for cooperation with the rest of the world. However the power struggles within the CCP evolve, CCP rule as such seems firmly entrenched.

In abandoning the two-term limit, Xi, like Trump, has put his personal interest over the national interest. Deng's system had solved what is a classic handicap of most authoritarian states: the absence of a system of succession. When the president dies or is otherwise incapacitated, a struggle for power often ensues that can paralyse government for a considerable period of time, or that results in a radical overturn of all existing policies. Even in absolute monarchies, a peaceful succession is not guaranteed: exactly because the prize is absolute power, more than one family member of the deceased monarch may feel called upon to assume the throne. The history of the Roman Empire in the west shows us what happens when 'he became emperor who could make himself emperor'.[19] Meanwhile, some republics have become quasi-monarchies where the presidency is handed over from father to son, even in supposedly communist North Korea. A dictatorship is thus inherently unstable, and that can influence its strategy. 'Totalitarianism is its own true enemy, and that is the secret it keeps from itself by attacking others', writes Timothy Snyder.[20] This holds true for Russia in particular, which does not appear to have any system of succession at all: nobody knows who will succeed Vladimir Putin, just like Putin himself was produced seemingly out of the blue to succeed Yeltsin. Putin has copied Xi, however, amending the constitution so as to accord himself the possibility of running for two more six-year terms as president; the changes were approved by a constitutional referendum in the midst of the corona crisis in June 2020. This implies that Russian grand strategy, which as we have seen has shown a lot of tactical agility and opportunism that not always benefits Russia's long-term strategic interests, will likely steer the same course for some time to come.

Amazingly, Donald Trump managed to create doubt about the system of succession in the US, which ought to be perfectly stable and predictable (even though the particularities of the system mean that the candidate who wins the popular vote does not necessarily win the presidency – Hillary Clinton gained 2.87 million more votes than Trump in 2016). In the course of the 2020 presidential campaign, Trump repeatedly hinted that the elections would need postponing or, worse, that the election procedures were fraudulent and that he would not automatically accept the results. When the media proclaimed Biden the winner a few days after the election, Trump refused to gracefully acknowledge defeat, as is customary. Incited by Trump's inflammatory speeches, on 6 January 2021 his supporters stormed the Capitol, where Congress was about to confirm Biden as president. That was nothing less than an attempted coup d'état. Fortunately, it failed, and Biden was sworn in on 20 January. But the damage to the prestige and power of the US was enormous, for this went to the core of the American way of life. And a state that is no longer sure of its own way of life, cannot be but an erratic international player – which is something very different from an agile player.

The EU offers the opposite image because the supreme political leadership is not directly elected. Every five years the elections for the European Parliament are followed by a period of intense wrangling between the member states, the European Parliament, and the European political parties (in which the national parties of the same conviction are grouped) for the allocation of the top jobs. The budgetary cycle, somewhat bizarrely, does not coincide with the electoral cycle: the EU budget is allocated for a seven-year term – that too demands intense negotiations between the member states and the EU institutions. Apart from these two moments (which can each last months, of course), the EU system, though not very agile, is fundamentally very stable, in spite of its complexity.

★★★

Agility must not only be balanced against patience – it also requires courage. If sometimes quick action is required, at other times it may be necessary to wait and see whether a developing situation affects one's interests. If it does not, then decision makers have to muster the courage not to act, and persist in implementing existing strategy, if necessary in the face of public opinion or interest groups clamouring for action. But if it does, it also takes courage to demonstrate agility and change a strategy that may have long standing. Without a minimum of daring, one cannot be a strategic player.

8

Courageous: Dare to Go In, Dare to Get Out, Dare to Stay Out

Making decisions on grand strategy takes courage: vital interests are at stake, so the consequences of failure may be grave, especially if one is engaged in active rivalry with another power. This is a different kind of courage than gallantry on the battlefield, of course; it is the courage to take responsibility, which is a requirement for strategic success, as Sir Hew Strachan notes.[1] Every decision is based on imperfect information, and one can never fully know the intentions of the other powers – the fog of diplomacy is as real as the fog of war. Accepting a degree of risk is inevitable, therefore, or one would never make any decision – and indecision and inaction have consequences too. The French and British policy of non-intervention in the Spanish civil war (1936–39) in practice amounted to a weakening of the legitimate Republican government, for Italy and Germany did militarily support Franco's rebellion, and London and Paris had no intention of stopping them. In such cases one must agree with Talleyrand, who defined non-intervention as 'a metaphysical and political term that means more or less the same as intervention'.[2] Sometimes, of course, not acting really is the best course to take. But not acting must be a conscious decision, because one assesses that one's interests are not sufficiently at stake to warrant action; it must not be the result of inertia or mere risk aversion.

In grand strategy avoiding failure is not necessarily the same as success. By escaping from the European continent through Dunkirk, the UK between 26 May and 4 June 1940 narrowly avoided the destruction of the British Expeditionary Force. That was justifiably celebrated as a remarkable achievement, but as Churchill dryly remarked: 'Wars are not won by evacuations.'³ Real success means achieving one's ends, which one must define in a sufficiently ambitious way to safeguard one's interests in the first place. That end, in 1939, had been to defeat Germany and restore the independence of Poland; instead, by sitting tight in defensive positions during the 'phoney war' and leaving the initiative to Germany, France and the UK invited failure. 'The certain fact was that neither we nor the French were doing anything more warlike than dropping pamphlets over Germany', wrote General Spears, Churchill's liaison officer to French premier Paul Reynaud, 'What these contained, I did not know; the only thing we could be certain about was the use to which the Germans would put this paper'.⁴ Powers should heed Churchill's advice: ' "Safety first" is the road to ruin in war, even if you had the safety, which you have not' – a rule that applies in peacetime as well.⁵ Strategists must therefore be prepared to do what they *have* to do to defend the interests of the state, rather than what they would *like* to do. For, to quote Churchill again: 'One thing is absolutely certain, namely that victory will never be found by taking the line of least resistance.'⁶

The most sensitive decision that a state can make is to threaten or to use force or, in other words, to threaten or to go to war. Because it is so sensitive, both vis-à-vis other states and their own public opinion, states often prefer to veil this decision and refuse to name war for what it is. Instead they purport to undertake imperial policing, constabulary operations, humanitarian intervention, crisis management, peace enforcement, kinetic action and so on. It is ironic how in 2021 many governments are more prone to use martial language to talk about the coronavirus than about actual military operations. The words that states use change, but the meaning remains the same: war. And war means killing and being killed. As the Duke of Wellington, reflecting on the fallen and the wounded, wrote in his despatch to London from the field of Waterloo, where on 18 June 1815 he had just defeated Napoleon: 'Nothing except a battle lost can be half so melancholy as a battle won.' Preserving human life is an absolute value. In principle, therefore, states do not threaten war lightly – not unless they are willing and ready to act upon the threat if it is not heeded; and they go to war with the utmost restraint, not putting their soldiers' lives at risk unless the vital interests of the state are at stake. Different states have different ways of life, however, and each society assesses the tipping point, at which duty or honour demands that citizens risk their life for their country, differently.

Even when the strategic community is inclined to show restraint, the pressure from public opinion to intervene militarily can be great. Emotions are never far away: people care about the plight of other people, or they feel that national honour is at stake, or that a crime is being committed and justice must be served. 'Do something, General!' is a recurring refrain in international crisis situations, as my Belgian colleague Brigadier General (Ret.) Jo Coelmont testifies. Moreover, precisely because the armed forces are a readily available instrument to be deployed overseas, from which some immediate effect can usually be expected, the temptation is often there to use that instrument within easy grasp. Other instruments often need more time to be mobilised. Powers that possess military preponderance are more prone to give in to this temptation then others – and then just as often overreach. But resisting this pressure and temptation when the national interest dictates that no military action is warranted, can be difficult. 'One of the hardest things to decide is to do nothing', writes Sir Lawrence Freedman, because it creates a perception of indifference or helplessness.[7] It is easier to start a war than to end one. Thucydides already noted that 'At the beginning of an undertaking the enthusiasm is always greatest'.[8] But even if the primary objective of a war is clear, second- and third-order effects of war are extremely difficult to predict; war often generates new problems. Therefore, and because people value human life, for most states war is an instrument of last resort: one that they will revert to only when no other instruments can reasonably be judged effective to safeguard their vital interests.

The military instrument can, of course, also be used for actions short of war: deterrence, military diplomacy (dialogues, port visits, exchange of military students and faculty), training the armed forces of partners and allies, monitoring sanctions regimes, peacekeeping with the agreement of all parties before or after a conflict. Any such action that involves an overseas deployment, however, carries with it the risk that the force is targeted, and must be withdrawn, or reinforced in order to retaliate – in other words, whoever deploys the military, even for a peaceful purpose, must be ready to make decisions about war.

★★★

'I have no doubt that, if the cost of the war continues at its present level, we will not be able to sustain it; but it would be a great shame if, having spent so much, we lost any chance that spending a little more might recover everything.'[9] This statement by King Philip II of Spain on the Dutch revolt is a classic example of the kind of circular reasoning that states often fall victim to once they are committed to war. So much blood and treasure have already been spent, that it cannot be in vain; so we must spend more blood and treasure, until we win. So the war goes on – until one loses. The refusal to see reality often leads to defeat. Other historical examples abound. Napoleon's grand strategy failed, because the war economy that his conquests created had to be fed by ever new conquests. Rather than consolidate his empire and conclude mutually acceptable peace treaties with the other parties, he imposed punishing settlements and embarked upon new wars, until he overreached by invading Spain, where a guerrilla war became a permanent sore, and Russia, where the Grande Armée was destroyed.[10]

The US' unwillingness to cut its losses in Vietnam can be compared to the futile effort to hang on in Afghanistan from 2001 until 2020, when the Trump administration in the end made a deal with the Taliban. The (horrible) irony is that when, after the end of the Second World War, France fought a war to maintain its colonies in Indochina, the US initially tried to dissuade it. By the time France conceded defeat, after it lost the battle of Dien Bien Phu in 1954, the US had espoused the domino theory, however, fearing that if communists would come to power in one country, they would inevitably seek to take over the next one, and so on until all of Asia would be under communist control. Thus the US took over and poured in ever more troops.[11] Even when Nixon and Kissinger ultimately decided to get out, they felt they had no option but to first escalate the war in order to end it.[12] Just like in Vietnam, in Afghanistan many American and allied soldiers were killed or wounded long after it had become clear that their sacrifices were no longer making any difference; that the war was, in Theo Farrell's word, unwinnable.[13] In 2007, an American three-star general confidentially analysed the Afghan war for me: its most concrete result up to then, he said, was that the war had spilled over to Pakistan, which was obviously of far greater importance to the US than Afghanistan. So the general asked me: what are we still doing in Afghanistan then? Afghanistan will without any doubt remain a fractious and violence-ridden country for years to come – but American and European troops could not stay there forever. The question was not, or not only, what the Afghan interest was; the US and its European allies invaded to defend *their* interests. Gradually, however, the broad objective of state-building superseded their initial precise objective of destroying al-Qaeda and capturing Osama bin Laden. But from at least 2006 it was clear that this new broad objective was unachievable. The coalition ought to have asked itself much earlier whether its interests were still served by continuing the war in Afghanistan. But the US refused to acknowledge reality, while the Europeans simply stayed as long as the Americans stayed. Out of loyalty and out of calculation (not willing to undermine NATO) the Europeans did not even try to influence American strategy.

Pretending that one is winning when one knows one is losing, and neglecting to take the decisions that one's interests demand, is not only hypocritical – it is criminal, for soldiers die implementing orders that the leadership knows have become meaningless. 'You are a man! For you know how to say: "I was wrong"', De Gaulle said to Eisenhower in December 1944, after convincing him to rescind the order to withdraw from freshly liberated French territory in order to concentrate troops against the surprise German offensive in the Ardennes.[14] Alas, many are not courageous enough to admit their mistakes. With Colin Gray, one must deplore that 'it is a sad feature in the nature of strategy and strategists that poor performance often encourages renewed effort, rather than discouraging and (if possible) terminating adventures that are failing'.[15]

★★★

Even more than other strategic decisions, the choice to go to war requires a precise definition of the ends in relation to the national interest. Christopher Coker created a fictional Clausewitz in order to convey the great strategist's thinking, and had him state this very clearly:

> You have to define what you understand by victory and thus know when to end the war and so design a post-war settlement that will make victory long-lasting. For even when you win a victory, you have to know how to use it, that is, to translate it into political capital, and that's often the most challenging task of all.[16]

Of today's great powers, the US and the EU struggle with this more than Russia and China, because of their inclination to present every war as a fight for the universal values of democracy, human rights and the rule of law, rather than as an intervention to defend their own interests. Indeed, the public debate about strategy in America and especially in Europe has been deformed to the extent that many reject any use of force that is ostensibly in the national interest – as if acting to defend one's own interests were a bad thing. Occasionally, intervention does have a purely or at least primarily humanitarian purpose. When Europeans deploy peacekeeping forces in Central Africa, for example, they contribute to upholding the Charter of the United Nations, which indirectly serves their interests as well, or they join an operation to gain credit with the state that proposed it. For most participating states few or any national interests are directly at stake – with the exception, usually, of the former colonial powers. In 2005 the UN General Assembly enshrined the Responsibility to Protect (R2P), which epitomises the idea of intervention to protect others. The principle of R2P holds that if a state is unable or unwilling to protect its citizens from war crimes, crimes against humanity, genocide or ethnic cleansing, or is itself the perpetrator, the Security Council may decide to supersede that state and authorise military intervention. Such altruistic acts are the exception, however. Whatever the official narrative, war is normally made to defend the national interest. Interests can coincide, of course: an intervention to defend the national interest can at the same time benefit the local population. The humanitarian motive may be as sincere as the aim of defending the national interest; but if the latter were not at stake, the operation most likely would not have been undertaken for humanitarian reasons alone.

The problem is that by nonetheless cloaking most interventions in the language of values, Europeans and American create confusion about the ends of a war. And when the ends are not clear, it is not clear when operations must be halted or reoriented. The ends of a war are either limited or unlimited. Unlimited war aims at the total military defeat of the enemy state (or non-state actor) and, more often than not, replacement of its government by a new, friendly regime. Limited war aims at ends that can be achieved short of total defeat and regime change. European or American interests, when they do require military intervention, can almost always be safeguarded short of replacing the incumbent regime with European or American-style democracy in the target state. But if democracy is the avowed purpose, how to legitimately end the war in the eyes of one's own public, media and parliament?

★★★

This issue is more acute for the EU than for any of the other great powers, because only the EU is confronted with a very instable periphery, to its south, from where security problems may easily spill over into Europe, and where military intervention might therefore be required. There has not been a year without war somewhere in North Africa, the Middle East or the Gulf since the beginning of the century. Neither the US or China, nor Russia, by contrast, are faced with conflicts or disputes on their borders that might threaten their vital interests; the conflicts and disputes that do exist in their peripheries, are, in fact, mostly of their own making. The great powers all play a role in the regions on Europe's southern flank, though; hence the 21st century history of war and intervention there provides a good illustration of the need for courage when deciding about war and peace.

After the American invasion of Iraq in 2003, the next intervention by a great power in the region took place in Libya in 2011. Why did Europeans and Americans intervene? There was a genuine humanitarian concern, as the Qadhafi regime was about to crush the uprising by the opposition, and many feared for brutal reprisals. The Libyan opposition's call for assistance was supported by the Arab League, in light of which Russia and China, who usually resist intervention (and hold a veto), abstained and thus allowed the Security Council to activate R2P for the very first time. Perhaps the main end that Europeans and American pursued was to safeguard their political influence in the region, which was waning after their slow reaction to the 'Arab Spring', the revolutions that had toppled the authoritarian regimes of Presidents Ben Ali in Tunisia and Mubarak in Egypt. Both had been supported by the West, which hesitated to choose the side of the opposition. Was this sufficient ground to intervene? The intervention resulted in victory for the opposition, but that was not formally its objective: the UN mandate was to protect civilians. Many argue that regime change had been the actual, though non-avowed, European and American end from the start. Probably, the dynamic of the civil war would always have led to this result: once outside powers intervened, they could not allow the opposition to lose; hence the only possible outcomes were a compromise agreement between the opposition and Qadhafi, a palace coup ousting him or, as eventually happened, his death.

Europeans and Americans then declared victory and pulled their hands off Libya, with the result that they quickly lost any permanent benefits that they might have counted on resulting from their intervention. A permanently instable Libya became a gateway for large-scale migration to the EU, and a theatre where other powers pursued their geopolitical rivalry. This included Russia, which saw and grasped an opportunity to pursue a potential strategic outcome – a permanent military presence on the central Mediterranean coast – at relatively low cost; at the very least, by fuelling the civil war, Russia would distract the EU from its eastern periphery. Moscow maintained deniability by operating through private security contractors – mercenaries. The EU from 2020 started to try and wrest back the diplomatic initiative, but for lack of engagement with the military situation on the ground, its leverage remained limited. The EU as well as NATO did deploy maritime operations in the central and eastern Mediterranean respectively, but their ends were extremely vague. Formally, EU operations focused on enforcing the arms embargo against Libya, but they were also declared to contribute to the fight against human trafficking – though in reality they did not; NATO operations mostly just focused on creating situational awareness. Neither the EU nor the NATO maritime operations had any significant impact on the security situation of the region; their real end seemed to be to show resolve to their domestic audiences.

One of the factors that contributed to the decision to intervene in Libya was the assessment that, as Qadhafi had no real allies, the war would not spread beyond Libya. In fact, in a typical example of unforeseen second and third-order effects, the opposite happened. First, Qadhafi's defeat pushed many combatants, who were foreign mercenaries and had no future in Libya, into Mali, where they swelled the ranks of an existing rebellion that now threatened to destroy the Malian state. Thereupon France, one of the initiators of the intervention in Libya, decided to intervene in Mali as well, in 2012, and managed to stabilise the situation. At the start of the 2020s, the Europeans had achieved their end of containing the security situation in Mali and avoiding spill-over to the region as a whole and to Europe, but only through a permanent military presence, with a 5,000-strong French force as its backbone. The EU as such had deployed several hundred personnel on a military training mission and two civilian capacity-building missions (including one in Niger) to train the internal security forces, and there were 15,000 UN peacekeepers in operation MINUSMA, while the US supported the Europeans with specific assets. Having economic interests in the region, and seeking to increase its influence, China contributed several hundred troops to the UN force and, like the Europeans and Americans, funded the G5 Sahel, the cooperation between Burkina Faso, Chad, Mali, Mauritania and Niger to stabilise the region. The Malian state remained very fragile, however; and in 2020 was shocked by a military coup. Moreover, even the semblance of success in Mali remained dependent on uncertain external factors, such as the continued European security cooperation with Algeria, itself on the brink of instability.

Another unforeseen second-order effect of the Libya campaign was that it contributed to the decision of the Syrian opposition to rise up as well, in the hope that they would also gain western military support. But because the Syrian regime did have determined allies in Russia and Iran, Europeans and Americans decided not to intervene, for fear of escalation, though they did support those opposition groups that they judged amenable to their interests (notably the Kurds) with arms and training. In 2014, in a third-order effect, ISIS, which had been able to rise in Iraq in circumstances that could still be traced back to the botched American invasion in 2003, struck into Syria as well, and launched a terrorist campaign in Europe. President Obama then created the international coalition that intervened against ISIS; but the US still stayed clear of direct military action against the Assad regime, with the exception later of missile strikes under President Trump in retaliation for the use of chemical weapons. Europeans and Americans also provided arms and training for the Iraqi armed forces. Meanwhile, Moscow and Tehran did intervene directly on the side of their ally, and achieved their end of maintaining President Assad in power. One clear end that Europeans and Americans achieved was the destruction of ISIS – an unlimited war aim. Neither had a clear end-state for Syria in view, however, which entered the 2020s still in a state of domestic strife. The US did pursue a regional end: helping Saudi Arabia gain regional dominance, and curtailing the influence of Iran (which had gained a military presence in Syria as well as Iraq and Yemen). The EU had the clear end of preventing Iran from acquiring nuclear weapons, which led to a divergence with the US when Trump withdrew from the nuclear deal that the EU considered to have achieved that objective. For the US, that was part of its regional strategy in support of Saudi Arabia; the EU did not have a regional strategy or a view of the desired regional order.

Mali and Syria might very well have ended up in a crisis situation anyway (and Iraq never really emerged out of the crisis since 2003), but the fact is that the European-American intervention in Mali was a primary factor in triggering escalation. Were the benefits of the intervention worth these negative effects? The answer can only be: no. Libya represents a failure of European and American strategy. At the time in 2012, I was strongly in favour of intervention; with hindsight, that was an obvious mistake, because no vital or essential interests were at stake. Developments in Libya did not threaten the EU or the US; had they not intervened, the Libyan opposition would have perished – but European and American security would have been unharmed. They did stand to lose status and influence by not intervening; but what prestige they won by acting, they quickly lost by leaving Libya to its fate afterwards. Moreover, Russia and China heavily criticised what they saw as abuse of R2P, as did many Arab and African states (including, rather hypocritically, many that had called for intervention). EU (if not US) interests were directly at stake in the migration and refugee crisis that resulted from the war, which arguably would have warranted military intervention, as part of a comprehensive strategy, in order to stabilise the situation, create a window of opportunity for a political solution and bring the Libyan borders back under control. But when it did prove necessary, Europeans were unwilling to intervene.

The conclusion, that EU and US interests would have been better served by not going to the rescue of the Libyan opposition, seems harsh. But only to Europeans and Americans, who have been raised in a strategic culture that holds that they have both the responsibility and the capacity to protect the citizens of other states from harm. This 'humanitarian interventionism' goes back to the 19th century; but one should not be ignorant of the selectiveness of the causes promoted (inevitably, some peoples were deemed more worthy of salvation than others) nor to the hardcore interests that the liberal impulse often obscured. It is in any case entirely absent from Russian and Chinese strategic culture; Moscow and Beijing have no compunction acting, or not acting, according to the national interest (though Chinese strategic culture is much less favourable to military action). The point of grand strategy is to preserve one's way of life; interests dictate that, a priori, war should not be made and lives put at risk for any other purpose, and even then only as a last resort, in view of the risk of second- and third-order effects putting even more lives in peril. Many use the term 'war of choice' for any war not in defence of the national territory in response to a direct attack. This wording not only suggests an undesirable frivolity in making momentous decisions, as Sir Hew Strachan rightly remarks;[17] it is also thoroughly misleading. If from the point of view of the national interest not going to war is as viable as making war, that really is not a choice at all: in that case, one should always avoid war. In Donald Stoker's words: 'If it is not important enough to win, it is not important enough to go to war.'[18] If interests do demand military action, the ends of the war should be clearly defined at the outset.

★★★

For the EU, at the start of the 2020s the main challenge in this regard remains the growing instability in North Africa, the Middle East and the Gulf; unlike for the other great powers, for the EU this presents direct risks for its territory and for its connectivity with the world. The security situation in these parts of the world is much more likely to get worse than to get better as the COVID-19 pandemic interacts with the existing climate, economic, demographic and security challenges in the region.

Europeans disagree, however, on how best to safeguard their interests. Because of the enormous number of people that have tried to move to Europe ever since the wars in Libya and Syria started, many in the EU have come to see the Mediterranean as the border – and some want that border (and the land border in South Eastern Europe) closed. But withdrawing from the African continent and Near Asia, and 'holding the line' in the Mediterranean, is not an option: the risk of negative spill-over effects of security crises is simply too great, and when Europeans and Americans move out, others move in. The EU must be careful what is wishes for: it may not wish to commit itself, and it may call upon other powers to play a 'responsible' role – but Brussels cannot allow Russia, Turkey, the various Gulf states or even China to steer the policies of its southern neighbours in a direction that is detrimental to its interests. As Sir Halford Mackinder posited:

> A vast belt of almost uninhabited, because practically rainless, land extends as the Sahara completely across Northern Africa into Arabia. Central and Southern Africa were almost as completely severed from Europe and Asia throughout the greater part of history as were the Americas and Australia. In fact, the southern boundary of Europe was and is the Sahara rather than the Mediterranean.[19]

Other Europeans therefore feel the need to engage militarily in North Africa and the Middle East, which they see as a forward line of defence: this is where security problems have to be contained so that they do not affect Europe. Others still seek to pursue much more ambitious objectives and aim to fundamentally reform the states on the EU's southern flank (which in the definition of the EU Global Strategy reaches as far south as Central Africa). But the reality is that the EU has neither the means nor the leverage nor even the legitimacy to democratise and entirely remodel these countries. As we shall see in the next chapter, democratisation cannot be engineered from the outside.

It appears that the EU has no realistic option but to pursue limited ends in its southern periphery: ends that would be sufficiently ambitious to safeguard Europe's interests yet that the EU could achieve with the resources that it could commit itself on a long-term basis. EU interests do not require EU-style democracy to be created. Rather, as a first end, the EU could aim at building a ring of states on Europe's southern flank that provide sufficiently effective and inclusive government to appeal to their own broad population. That would be a precondition for the second end: to build local security and defence forces that are able and willing to uphold an acceptable degree of internal security, in order to maintain public support for the state – the people should support the state, and the soldiers should be willing to fight for it. That, in turn, should ensure the ultimate end: to prevent the emergence of security problems that could threaten the European interest. As General Sir Rupert Smith concludes, such limited ends call for a different definition of success. Wars in the region have tended to be 'wars amongst the people', pitting various groups within a country against each other, with different external powers supporting different factions or trying to mediate; at war's end, these domestic groups have to live together again. What the EU should seek to promote, therefore, is not necessarily a resounding victory of one party over the other, but a compromise between rivals that allows people to live and to prosper.[20] Rather than seeking to impose one's will, Beatrice Heuser writes, one must try to create the willingness to accept an outcome in which all parties have a stake.[21]

Even these limited ends would demand a European military presence in the region, which will likely be as good as permanent. But the EU could pursue a primarily 'indirect approach', the strategic maxim that Sir Basil Liddell Hart favoured, very much like its ongoing involvement in the Sahel.[22] The main military instrument could be capacity building and mentoring of the national security and defence forces of the states concerned, so that these could undertake autonomous military operations and defend the state against internal and external threats. If the local forces would nonetheless require outside assistance, the states of the region should be called on first; they would, after all, feel the consequences of a collapsing state in their midst much more immediately than the EU. The use of European forces for direct interventions and the use of force could be reserved for crisis situations in which there would be no other way of maintaining an acceptable degree of stability and preventing threats to Europe itself. This is why France acted in Mali in 2012. Examples of 'triggers' that could warrant direct military action are conflicts that would threaten to spill over onto European territory, to cut off Europe's connectivity, to generate terrorism against Europe, to let a party with hostile intentions against Europe occupy the ground, or to generate migration to Europe on such a scale that only restoring peace could prevent it. In all other scenarios, when its interests are not directly at stake, the EU would be well advised to abstain from direct military intervention. That is not to say Brussels should stand idly by when war causes a humanitarian crisis in its periphery: it has a range of political and economic instruments that it can use, as well as indirect military instruments (such as enforcing an embargo). Only when a humanitarian crisis is so dire that the Security Council activates R2P should the EU contribute with forces even when no direct European interests are at stake. The EU was instrumental in creating this mechanism, and ought to promote its active use by the Security Council. The divides between the permanent members of the Security Council make it highly unlikely, however, that R2P would be activated anytime soon; its alleged misuse in Libya has only deepened those divides.

The EU, the US, and NATO have all come to rely heavily on the 'indirect approach' of capacity building, in the Sahel, in Iraq, in Afghanistan. Yet this approach is not without its problems, as the coup in Mali by the army that the international community had been training amply demonstrates. If a security threat to the EU, or the US, can be averted by training up the forces of a partner country, so that they can address it, that can, of course, be a cost-effective solution. But effective capacity building often takes many years; European or American troops risk overstaying their welcome before they can have sufficient impact. Training troops without supplying arms and equipment is useless. This has been problematic for the EU: legal rules have stood in the way of providing weapons to partner countries. But troops cannot go into combat unarmed; if Europe cannot supply lethal equipment, its partners will turn to someone who will. Finally, capacity building aimed at tactical and operational proficiency will have but limited effect if the partner state does not adopt an adequate strategy. This requires engagement with the country's strategic establishment as a whole, including not only the senior levels of the security and defence forces, but also the political leadership, who may not always be happy with the role assigned to it in European or American strategy. No country likes to be a buffer state, unless there is ample compensation.

★★★

Many feel that the US ought to heed the same warning: do not make war when no vital or essential interests are at stake – it seems to be the obvious lesson from the disastrous invasion of Iraq in 2003. The main issue is not *how* to fight that and other wars, as authors like Sean McFate pretend,[23] but *which* wars ought to be fought in the first place, and why. Moreover, 'western interventionism' continues to be seen as highly disruptive in many parts of the world and greatly damages the American and European image[24] – although the same critics rarely decry Russian interventionism or China's de facto military annexations in the South China Sea with anything like equal fervour. The ideological stance of the Trump administration repeatedly seemed to bring the US close to launching yet another war without obvious cause, against Iran. At the same time, in 2019 the US did to a significant extent disengage from ongoing military operations in the Middle East, notably reducing its forces in Syria to less than 1,000 (though in 2021 close to 50,000 troops remained in permanent bases across the Middle East and the Gulf). Under Trump, the US thus constantly seemed to oscillate between military posturing and isolationism; for both its allies and its adversaries, American strategy became very difficult to read.

This has left the EU (but also NATO) in a quandary. Many Europeans are suspicious themselves of American interventions and often fear that Washington will unduly escalate a dispute. A 'wargame' in which I participated as one of the EU team quickly revealed this. The scenario was an incident with China in the South China Sea. The EU team released a declaration and, when that did not score much effect, crafted another, more strongly-worded declaration. The US team, after some diplomatic movements, quickly began to move aircraft carriers around – and the EU team began to worry about the US more than about China. There certainly is no reason for Brussels to support an American war against Iran, for example, unless Tehran launches into it itself, even though this would likely put Brussels in the position of de facto siding with China and Russia (who could not prevent such a war, nor would they join it, but they would probably provide political and economic support to Tehran). Yet the Europeans need American support for those operations that they do judge necessary, against insurgent groups in the Sahel, and in order to stabilise Syria and Iraq, so as to prevent a new wave of terrorism against Europe. The EU could, with serious effort, take the lead itself in the Sahel; but it could not, with the capabilities at its disposal as it enters the 2020s, do the same in the Middle East or the Gulf, even less so simultaneously. The EU could also not maintain its global connectivity by itself. In the maritime sphere in particular, the European navies are already stretched by the need to continue to operate in the western Indian Ocean, in order to prevent a resurgence of piracy, while running the EU and NATO operations in the Mediterranean. Europeans play but a minor role in FONOPS in the South China Sea. Keeping open shipping lanes worldwide, a challenge that has become prominent on the EU agenda, is beyond its means. As we have seen in Chapter 5, for lack of sufficient expeditionary capabilities of its own, the EU remains militarily dependent on the US – and thus on America's strategic choices.

US grand strategy focuses on China, and America's force posture has increasingly come to reflect this. America's Asian alliances serve to deter China, just like its continued military presence in Europe (after all the reductions, still over 70,000 troops in 2021) is meant to deter Russia. America's allies in Asia do not need to fear ill-judged wars to the extent that Europeans fear them in the Middle East and the Gulf, though wars there would, of course, distract the US from Asia, just like invading Iraq led it to momentarily shift attention away from Afghanistan (with probably irredeemable consequences). Even the North Korean nuclear issue is unlikely to lead to military intervention, as long as Pyongyang does not itself launch an attack, precisely because it is a nuclear weapon state, and in view of its alliance with China. Nevertheless, the Chinese and American military build-up, in particular in the South China Sea, does create a risk of accidents and incidents, which would undoubtedly increase tensions further.

As a great power, the US needs to defend its interests globally. For Washington, this is not a matter of abandoning one or the other part of the world, but of prioritisation. In view of its historical involvement in the Middle East and the Gulf, and of its alliances with Israel and Saudi Arabia in particular, the US is unlikely to abandon its role in the region anytime soon. But future US administrations may wish to reconsider the nature of its role. Do American interests actually demand supporting Saudi Arabia in its geopolitical competition for Iran? Or can one conceive of alternative strategies that are less likely to lead to proxy wars in the region, and thus necessitate less American military involvement? Focusing on China may require refocusing strategy for the Middle East and the Gulf.

***

China's global presence has obliged it to review its traditional policy of non-intervention, if only because, as we have seen, the government is responsible for protecting Chinese citizens and assets abroad that may be threatened by civil war, terrorism or crime. Many Chinese investments are indeed located in some of the most instable countries. Mikko Huotari and his colleagues at MERICS have analysed the emerging Chinese thinking on the use of force: Beijing may join a multilateral military intervention, but on the conditions that every state retains the primary responsibility for its own security; that there is an imminent threat to peace and security; that the UN Security Council mandates the intervention; that the host country consents; and that the relevant regional organisations support it too.[25] For the time being, at least, China remains very suspicious of unilateral interventions, and it is unlikely to go to war itself, except for the control of what it considers to be its sovereign territory (which is, of course, a matter of dispute with other states).

Perhaps this Chinese attitude opens up opportunities for military cooperation. The other powers are understandably wary of China's growing military reach. As noted in the introduction, the opening of a Chinese navy base in Djibouti in 2017 was an eye-opener for many. Chinese diplomats, in an effort to counter the concerns, maintained that it was a naval 'station' rather than a base, though the difference seems rather ephemeral. In any case, in and of itself it is not more or less legitimate that China builds a base or a 'station' in Djibouti than that the US, the UK and France do so. The other powers, of course, need not encourage China to open more bases. But they must realise that, short of conflict or at the very least grave tensions, pushing China out once it has established a military presence will be impossible. Instead, it might be wiser to try and engage China in security cooperation in areas where interests overlap. The EU in particular, which does not regard China as a security threat in the same way the US does, could pursue such cooperation, which might be a confidence-building measure. The primary area of focus could be Africa, where Brussels and Beijing share an interest in security and stability. By cooperating, the EU could try to ensure that China's military engagement does not run counter to its interests, and respects the same norms that it seeks to uphold itself. There is a precedent: the EU's naval operation Atalanta, in the western Indian Ocean, coordinates with the Chinese naval presence in the same area. Military cooperation with China might seem outlandish to some, but it was the Ronald Reagan administration that authorised selling US military equipment to China in 1984, in a further move to isolate the Soviet Union following the gradual normalisation of US–China relations since Kissinger's and Nixon's visits in 1971–72.

However, if for now China remains uneasy at the thought of going it alone in operations, it also remains very reticent to engage in concrete military cooperation with the West, in spite of its rhetoric to the contrary. Or, as a Chinese diplomat once regretfully told me: China itself would be very interested in cooperating with the EU in Africa, but its 'African brothers' were very uncomfortable at the thought, and China could, of course, not go against them. A more likely reason probably is mere lack of trust. What could play as well is China's reluctance to reveal the limited operational effectiveness of some of its deployments. Many Chinese blue helmets in countries like Mali hardly leave their barracks, for example. The performance of the Chinese armed forces can only improve, of course, and it will. More active participation in multilateral operations would exactly be a way of enhancing experience and expertise – and of building confidence at the same time. The choice for cooperation, however, demands courage too.

★★★

Many in the US strategic establishment still defend the invasion of Iraq, and publicly at least most in the US and Europe continue to stand behind the intervention in Libya. Russia too is unapologetic about its interventions since the turn of the century, in Georgia, Ukraine and Syria. As we have seen, though, the balance sheet of these interventions is not necessarily positive for the Russian interest in the long term. Moreover, Russian public opinion does not always wholeheartedly support 'interventionism'. It is very revealing that Moscow covered up the number of casualties in Ukraine, for example. In the Central African Republic and Libya, Russian private military companies are in the forefront rather than the Russian armed forces: this modus operandi creates deniability towards other states, but also towards the Russian public itself.

When in August 2020 election fraud in Belarus triggered large-scale demonstrations against President Alexander Lukashenko, the limitations of the use of force that had become apparent in Ukraine manifested themselves again: Russian military intervention was the best way of pushing an even larger share of Belarussian public opinion into opposition against the regime, and into seeking closer relations with the EU. Moscow had been pursuing the same strategy that ultimately failed it in Ukraine: it had allowed its influence in Belarus to depend almost entirely on the power of one particular president. Paradoxically perhaps, the strategy of relying on force to maintain a sphere of influence seems to have neared its end in Russia's immediate periphery, while it has more scope further afield, in the Middle East and (North) Africa. In the former Soviet republics, Russian 'interventionism' has probably reached the point where it does more harm than good, since it antagonises local public opinion, which goes against the objective of permanently integrating these states into a network of close relations with Russia. Furthermore, China is ever more present in these countries. Beijing welcomes Russian interventions in response to actual security crises, as in the 2020 war between Armenia and Azerbaijan, but it is more pragmatic where the nature of the governments it works with is concerned, as long as its economic interests are guaranteed. Beijing would therefore likely discourage Russia from intervening for purely political reasons, in order to threaten or even to dispose of governments that Moscow sees as too western-oriented, if such interventions would cause great economic disruption.

In the Middle East and Africa, in contrast, Russia does not necessarily seek permanent ties (except in Syria): The primary aim may be to create leverage vis-à-vis the EU and the US.[26] Interventions may thus be an expression of Russia's nuisance power, thwarting European and American plans rather than pursuing any plan of its own. To that end, Russia opportunistically plays into local dissatisfaction with Europe or America, or with 'the West's own unfinished business'.[27]

What Russia does not have the courage to confront is its 'unfinished business' with China: its own 19th century territorial aggrandisement at the expanse of the Qing empire. As Niklas Swanström puts it: 'There is a fear that Russia's Far East could at some point be viewed as a 'near north' by China.'[28] In the current constellation of power between the four great powers, there is little reason for China to act on this and alienate Russia. But in a scenario in which China would grow significantly more powerful, either by confronting the US or by seeking reconciliation with it, Beijing might just remember the last of the 'unequal treaties' to be rectified.

★★★

Russia and the US resemble each other in the sense that both have a strategic culture that sees the use of force as a 'normal' instrument of strategy, to be used when interests demand it, without any moral qualms. Both Moscow and the US have experienced, however, that overly relying on the use of force may backfire. China and the EU are much more reticent. Beijing has as yet little experience with the use of force; its last combat operations date back to the war with Vietnam in 1979 – and those were not very successful. China's military expansion in the South China Sea has taken place with hardly a shot fired in anger. Nationalist forces and hawks in the military and sections of the party might yet put China on a more aggressive track, but its strategic culture has so far acted as a break on the use of the military for other purposes than to defend what for China is its national territory. Some EU member states, notably France, are more ready to use force than others, but overall Europe has developed a strategic culture that is more conscious of casualties and really does see war as a last resort. The EU Global Strategy pretends that Europe will use force primarily to protect citizens of other states that are trapped in conflict, but the reality is, of course, that when the EU or its member states do go to war, they do so to defend their own citizens and interests. The EU institutions have come a long way in terms of thinking about the role of the military instrument. But as long as the EU maintains the official fiction that the purpose of its CSDP is akin to R2P, the Europeans cannot have an effective strategic debate on why and when they may have to use force. Like all players in international politics, Europeans have to come to terms with the fact that one cannot engage in grand strategy without getting one's hands dirty.

Dirty: No Great Power Can Keep its Hands Clean

Everyone involved in making strategy must accept that inevitably they will have to face circumstances in which there are no 'good' options: a situation in which every course of action, as well as inaction, risks to produce specific negative effects for one's interests. The strategist will still have to make a rational choice, and identify the lesser evil: the option that presents the best chance of safeguarding the vital interests of the state. The reticence to make stark choices even though the situation demands it is understandable, for the decision makers will be held accountable for the potential negative consequences – but it goes against the precepts of grand strategy. A state cannot retreat from international politics and fence itself off from the world: it will have to play its part. Even if a state foregoes an active role, it will for sure be the object of the strategies of its competitors and rivals.

The history of my own country, Belgium, exemplifies how it is an illusion to think that one can escape from reality. In 1830 the great powers recognised Belgium's independence from the Netherlands, but imposed neutrality on the new state. The powers did not trust one another: by forbidding the Belgians from entering into an alliance, they made sure that none of them would dominate the kingdom. Neutrality shielded Belgium from the Franco-Prussian war in 1870. Afterwards, neutrality was raised into a dogma: the Belgian strategic establishment became convinced it would protect the kingdom forever – but in 1914 Germany violated neutrality and invaded. Following the war, the Treaty of Versailles did away with compulsory neutrality, and Belgium concluded a military agreement with France. Yet in 1936, when the threat of war was clearly rising as Nazi Germany was rearming, the country opted for neutrality again, voluntarily this time, in the vain hope that the war that by then everyone expected would pass it by. The experience of the Great War ought to have taught the strategic establishment that this was not a realistic strategic option: it was clear that any German offensive against France would once again seek to pass through Belgium. The kingdom could not stand aside from the world, and so the result of retreating into its own bubble was still the same: in 1940 Belgium was invaded a second time. Had it stayed allied with France, it would most likely also have had to face invasion, but both countries would have been better prepared; whereas by withdrawing from the Franco-Belgian military agreement, Belgium undid some of the key assumptions of French defence planning.[1]

Grand strategy, as we have seen in the first chapter, cannot aim for perfection: waiting for options that perfectly guarantee one's interests is a recipe for paralysis. It is, in fact, a form of cowardice; assuming responsibility and making choices even when all options carry risks, requires courage, as the previous chapter explained.

★★★

While often there are no 'good' options available, that would not have any negative effect on one's interests, many times no available course of action is entirely 'clean' either: all options may to some extent clash with one's values. If those values are deeply held, a decision maker will feel uncomfortable violating them, and public opinion may condemn them for it. No power can long pursue a strategy that violates its own values: the public will reject it, as, eventually, will members of the state apparatus who have to implement the strategy. In the end even members of the strategic establishment who have crafted the strategy may turn against it. At that point, the state will find itself obliged to alter course. The escalation of the US' military involvement in the war in Vietnam is a classic example. Having so many American soldiers killed and wounded for an unconvincing purpose, seeing so many villages destroyed to 'save' them from communism and feeling that the war as it was being waged could last forever led to large-scale anti-war demonstrations. In 1971 a member of the strategic establishment, Daniel Ellsberg, leaked the Report of the Office of the Secretary of Defense Vietnam Task Force, better known as the Pentagon Papers, which revealed that escalation of the war had gone much further than the US government had admitted. In the face of domestic opposition, the US could not sustain a war whose purpose no longer seemed to further American values (and interests), and whose methods of warfare continuously went against those same values.

Grand strategy demands that states stay true to their own values, therefore – but one must be realistic about what exactly that means in international politics. Values are the point of grand strategy: its overall end is to preserve one's way of life, that is one's form of government, the way society is organised and the values on which it is based. Every state has its own way of life; between some states, there are large similarities; between others great differences, if they hold different basic values. A state that holds different values is not ipso facto a rival: states with widely different values may still share interests and thus choose to cooperate. At the same time, even states with nearly identical values will still be competing for markets, resources and influence, given the inherently competitive nature of grand strategy, and may have different interests; they might even be active rivals.

Every state, no matter which way of life it adopts and which form its government takes, ought to respect human rights as enshrined in the Universal Declaration of Human Rights proclaimed by the UN General Assembly in 1948. The Declaration does state that 'Everyone has the right to take part in the government of his [sic] country, directly or through freely chosen representatives' (Article 21.1) and that 'The will of the people shall be the basis of the authority of government; this will shall be expressed in periodic and genuine elections which shall be by universal and equal suffrage and shall be held by secret vote or by equivalent free voting procedures' (Article 21.3). But at the same time the UN Charter, which is at the heart of international law, is based on the principle of non-interference in domestic affairs, and does not therefore set democratisation as an objective. In practice, therefore, one must distinguish between overall human rights promotion and democratisation in particular. For the democratic powers, staying true to their own values means that they must not only respect human rights themselves; they also have a duty to urge other states to respect human rights, and to consistently criticise all states who do not. In situations in which democratic powers have sufficient leverage (which will also depend on the presence or absence of other powers), they can promote respect for human rights by making it a precondition for certain forms of cooperation. To stay true to their values, the democratic powers, however, do not have to limit their cooperation only to states that fully respect human rights, nor are they obliged to go beyond human rights promotion and attempt democratisation.

If a value-based strategy meant that one could only cooperate with other states that, by and large, share the same values, the democratic powers would quickly find out that this would leave them with preciously few potential allies and partners. But even states that share similar values, be they democratic or authoritarian, often have such divergent interests that cooperation is limited or even impossible. During the Second World War, for example, Spain remained neutral, in spite of Hitler's attempts to convince Franco to join the war. Franco had won the civil war thanks to the military support of Nazi Germany and fascist Italy, and shared their values – but not their interests. The UK, meanwhile, was very suspicious of neutral Ireland, although it was a fellow democracy; Churchill even considered a pre-emptive military occupation of Irish seaports. During the Cold War, the Sino-Soviet split was a clear example of how two powers, which many in the western camp saw as a monolithic bloc, actually developed a very different outlook, in spite of both being communist states. On the other hand, cooperation with states that have a different way of life may in itself further one's interests. Pursuing shared interests with a state that, because of its different values and outlook on the world, may be suspicious of one's intentions, serves as a confidence and security-building measure.

Respecting one's own values can also not mean that one must actively seek to export them, and try and convince every other state to copy one's way of life. The democracies do have an interest in democratisation, because well-governed democracies that provide for their citizens generate domestic stability, which in turn serves peaceful and stable international relations. That is why the democratic powers usually support democratisation when it occurs – but they cannot trigger it. Not even the great powers have the leverage to change another state's way of life. The oft-quoted examples of Germany and Japan are not models, but the exceptions that prove the rule. After their total defeat and utter destruction in the Second World War, which entirely delegitimised the previous way of life in the eyes of the large majority of their population, the allied powers successfully helped them to embrace a new way of life, which meant in some way to return to the way of life that had already existed before the advent of dictatorship, and to grow a new strategic culture. Those specific circumstances are unlikely to be replicated; so far pretty much every other attempt has failed. Incentives, such as the EU offered to its southern neighbours under the ENP, do not work: there is little that one can offer to a leader that has absolute power to entice him to change his ways. Sanctions rarely work either: more often than not, they unite the country against foreign interference, no matter how unpopular the leadership. Military occupation has been singularly unsuccessful: after nearly 20 years of western military presence, Afghanistan still feels as if it will revert to its previous ways the day the last foreign troops leave. The Soviet Union militarily occupied its satellites in eastern Europe for 45 years, but the imprint it left on their desired way of life turned out to be very superficial. Finally, when an authoritarian regime does fall, democracy is not necessarily the natural successor. In many cases, one authoritarian regime is succeeded by another, less repressive one. Russia itself is the primary case in point: communism led, via the chaos of the Yeltsin years, to Putin. As Churchill put it rather colourfully: 'Democracy is no harlot to be picked up in the street by a man with a tommy gun.'[2] A way of life cannot be engineered from the outside; it can only be changed from the inside, organically or through a revolution – but only if the people themselves are carriers of change.

Moreover, if a state proclaims the purpose of its grand strategy to be to bring other states' way of life in line with its own, it will only antagonise others and render cooperation more difficult even when interests do coincide. Once again, aiming for perfection can be counterproductive. As seen in the previous chapter, it is in the EU's interest to foster states in the Sahel that may be relatively authoritarian, but sufficiently inclusive and effective in providing public goods to count on the support of their citizens and armed forces, so as to ensure stability. Pushing for faster and further reforms may actually create instability, while turning the incumbent government away, and potentially pushing it into the arms of other partners who care much less about values.

What counts, therefore, is not *who* one cooperates with, but *what* one cooperates on and *how*. Staying true to one's values means first and foremost not undertaking any action oneself that violates those values. In international politics, a state can thus legitimately cooperate with any other state that shares the same interests, regardless of the other's values and way of life, on the condition that in doing so, it does not become party to any violations of its own values that the other state may commit. A democracy can cooperate with an authoritarian state on foreign, security or defence policy without losing legitimacy, as long as it does not itself become party to human rights violations. Whether acting alone or in cooperation with others, democratic values will, however, proscribe the use of certain instruments, such as torture, or the indiscriminate use of force without regard for civilian life. Grey areas do exist. During the Second World War, even Churchill doubted the wisdom of carpet-bombing German cities, killing hundreds of thousands of civilians, in spite of the atrocities that Nazi Germany committed – though eventually those doubts were pushed aside. In the fight against terrorism today, European and American security services cooperate with the security services of states who they know do not (fully) respect human rights and the rule of law – but they use the intelligence that they share anyway. As a Belgian judge once reported his dealings with the justice system of a North African country to me: all suspects confess; those who do not confess upon arrival are taken to the basement, and end up confessing as well. Grey areas are inevitable, alas, but the overall guideline for grand strategy stands: as long as you do the right thing in the right way, it does not matter who you do it with.

The only exception to this rule would be governments that are guilty of the crimes that would warrant activating the Responsibility to Protect: war crimes, crimes against humanity, genocide and ethnic cleansing. Any cooperation with such regimes would surely constitute a violation of the values of nearly any other state. Only the Security Council can activate the mechanism and mandate action to put an end to such crimes. But any state can judge for itself, and ought to terminate cooperation with a regime that has perpetrated any of these crimes. That would mean, for example, that no cooperation should be allowed with the Assad regime in Syria. Powers that do not observe this rule, such as Russia, clearly have difficulty legitimising their course of action vis-à-vis the international community. Putin may judge, however, that the interests at stake are worth the price. Ultimately, in international politics every state will decide for itself where precisely to draw the line between its interests and its values. If the offending state is a great power or a major economy, that inevitably will influence that decision.

★★★

The irony is that while the US and many in the EU constantly accuse China and Russia of seeking to impose their way of life on other countries, it is actually America and Europe who habitually see democratisation and human rights promotion as the purpose of their foreign policy, and who feel that no non-democratic state can really be fully legitimate. Americans and Europeans often behave, as Kissinger points out, as if 'a significant portion of the world lives under a kind of unsatisfactory, probationary arrangement, and will one day be redeemed'.[3] Redeemed by the US or the EU, that is – not surprisingly, this leads to rather adversarial relations. Russia does seek to create a sphere of influence in its periphery consisting of states that emulate the Russian model, out of fear that successful democratic states would push its own population to demand regime change. China, on the other hand, pragmatically works with any state, including notably a series of EU member states, in order to further its interests.

There is a strong tendency to present international politics as a confrontation between democracy and authoritarianism. But that is a misconception. International politics is about states who pursue their interests. They cooperate and compete with other states, depending on whether interests coincide or clash, but quite regardless of their way of life. Reading international politics in general, and great power relations in particular, through the lens of democracy versus authoritarianism will generate a distorted picture, therefore. Founding a grand strategy upon that distortion will lead to faulty decisions. Most dangerously, this prism, by refusing to see non-democracies as potential partners, risks bringing into being precisely the hardening of two opposed blocs that certainly the EU seeks to avoid.

The basic values of a state do shape its grand strategy. But the fact that a state is authoritarian does not mean that it is out to conquer its neighbours or to overturn the world order. The form of their political institutions and the methods of repression that various authoritarian states use may be similar, but their values and their general outlook on the world can still be very different. Some authoritarian states do indeed espouse an ideology that centres on conquest, such as Nazi Germany and its quest for Lebensraum in Europe. Soviet Russia initially sought to fuel world revolution, but when that strategy failed, Stalin crafted the ideological principle of 'socialism in one country'. As we have seen, that did not prevent Stalin from demonstrating great strategic agility and acquiring a buffer zone on his western border, first in collusion with Nazi Germany and then as a result of its defeat. But after the Second World War, the USSR did not seek further military expansion in Europe. It did resort to force to put down opposition in its European satellites, and (like the US) was engaged in many coups and schemes in 'the third world', but it did not invade any other state until Afghanistan in 1979, and that turned out to be a serious strategic mistake, which contributed to the erosion of communist rule. Today's Russian strategy is also to some extent inherently expansionist, as Moscow dresses up as the protector of Russian speakers who allegedly share or aspire to the same way of life whichever state borders they live behind. In Czarist times, Russia claimed the right of protection over the orthodox Christians in the Ottoman empire, always with the same objective: acquiring a buffer on Russia's western borders.

Other authoritarian states, however, value internal stability and consolidation, and do not seek expansion. Some may simply be too weak, of course, to risk any foreign adventures (although domestically weak regimes sometimes engage in intervention abroad to distract public opinion from the country's own problems). China's values attach more importance to domestic stability, harmony and development than to expansion of a country that, like in imperial times, is anyway seen as the centre of the world: the Middle Kingdom. The CCP aims to consolidate China's territorial sovereignty; the problem is, of course, that its interpretation of where that sovereignty extends clashes with that of most of the rest of the world. One can certainly not rule out that the shifting balance of power may create opportunities that the Chinese strategic establishment may be tempted to exploit. But China's values and ideology are not inherently expansionist. Authoritarianism does not always equal revisionism, therefore. When one uses the term 'systemic rivalry' vis-à-vis China, as the EU does, one should clearly understand that this refers to rivalry for influence in the international system – not to the fact that China has a different domestic system from the EU and the US. 'Systemic rivalry', moreover, is not systematic: it does not exclude cooperation when interests coincide.

The sad reality is that not all democracies always respect democratic values in their domestic politics themselves, nor do they always abide by the rules-based order in international politics. China has militarily occupied most of the South China Sea with total disregard for international law, just as Russia illegally invaded and annexed the Crimea – but the American invasion of Iraq was equally illegal. In China, the Uighur people suffer a horrible fate in the militarised province of Xinjiang. But some of the policies of India vis-à-vis its Muslim population go in the same direction, as elements in the government incite violence against Muslims, and the province of Kashmir is being treated as if under military occupation. As a result of the policy of mass incarceration, 2.3 million Americans were in prison in 2020 or 655 per 100,000 inhabitants. The number for China was an estimated 3.2 million (1.7 million in prison, and 1 million Uighurs and half a million others in various detention centres), or 228 per 100,000 citizens.[4] The US does not purposely target a population group as China targets the Uighurs, of course, but it is a fact that mass incarceration disproportionately hits African Americans: they make up a third of the prison population but only 12 per cent of the total US population. Those who unjustly fall victim to the policy likely do not see the US as a beacon of human rights. The EU callously ignores the plight of the hundreds of thousands who try to cross into Europe from North Africa and the Middle East; many lose their lives in the process, or end up being maltreated in one of the many refugee camps in the states that border on the EU or even inside the EU. But as long as people do not make it across the border, or stay confined in refugee camps, Europeans can easily look away. The US too has a policy of locking up 'illegal immigrants' who cross the border from Mexico; for a while it even separated children from their parents. Chinese diplomats often do not seem to understand that for any European or American with the slightest knowledge of the Second World War, the very notion of imprisoning people in a 'camp' is abhorrent; the footage of Uighurs shoved into trains was too similar to the images from the Holocaust not to cause consternation. But somehow Europeans and Americans turn a blind eye to the camps that they create themselves, or fund others to create.

This is not to suggest any precise degree of moral equivalence between the behaviour of different states – comparing atrocities shows bad taste, and is anyway useless. Nor does it serve to excuse any state that others too violate human rights: one should judge each state by its own actions, not by what others do. The point is just to demonstrate that a black and white picture of 'virtuous' democracies versus 'evil' dictatorships is not the reality of international politics.

Moreover, the democracies often condone in one authoritarian state what they condemn in another. The US allies with Saudi Arabia in its geopolitical competition with Iran, yet in terms of political participation the latter is more democratic: in Tehran there is an elected president alongside the religious leader, whereas an absolute monarchy rules in Riyadh. If one condemns Iranian military interventions across the region, then one must condemn Saudi interventions as well. The proxy war that saw them pitted against each other in Yemen, for example, saw all parties ignoring the safety of civilians caught up in the conflict. For the US to pose as the champion of democracy and human rights while it entertains an alliance with Saudi Arabia is not very convincing; instead, it undermines Washington's credibility in many parts of the world, Europe included. But the EU too conveniently overlooks human rights abuses in Egypt, for example, where in 2014 Brussels and Washington quietly condoned the military coup by General El-Sisi, because he seemed to promise more stability in the region than the government of the elected president, Morsi, whom he ousted.

Interests will regularly require the democrats to partner or even to ally with some of the dictators, as we have seen in Chapter 4, and most democracies too at times violate the democratic values and the rules-based order even though they are sincerely committed to them. Depicting international politics as a fight of democrats against dictators, in spite of this reality, inevitably leads to double standards. One ends up explicitly condemning authoritarian states that are seen as rivals for courses of action that are but legal and legitimate uses of statecraft, while one quietly condones illegal and illegitimate actions by authoritarian states that happen to be allies or partners. Yet can one judge the same act differently depending on who undertakes it? Is China necessarily setting a 'debt trap' for another country whenever it invests in a harbour or a railway line, while any European or American investment promotes sustainable development? Is the US automatically strengthening peace and security when it 'invites' an ally to buy American weapons, while growing Chinese arms exports must of necessity undermine stability?

★★★

It is in dealing with China that Americans and Europeans are most uncomfortable, because China is both an authoritarian state and a great power.

Human rights violations in China are very visible, notably the repression of the Uighurs in Xinjiang and of democrats in Hong Kong. In 2020, repressive policies triggered unrest in Inner Mongolia as well. The negative publicity that these policies create is obviously unwelcome to the regime; arguably, they also are counterproductive for the Chinese interest. China's avowed purpose in Xinjiang is to fight terrorism, but many would argue that repression provokes radicalisation and, ultimately, violence. If it would come to that, history shows that foreign military occupation usually cannot be maintained in the face of a locally-supported insurgency. However, Xinjiang has been part of China since the Qing dynasty, and nine million Han Chinese now live there alongside 10 million Uighurs, whose treatment does not seem to overly concern the majority of the Chinese public. China's policy is therefore likely to achieve its objectives. In Hong Kong, the transition regime will come to an end in 2047, 50 years after the 1997 handover that had been agreed in 1984. That works both ways: arguably, Beijing could just show patience, and indulge some of the demands of the pro-democracy campaign; but Europeans and Americans also know that whatever might be achieved will likely only be temporary anyway. Moreover, they conveniently tend to forget that the UK introduced most democratic reforms only after 1984; before that, Hong Kong was administered as a colony in a very top-down fashion. The CCP cannot tolerate a fundamentally different form of government on its territory. Furthermore, Xi likely saw the massive protests as a personal loss of face, and thus decided to put an end to them, which the lockdown to halt the spread of the coronavirus helped to achieve. In Hong Kong too, therefore, China is set to achieve its ends.

Domestically, China thus is a massive human rights abuser; in international politics, it has become a peer competitor. For the vital interests of the US and the EU, it is the second fact that matters much more than the first: that China is a great power. If China were to become a democracy and fully respect human rights, it would still be a great power, pursuing global interests, which would often compete with European and American interests. A democratic China would still seek more weight in the multilateral architecture; it would likely still see reunification with Taiwan as a desirable goal; and it might even uphold its claims to the South China Sea (which were first advanced by the Republic of China in the 1930s). The US, for its part, would likely still aspire to global leadership as the greatest of the great powers. As stated in the introduction, Washington would not simply cut the cake in two and divide the world between itself and a democratic China, like Spain and Portugal divided the 'new world', the Americas, among themselves by the 1494 Treaty of Tordesillas, which demarcated their respective spheres of influence. (Not even the EU, and certainly not Russia, would likely figure in American calculations at that hypothetical point.) US and EU grand strategy, therefore, must logically focus on China's actions as a great power in international politics rather than on its authoritarian domestic policies. This does not mean that the US and the EU should not care about authoritarianism in China and elsewhere; it does mean that they must be aware of where the true interests of all parties lie, and of the constraints that this imposes.

China, like every other state, is free to choose its own political organisation, As seen above, a way of life, of which the form of government is a core aspect, cannot be engineered, let alone imposed, from the outside. One state has but limited legitimacy to try to change the form of government of another. Towards a great power, no state will anyhow have the leverage to attempt this, and such efforts may even backfire.[5] Many feel that engagement of China, and including it in the WTO, has failed, because it has not led to democratisation. Indeed it has not, but neither was that the original purpose of Nixon's and Kissinger's recognition of the PRC. They sought China's support against the Soviet Union in the context of great power politics; they did not seek to change China's way of life. That idea took hold only after the end of the Cold War and the demise of the Soviet Union, when many felt that CCP rule too would soon come to an end, without too much regard for the specificities of the country. The US and the EU certainly do not have to like the Chinese form of government; but they better come to terms with the fact that only the Chinese people can change it (and the same applies to Russia).

Europe and America likewise have limited leverage to promote human rights in general in China. For the Chinese government, control of both Xinjiang and Hong Kong is a vital interest. Neither EU nor US vital interests are at stake, which is why they will fail if, nonetheless, they make it their end to change Chinese policy, since the CCP cannot compromise on its vital interests, even in the face of economic sanctions. Furthermore, most Chinese people are not waiting to be liberated by America or Europe. The average member of the new middle class is not suffering permanent oppression but leads a normal life, aware of the limits placed on the freedom of expression, but confident, at least until the corona crisis, in the economic future, and in the fact that the government provides security – the streets of Beijing are safer at night than those of Brussels. The number one challenge for the CCP is to continue to guarantee rising levels of prosperity, in order to maintain legitimacy. People are proud as well of China and its position as a great power (and the government has for many years been waging an active nationalist propaganda), which makes them see foreign interference in a negative light.

The European and American way of life is, however, based on respect for human rights, and that creates a moral obligation to promote human rights everywhere. If one is committed to human rights, one must commit to their universality – otherwise they would not be human but western, European or American rights. Regardless of how they frame their demands in political terms, people everywhere seek freedom from want and freedom from harm. There is no point, though, in incurring the cost of economic sanctions or other instruments in circumstances when one can reasonably assess in advance that they cannot be effective. But the EU and the US can legitimately criticise every violation of the Universal Declaration of Human Rights and demand that states respect it, in order to uphold the discourse of human rights, and to systematically stress that respect for human rights is the norm – ergo, that violating human rights is abnormal. This may also provide moral support and strengthen the legitimacy of local human rights campaigners. In many cases, one regrettably cannot hope for any short-term or concrete impact. The Soviet Union did not alter its domestic policies, in spite of 45 years of western pressure to do so, and neither, probably, will China. But in this area 'one need not hope in order to undertake nor succeed in order to persevere', as was the motto of William the Silent, the main leader of the Dutch revolt against Spain.[6]

The US and the EU do have leverage when it comes to China's behaviour in international politics, which has a direct impact on their own interests. Rather than wasting their energy on trying to actively change China's domestic policies, which will be well-nigh impossible, they ought to reserve their potentially most effective instruments to push back against China when it threatens their interests in international politics. Paradoxically, though, Europeans especially are much more vocal about human rights issues in China than about the Chinese annexation of the South China Sea or about Chinese cases of subversion inside the EU. Yet, to put it starkly: the vital interest of the EU and the US is not how China treats the Chinese (or Russia the Russians), but how China (or Russia) treats them, in its foreign policy. Short of China's or Russia's domestic policies leading to a revolution, that is what matters for European and American grand strategy.

★★★

This stark reality also applies to the concept of order in international politics. The core of any international order are the rules that the large majority of states accept as guiding relations *between* them. How they behave within their own borders basically remains every state's prerogative. Hence the emphasis of the UN Charter, which codifies the core rules of the current international order, on state sovereignty and non-interference. The mechanism of the Responsibility to Protect is the exception, and there is a very high threshold before it can be activated. Since the Second World War, states have created an ever more dense network of specialised international organisations, to regulate specific dimensions of their relations, such as trade, and to address global challenges, such as climate change. States have endowed some of these organisations, such as the WTO, with the capacity to enforce the decisions that their members arrive at; in other areas, climate in particular, the enforcement capacity remains limited. What the rules of the international order definitely cannot purport to achieve is to change the form of government or the overall way of life of a state.

Yet that is how many who talk of a *liberal* international order understand the purpose of the rules. The reality is, however, that to the extent that a liberal international order came into being after the Second World War, it never covered the globe. Rather, as John Ikenberry explains, 'It was built "inside" one half of the bipolar Cold War system. It was part of a larger geopolitical project of waging a global Cold War.'[7] A liberal international order in the sense of promoting a specific democratic way of life only ever existed within the US led bloc. But even within the western bloc, this was applied very selectively. The core members of the bloc, the US, its Western European allies, the 'Five Eyes', and Japan, were democracies, but they actively supported many authoritarian regimes as long as they were opposed to the communist bloc, and even purposely brought down various democratic regimes that they saw as too close to the Soviets.

Joseph Nye rightly advocates to discard the term 'liberal', and refer instead to a 'rules-based' international order.[8] In the current context of increasing competition and rivalry between the great powers, maintaining a set of key rules that all powers can agree on is crucial to maintain peace and stability. China, Russia and others will never consent if the rules are seen to favour one specific form of government only. Once again, the EU and the US need not accept the Chinese or Russian way of life – but they need to accept that it is not up to them to change it. What they can aspire to change is the rules for relations between states. Pretending otherwise can only deepen the divides between the powers and contribute to the creation of two opposed blocs – which is perhaps what certain hawkish strategists in Washington and Beijing seek. Overloading the notion of international order will divide the world rather than unite it, and will weaken rather than strengthen the rules-based order.

★★★

Since the democratic powers cannot change the way of life of other states, they ought at least to stay consistent with themselves, and always respect their own values in their own actions. As George Kennan wrote: 'The man who makes it a point to behave with consideration and dignity in his relations with others, regardless of his inner doubts and conflicts, will suddenly find that he has achieved a great deal in his relations with himself.' Changing another state's domestic policies may not be an achievable end, but Kennan continues: 'Where purpose is dim and questionable, form comes into its own.'[9] This may come across as smug or even cynical: knowing that one cannot prevent or end human rights violations in other countries, and that one has no choice but to cooperate with authoritarian regimes on shared interests, one continues nevertheless to talk in the language of human rights if only to satisfy one's own need for consistency and for feeling that one has done something – like signing an online petition. Yet for the EU and the US consistency in condemning human rights violations elsewhere and in respecting human rights in their own actions is important.

For one, it would prevent them from ending up in the situation that they found themselves in during the 'Arab Spring' in 2010–11: people in Tunisia and Egypt felt that they had made a revolution in spite of, not thanks to, the EU and the US, who were seen as uncritically supporting and cooperating with the local dictator, and thus lost a great deal of influence. Europeans had indeed muted their criticism of the regimes in question, and even congratulated them for obviously fabricated election results. One might reject a policy of condemning a regime for its actions in one area while working with it in another as betting on two horses, but if and when over time internal change does occur in a country, it puts the EU and the US in a much better position to defend their interests. As De Gaulle wrote of his refusal to recognise the Lublin Committee, the puppet government that Stalin sought to impose on Poland: 'The future lasts a long time. Everything can happen one day, even that an act made with honour and honesty appears, in the final reckoning, to have been a good political investment.'[10] Moreover, such compartmentalisation of relations is, as we have seen, precisely a mechanism of mitigation; if, on the contrary, every disagreement in one area would lead to a total breach of relations, there would be little international relations left.

If compartmentalisation of relations with non-democratic states should not be condemned as hypocrisy, the EU and the US should avoid doublethink, though, to which they both fall victim. 'The Anglo-Saxon is gifted with a limitless capacity for excluding his own practical requirements from the application of the idealistic theories which he seeks to impose on others': Harold Nicolson's judgement applies to both the US and the EU.[11] Americans often are convinced that their national interest and the interests of the world coincide, Europeans that they are not pursuing their interests at all. Members of the US strategic establishment exhibit doublethink when they sincerely believe that the US even when pursuing its national interest only acts in the interest of world peace, democracy and human rights, and, moreover, that well-thinking people in other states believe that too – only those opposed to humanity's wellbeing could oppose the US. At the same time they know fully well that specific US policies are resisted even by the US' democratic allies, and that on several occasions the US has not hesitated to go to war, break treaties, bring down democratic regimes and violate human rights in the pursuit of its interests. Yet I heard a senior official from the State Department explain to an audience of European strategists at a conference in eastern Europe in early 2020 that the US had withdrawn from the Iran nuclear deal in order to protect Europe's security – which is exactly the opposite of what his European audience thought.

Doublethink in Brussels meant that for a long time the EU was convinced that its diplomacy was not interest-based at all but pursuing a purely altruistic agenda, and that the world therefore saw the EU as a benign actor in a different category from traditional great powers. Yet at the same time the EU pursued international economic policies that were very much interest-based, and did not hesitate to drive a hard bargain in the process, as states on the receiving end would testify. The mindset in Brussels has shifted, culminating in Commission President Ursula von der Leyen's announcement in 2019 that hers would be a 'geopolitical Commission'. But even so, the idea that somehow EU grand strategy is different and less defined by interests than that of the other powers lingers. Many in the European Parliament in particular look at foreign policy almost exclusively through the prism of human rights, as if that were its sole purpose. When in June 2020 I had the opportunity set out my views on the 'dirty' nature of grand strategy in the European Parliament, the chairman of the foreign affairs committee thanked me for my Realpolitik – and he did not mean it as a complement.

★★★

Yet Realpolitik is precisely what is called for – but in the original meaning of the term. A simplistic understanding of Realpolitik is that the ends justify the means. But they do not: as we have seen, a state cannot sustain a grand strategy that violates the values on which its own way of life is based. If it did, it would in the end corrupt its values and affect its own way of life, while the purpose of grand strategy is to defend it. If wars of aggression like the invasion of Iraq were to become a permanent feature of American strategy, that could not but affect the organisation of the state, the mindset of the strategic establishment and, ultimately, society as a whole. The same applies in domestic security: a democratic state that permanently curtails liberties as a response to terrorism ceases to be a democracy, which might exactly be the purpose of terrorists seeking to promote authoritarianism. That is not Realpolitik. Ludwig von Rochau, the German liberal who coined the term in 1853, was writing about domestic politics; his point was that to bring one's values into practice, one needs power.[12] Without a strategy to gain domestic political power, thinking about values and how to organise society is not a political programme but mere utopianism. Translated to international politics, Realpolitik means that a state also needs power in its relations with other states, in order to uphold its way of life, but should do so through a grand strategy that is in accordance with its own values – the alternative would be self-defeating. In international politics, Realpolitik also means, however, that one must be realistic and accept that one cannot change other states, and can therefore cooperate even with states that do not share one's values, as long as one does not violate them oneself.

International politics is not immoral, therefore – but it is a meeting of different moralities. Every state acts in a moral manner by staying true to its own values. It is a moral duty to criticise other states who do not live up to the universal standards that they have committed to, in particular the Universal Declaration of Human Rights. But morality does not require a state to actively try and change another state's way of life, for that, in most cases, is only possible by coercing it and, ultimately, by going to war. As we have seen in the previous chapter, war often creates more suffering, and generates more problems than it solves. Again, the Responsibility to Protect is the exception, or the emergency brake in the system: the UN have defined the crimes that are so immoral that the Security Council may legally and legitimately authorise the use of force to halt them.

In general though, moralising – dividing the world in good and evil – has no place in international politics. Not because all states at times act against their own values or violate the rules of the world order, for it is true that some states sin systematically and others only occasionally – although the tone of righteous indignation that Pompeo, as Trump's secretary of state, used when speaking of the 'evil' of Chinese communism was particularly irritating to those aware of the Trump administration's own permanent violation of American values. As part of this tactic, the Trump administration stopped talking of China and referred only to the Chinese Communist Party, while it also habitually accused its domestic opponents of being 'socialists'. But if the terms 'socialism' and 'communism' may still cause a frisson in many American quarters, in the EU socialism is one of the mainstream political forces, and in many EU member states even communist parties are represented in parliament. If Pompeo were consistent, he ought also to have stopped talking about Saudi Arabia, and speak of 'the house of al-Saud' instead, for the kingdom is not a one-party but a one-family state. What in its ignorance of the reception in Europe the Trump administration was doing, just like Reagan when he spoke of the USSR as the 'evil empire', was to close down the avenues for cooperation with China, leaving open only competition and rivalry – for, surely, one cannot partner with 'evil'. Moralising thus makes it more difficult to compartmentalise relations with other states, cooperating on one issue while disputing another, and contributes to the creation of two exclusive, mutually opposed blocs. International politics in the 21st century is neither a moral nor an ideological confrontation. In the end, in international politics, moralising, like ideology, obscures reason, and that amounts to obscuring strategic thinking itself.

In fact, the Trump administration merely instrumentalised morality and human rights. As argued above, the objectives of US grand strategy as pursued by both Obama and Trump would not be achieved if China were a democracy but also still a peer competitor. Conversely, a China that would remain authoritarian but lose its power and abandon its global ambitions, would most likely satisfy the US strategic establishment. The US would still condemn human rights violations in China, but it would most probably not attempt to build a global coalition to rival Beijing in all dimensions of international politics: political, economic and military. Quod erat demonstrandum: international politics is about the pursuit of interests, not about the promotion of values.

Some of the conclusions drawn in this chapter may be uncomfortable. I myself would feel a lot more comfortable if I would be able to conclude that the EU and the US can democratise the world and enforce respect for human rights everywhere. But having looked at the facts, I cannot. The willingness to accept the conclusions of a rational analysis, even though they make one feel uncomfortable and, to some extent, 'dirty', is precisely one of the precepts of grand strategy. The alternative would be a recipe either for paralysis, for very rarely is any course of action entirely blot-free, or for disaster, for forcing others to change themselves can only provoke war, like the wars of religion that ravaged Europe in the 16th and 17th centuries. Once one does accept the limitations that reality imposes, on the contrary, one can craft a realistic grand strategy that one can proactively pursue.

10

Proactive: A Strategy for Action

Rarely has a state safeguarded its vital interests by passively waiting for things to come. As A.J.P. Taylor wrote: 'Those who really know what they want, get it – not necessarily of course in the way that they want, but they get it somehow. But those who hesitate between different objectives and seek only some compromise which will postpone difficulties, get nothing – not even the postponement they long for'.[1] A state may, of course, adopt a defensive grand strategy in the face of current and expected threats and challenges. Or it may opt for an offensive approach, grasp the initiative, and seek to change its environment. Either way, be it for offence or for defence, a state must prepare to act: those that are not proactive will be forced to react to the strategic moves of the others. In war, if one can get into the decision-making cycle of the enemy, that is make the next move before the opponent has even had time to digest and react to the previous move, success is nearly always guaranteed. In 1940, French command and control was methodical, but slow, geared to the speed of operations of the First World War. As a result, France was systematically outpaced – rather than outgunned – by the German armoured formations.[2] The American armed forces achieved a similar feat against their Iraqi counterparts in the two Gulf Wars, in 1991 and 2003. The same rule applies to grand strategy overall: the state that holds the initiative and sets the pace has the advantage over the others. Vice versa, once stuck in a reactive mode, it is difficult to focus on one's own ends.

The very definition of a great power implies proactivity: the ambition to have a global impact cannot be realised otherwise. Proactivity should not be mistaken for aggressiveness, however: rather than in undermining or attacking its rivals, a power can also be proactive in forging alliances and partnerships, and in improving its own competitiveness. Setting out a constructive agenda in the mutual interest of various powers takes as proactive an approach as launching a military intervention. If, however, the great powers ignore the opportunities for cooperation and focus exclusively on competition and rivalry, they risk bringing about a world ruled only by Thucydides' dictum: the strong do what they will and the weak suffer what they must.[3] Ultimately, the absence of cooperation can only lead to confrontation.

★★★

The last time that the great powers had to craft a proactive grand strategy to cope with a multipolar world, before the bipolar Cold War set in, was during the years in between the two world wars. The interbellum was also the first time since the apex of the colonial age that great powers other than the European ones had a determining impact on international politics. Some of these new powers actively engaged and confronted the established European powers; until then, they had mostly been the object of European imperialist strategies. And the interbellum saw the first attempt to guide international politics to permanent, institutionalised and encompassing multilateral cooperation, through the creation of the League of Nations, the forerunner of the UN, with its headquarters in Geneva. A resurgent and soon assertive Germany, an ambitious Italy, the new Soviet Union, and an expansionist Japan challenged the rules of the international order that the victors of the First World War attempted to build. France and the UK seemed to be at the height of their power, and their empires reached their largest extent, but in reality the cost of the Great War had already hollowed out their power base. The US, for lack of ambition to weigh on global affairs, remained a great power in waiting, as it had been before the war, rather than an actual centre of power. Analysing both the moves to destroy the international order of the interbellum and the rescue attempts is very instructive in assessing where the grand strategies of the great powers of the 21st century might lead us, and to understand the pitfalls and possibilities to build a sustainable order in the multipolar world of today.

A first insight from the interbellum is that any attempt by some of the great powers to create a world order for the express purpose of keeping another great power outside the system, is bound to fail. Only an inclusive world order can be stable: an order that all of the great powers benefit from and feel committed to, because they have more to gain from its survival than from its collapse. If one of the great powers of the day is pushed out by the others, that power will inevitably contest the legitimacy of the world order, and will likely attempt to undermine it, and/or seek to set up a parallel order with its own allies and partners. After the First World War, there was an understandable urge among the victorious powers to take revenge on Germany, particularly in France. When Germany could not make good on the reparation payments imposed by the Treaty of Versailles, France and Belgium militarily occupied the Ruhr area, the industrial heartland of Germany, from 1923 to 1925. But after a few years even Paris realised that this revanchism was counterproductive and that Europe could only be stable again if Germany were allowed to re-enter the club of European nations as a 'normal' state, with a revived economy. The powers similarly could not continue to ignore the Soviet Union, since it was a great power. One after the other they overcame their revulsion and established diplomatic and economic relations with the regicide Bolshevik regime, which had executed the imperial family, and which the western powers had first sought to bring down by intervening on the side of the 'Whites' against the 'Reds' in the Russian civil war. Indeed, while the Bolsheviks were excluded, a 'White' delegation had attended the Versailles negotiations.[4] Japan had joined the allies and was amply rewarded in Versailles. China, on the contrary, which was still in the throes of domestic instability after the overthrow of the Qing dynasty in 1912, was studiously ignored by the victorious powers.

Informed by the failure of the League of Nations to keep the peace, in September 1944 Field Marshal Smuts wrote to Churchill about the future United Nations: 'Should a World Organisation be formed which does not include Russia she will become the power centre of another group. We shall then be heading towards a third World War.'[5] The Soviet Union was duly given a permanent seat with the power of the veto in the UN Security Council. In the 21st century, it is difficult to see how to build a stable international order that does not include both the US and China, the most powerful of the great powers. An order that excludes Washington or Beijing would only ever be a partial order, covering part of the globe, and the other would likely be prompted to construct a partial order of its own. Abandoning the ideal of an inclusive world order thus risks triggering the emergence of two opposing, mutually exclusive orders, each centred upon one great power with its allies and partners. The result would be a new cold war-like permanent rivalry.

Building an inclusive order does not mean that all powers have to be kept on board at any price. A second historical insight is that if violating the rules of the order carries no consequences, the world order will be hollowed out and, eventually, collapse. The democratic powers were very reticent to act in the spirit of the League of Nations, and to make use of economic sanctions or military force to halt aggression. They were understandably war-weary, so soon after the Great War, and put their hope in granting concessions and in diplomatic combinations to curb the increasingly expansionist authoritarian powers of Japan, Italy and Nazi Germany. The strongest sanction that the League of Nations could impose was expulsion. But if the offender in question did not care, or even resigned from the League itself, like Japan in 1933 after its conquest of Manchuria, and Germany in the same year after the appointment of Hitler as chancellor, the League was powerless. The impression created was that 'The English [and, by extension, the other democracies] do not want to fight. They want to withdraw as slowly as possible, but they do not want to fight', as Galeazzo Ciano, Mussolini's foreign minister (and son in law) wrote in his diary on 12 January 1939.[6] In fact, Britain and France would soon resolve to finally take a stand, when Hitler violated the 1938 Munich agreement and in March 1939 dismembered all of Czechoslovakia rather than 'limiting' himself to the annexation of the Sudetenland border regions as agreed with the other powers. France and the UK declared war on Germany when in his next move Hitler invaded Poland on 1 September 1939.

In the 2020s as well, allowing every great power to take its rightful place in the world order does not amount to sheepishly accepting each and every of its policies. The other powers cannot possibly recognise China's sovereignty claims over the South China Sea, for example, for that would be the end of international maritime law, which is the foundation for the delineation of their own sovereign territory. China, and the other powers, ought to see the world order as a single whole: a state cannot just pick and choose those rules that happen to suit its interests. Very soon, there would be no reliable rules left, and the powers would not be able to usefully invoke the rules even when it would serve their interests. Objectively, all powers share an interest, therefore, in upholding a core of rules that enable stable international relations. States that violate those core rules ought to suffer political and economic consequences, but discretion and proportionality is called for. One cannot sanction a power simply for being successful in pursuing its interests if it does so in legal and legitimate ways; one might not like it, but one can only improve one's own strategy in response.

When a power does break the rules, one should not too easily resort to comparisons with the Munich agreement: one cannot speak of 'appeasement' of a power when it does not threaten the peace, as Nazi Germany did. When a power launches a war, or threatens to, severe diplomatic and economic sanctions are justified, and military measures may be taken against the aggressor or in support of its victim. Thus Russia was sanctioned after its invasion of Ukraine — and the

US was not after its invasion of Iraq. At the same time, Washington, Beijing, Moscow and Brussels will logically seek to avoid needless escalation between them, given the enormous risk involved in any direct confrontation between nuclear great powers. This is why the South China Sea issue is so delicate: almost without firing a shot, China has militarily occupied areas far beyond its territorial sovereignty. The US and the EU continue to signal the unacceptability of this violation of a core rule for as long as it lasts, but preferably also without firing a shot. Once again, the importance of 'compartmentalisation' stands out: measures taken in response to one dispute must not be taken to mean that one is seen as the enemy; loss of face on one issue must not lead to anger and resentment that infects relations in other areas.

If one wants the other powers to abide by the rules, one must follow them oneself. That is a third historical insight: a great power that refuses to invest in the world order cannot expect the others to do so, and will gradually see its credibility and leverage shrink. US President Woodrow Wilson included the creation of the League of Nations in his Fourteen Points, which he saw as the basis for the post-war settlement. The League was duly created, and many invested it with great expectations and a lot of enthusiasm, in the hope that the First World War would truly turn out to be 'the war to end all wars'. But in 1920 an isolationist US Senate refused to ratify America's accession. From the start, the League was greatly handicapped by this American refusal to join: the absence of one of the democratic great powers played into the hands of those who sought to subvert the international order and weaken the League. The US had signalled that it did not want to commit resources to upholding the rules. In the words of Joseph Nye: 'the United States replaced Britain as the largest global power but failed to take on Britain's role in providing global public goods'.[7] The Soviet Union too, once it had given up on its project of world revolution, played only a very limited role in the budding multilateral system. As two of the economic power houses of the interbellum steered a relatively isolationist course, the international order did not reflect the fundamental economic reality of the age.[8]

After the Second World War, the rules and institutions of the renewed attempt to create a global order were mostly an American creation too, but this time the US firmly took the lead. The resulting system could be described as a Pax Americana – from which under President Trump the US has started to withdraw. The strategy of the Trump administration was driven, as we have seen, by the assessment that other powers now benefit more from the current set-up than the US. Many condemn the decision to allow China to join the WTO in particular as a strategic error. Yet what legitimacy and effectiveness could the WTO have claimed if ultimately one of the three largest economies had stayed outside it? Obviously, once it did join, China ought to have faithfully adhered by the rules of the WTO: for the organisation to achieve its purposes, it needs to be inclusive, enforce its rules, and have buy-in from all key powers. By choosing to block the WTO, however, the US acted against its interest, creating a vacuum that China immediately sought to fill, and making it more difficult for the EU to counterbalance China's influence on the future functioning and rules of the organisation. Indeed, the US did not just undermine its own legitimacy by disinvesting from the multilateral architecture, but also that of other powers, who remained committed to the system. It becomes increasingly difficult for Brussels and its partners to stand up for the rules when China and Russia can always point to Washington and say: fix your friends first, before pointing the finger at us.

A final historical insight from the interbellum is that no state voluntarily submits to another: a world order that is only imposed and not accepted will not last long. Moreover, if they have a choice, states will naturally seek to entertain relations with various other states and powers simultaneously, rather than allow one great power to gain an exclusive hold over their international connections. After the democratic powers let Nazi Germany dismantle Czechoslovakia, even though it was an ally in the 'petite entente' with France, the other members, Romania and Yugoslavia, no longer could have much confidence in Paris. No alternative alliances were on offer; indeed, the Soviet Union secured Germany's agreement to occupy the Romanian region of Bessarabia. Bucharest and Belgrade thus ended up allying with Nazi Germany, for lack of other options. When in 1941 a coup ousted the pro-Axis government in Yugoslavia, Germany invaded and occupied the entire country. In Asia, Japan aimed to incorporate other countries in what it grandly called the Greater East Asia Co-Prosperity Sphere. One of the reasons why that project ultimately failed was that it was entirely based on conquest and repression rather than on real cooperation; in the end, Japan merely replaced western colonialism with its own form of exploitation. If certain Asian actors initially saw some merit in the project, that had a lot to do with the absence of any alternative as long as the western colonial powers had nothing more to offer than empty reforms and vague promises about independence in the distant future.

No state in the 2020s is volunteering to hide behind an iron curtain policed by one of the powers. Even governments which are closely aligned with one specific power tend to play a subtle game, keeping just enough distance to gain benefits from others powers as well, without letting them come so close as to invite reaction by the former. Powers that are seeking to establish an exclusive sphere of influence will be wary of push-back; if their strategy brings more disadvantages than benefits, they may think twice. States that feel themselves the target of powers trying to gain influence will look for other powers to put an offer on the table also. A lot depends, therefore, on the positive offer that the different powers are willing to proactively extend to potential partners, more perhaps than on the actions and countermeasures that they are ready to take against other powers.

Armed with these insights from the interbellum, one can take another look at the grand strategies of the four great powers of the 21st century, and analyse their intentions and their prospects of success.

★★★

Boosted by its enormous economic growth since the turn of the century, and grasping the opportunities created by the 2008 financial crisis and the temporary weakness of the US and the EU, China has pursued a very proactive grand strategy ever since. When assessing the grand strategy of a great power, it is important not to project one's own fears and ambitions onto it, or one's own history. In the past, whenever a European state amassed great power, it nearly always turned to conquest and colonisation. But that does not mean that today's China will do the same. Many fear that China will behave like a 19th century European power. Europe's unbridled expansionism led to the continent's destruction in two world wars, however, and the European states consequently ended up as secondary players during the Cold War. Given this precedent, might it not be at least as rational to assume that China might also draw some inspiration from the 21st century EU and seek to pursue its interests without provoking a major clash with one of the other great powers? If, that is, China perceives the latter as willing to work out an equitable way of peaceful coexistence within the basic rules of the international order.

Chinese strategic culture, as we have seen, suggests that territorial expansionism is unlikely. The exception are the peripheral waters in the East and South China Seas that China, contrary to international law, considers falling under its national sovereignty – in Chinese eyes, this is about consolidating, not expanding the national territory. In the South China Sea, military annexation has de facto already occurred. For what in its own interpretation is Chinese national territory, which also includes Taiwan, the regime can mobilise the public for a military confrontation – for years now it has been preparing it through a

199

campaign of nationalist (rather than communist) propaganda. This has been the focus of Chinese military strategy since 1993.[9] As multiple incidents with commercial, coast guard or military vessels have already shown, China does not shy away from demonstrations of force. The border clashes with India in 2020 and again in 2021 demonstrated that this pertains to China's land frontiers as well. The risk is great, therefore, that a future incident might trigger escalation, in particular if it were to involve an American ship or aircraft engaged on 'freedom of navigation operations'. It seems unlikely, though, that China would purposely seek escalation and opt for a strategy of military aggression, while its strategy of creating a fait accompli and gradually consolidating its hold over the waters it claims has been so successful.

The tactics that China employs to pursue its strategy in the South China Sea are, of course, very offensive. But for the regime, these are all components of a grand strategy that is basically defensive in orientation. To quote Khan's phrase again, the CCP still is 'haunted by chaos'.[10] Because the regime feels uncertain and under threat, it lashes out against all perceived internal 'enemies', and seeks to prevent any external adversaries from achieving a position from which they might threaten the party's survival. The fears and ambitions of the CCP are inseparable, as General MacMaster writes.[11] Seen in this light, the claim to the South China Sea is China's Monroe Doctrine. In 1823, US President James Monroe asserted that the US would not tolerate any interference in the Americas by the European powers, at a time when the US was much less powerful relative to the other players than China is today.[12] China has now proclaimed a sphere of influence from which Beijing wants to ban all foreign militaries, so that no other power (read: the US) would be able to cut off its connectivity with the rest of the world by severing the vital maritime trade routes. Furthermore, it has postulated that all territorial disputes should be settled bilaterally, without interference from any third parties.[13] The overland routes of the BRI are the accompanying measures to this main effort. Internally, the brutal repression of the Uighur population, Hong Kong democracy activists, and others, serves the same purpose: to ensure the survival of the regime.

In no way does this analysis justify Chinese actions that violate international law and universal human rights; it serves only to assess China's intentions. That assessment is that, with the exceptions stated above, territorial aggrandisement does not appear to be an objective of China's grand strategy.[14] Nor does Beijing seem to consider the threat or the use of force an apt instrument to pursue ends other than its 'territorial consolidation'. 'The priorities for which military force is relevant for as far as Xi can see are local and regional – not global', says Allison.[15] Chinese military strategy is evolving, and China is building up a blue water navy and expeditionary forces that can operate globally, but for now, China adheres to non-intervention, except eventually to protect its own citizens and assets abroad and to maintain maritime security.

Repression alone cannot keep a regime in power forever, nor is the agenda of 'territorial consolidation' sufficient to generate public support. The CCP also needs legitimacy, which it has so far acquired by ensuring that citizens can look forward to ever growing prosperity. Gradually, rising prosperity should come to benefit all Chinese in all provinces; inequality is the regime's headache, and not only because it goes so obviously against the ideological façade of communism that the CCP studiously maintains. That is why, Dominic Lieven argues, one should perhaps compare China today less to Wilhelmine Germany (though they share a strident nationalism that, once created, the regime no longer fully controls), than to tsarist Russia: 'a vast and backward country developing at great speed but in a manner that puts the survival of its current regime in question'.[16] In addition, domestic legitimacy is associated with the regime's commitment to guarantee its citizens' safety and security, against health threats, pollution, crime and so on. Both major dimensions of legitimacy have been severely shaken by the regime's initial mismanagement of the coronavirus outbreak, and by the economic shock that followed it. This is the major internal challenge for the CCP and, therefore, continues to be the other main end of its grand strategy, next to territorial integrity: in all other areas of international politics, the economic interest comes first, because it is vital to the survival of the regime. This defensive orientation notwithstanding, the CCP has managed to advertise its grand strategy at home as aiming at positive objectives, for the benefit of the citizens, under the heading of the 'China Dream'.

China pursues its economic interests through a very pragmatic geo-economic approach. Rather than expanding, China oozes, as an American former diplomat phrased it to me. In a mostly non-confrontational way, Beijing has acquired great influence worldwide, even in the EU, through a targeted use of its economic sticks and carrots, and through a bilateral diplomacy that combines flattery and threats. Its flagship policy, the BRI, does not only seek to increase Chinese exports, but also to push the target countries to orient their economies on the Chinese market and its norms and standards. China does not seek to export its own political model, nor, with some exceptions, can it realistically aspire to create satellites and an exclusive sphere of influence (precisely because no other state wants to become another one of those exceptions). But China does aspire to create a political climate in its partner states that is permanently conducive to its interests, regardless of the political system in place. At the same time, targeted investments across the world aim at the acquisition of technology, and Beijing continues to favour Chinese companies, both state-owned and private, by refusing effective reciprocity in market access and the regulation of state subsidies.

At the multilateral level, China is strengthening its position within the existing institutions (notably the United Nations and its specialised agencies), in order to gain more leverage to shape the rules of the world order according to its standards and preferences. It has also created its own institutions, such as the AIIB, and tries to create the image of a commonwealth of China and its partners by convening a BRI Forum in Beijing. Trying to gain influence within the multilateral system is what every power does. The important thing is that China does not seem set on overturning the existing order.[17] It has risen to immense power under this order; and the domestic policy of continually increasing the standard of living, and hence the survival of the regime, is also heavily dependent on global stability, as Jisi Wang states.[18] Therefore, China is a disruptive power – given its size, it could hardly be otherwise, whatever its strategy – but not a revolutionary power: it seeks (significant) changes within the order, not its overturning.[19] China does apply the rules very selectively, however, so its role is rather ambiguous: where it sees an interest, it can effectively contribute to the multilateral architecture, but it does not hesitate to bypass and undermine it when that suits its interests better. Consequently, even though China is not actively trying to undo the international order, it does not contribute to its stability either. It is not quite the 'responsible stakeholder' yet that the EU and the US would like it to be. Some argue that it will never be since it perceives the international order as fundamentally US-centric.[20] Yet if on those Chinese demands that are legitimate, the other powers were willing to offer some concessions and amend the rules while respecting the foundations of the order, a 'grand bargain' might be possible.

The picture that emerges is one of a grand strategy that has successfully put China in a global position of influence, and has strengthened its capacity to pursue its interests. Graham Allison defines the ends thus:

> 'Making China Great Again' means: returning China to the predominance in Asia it enjoyed before the West intruded; re-establishing control over the territories of 'greater China', including not just Xinjiang and Tibet on

the mainland, but also Hong Kong and Taiwan; recovering its historic sphere of influence along its borders and in the adjacent seas so that others give it the deference great nations have always demanded; commanding the respect of other great powers in the councils of the world.[21]

That is not actually an expansionist or revisionist grand design. Nevertheless, many have come to fear that in reality China is set on a revisionist course. In part, those fears are triggered by the sheer size and rapidity of China's rise. They have also been provoked, naturally, by China's own rhetoric, notably Xi's aspiration for China to become a global leader and a first-tier military power, which clashes with the discourse of peace and harmony and the 'China Dream', and by China's military actions in the South China Sea. There is, in fact, debate within China whether a too assertive stance is not counterproductive: it provokes countermeasures by the other powers that could do so much harm to China's economy that they would undo any benefits that its assertiveness might have brought. The initial failure to address the coronavirus amplified that internal debate. This demonstrates that push-back by the other powers and states when China threatens their interests and steps outside the bounds of legality and legitimacy is crucial. If the CCP perceived that its assertive policies go unchallenged, the hawks within the Chinese strategic establishment might be tempted into even more assertive moves that could lead to a major escalation.

A balance must be found, however: in the face of the overly confrontational policies of the Trump administration, that made no distinction between legitimate and illegitimate Chinese aspirations and ways of pursuing them, no Chinese leadership could simply give in without losing legitimacy internally (in view also of its own nationalist propaganda). China itself, however, has been uncompromising even towards the EU, which does not perceive the same challenge to its status as the US, and has pursued a more conciliatory approach aimed at negotiating a bilateral investment treaty. By moving fast, Beijing might have played into the differences between the EU and the Trump administration; by dragging its feet, Beijing instead created the perception in Brussels that even with a bilateral investment treaty, China will never be sincerely committed to real economic reciprocity. This might have been the result of hubris on the Chinese side, or of the assessment that the EU is only a secondary player. Yet many in the EU strategic establishment still prefer to work with China, within the existing order – but if China does not give the EU something to work with, the Europeans will inevitably focus on the very prominent negative aspects of the CCP regime, such as the human rights violations in Xinjiang and Hong Kong, and will likely align closer and closer with the US. The more assertive China's strategy becomes, the more a new cold war-type confrontation is likely.

The other main reason why many have come to fear China is because they are afraid it is on the way from being an authoritarian to becoming a totalitarian state. A truly totalitarian regime, such as Nazi Germany, the Stalinist Soviet Union or North Korea today, is much less reliant on active buy-in from its public, if at all, because it is in total control of both the public and the private sphere. There are thus far fewer restraints on its grand strategy, and the risk of aggression rises accordingly. Some argue that China is a totalitarian state already, but that is not my experience. There still is scope for debate, there are demonstrations, and the climate in some cities is more open than others; even a foreigner who does not speak the language can feel the difference in atmosphere between Beijing and Shanghai, to name the most obvious example. That said, technology now enables totalitarianism more than ever before, if that were the intention of some of China's leaders. Such a move would certainly not find unanimous consensus within the CCP, however. The big question is whether the Chinese people would rise if they felt totalitarianism in the making; much depends on the answer – and the other powers have little or no leverage over it.

★★★

The US has waged a proactive grand strategy since the Second World War. Since 2001, however, its strategy has mostly been guided by vague, negative ends. The US successfully and justifiably retaliated against the terrorists behind 9/11, destroying the al-Qaeda organisation in Afghanistan and, eventually, killing its leader, Osama bin Laden. But as US strategy shifted away from this specific purpose and into a 'global war on terror', it quickly became counterproductive, spending massive resources on wars in Afghanistan and Iraq with no clear ends and no discernible benefits for the American interest. By 2020 the US had finally reduced its active military engagement in the broader Middle East to a minimum, but without having stabilised the region in any sustainable way. By then, however, the focus of US strategy had long shifted to China: the Obama administration had announced the 'pivot' to Asia in 2011. Under Trump, strategic rivalry with China became the mainstay of US foreign policy, to the extent that, rather than 'Make America Great Again', 'Keep China Small' seemed to be what concerned the administration most.

Once again, the ends of US strategy as it entered the 2020s were not as clear as they should have been. China is a great power, and except for an internal collapse, which seems unlikely, it will remain one; even if the regime would change, it would still be a great power. It is too late, therefore, to 'keep it small'. Maintaining American primacy as the most powerful of the great powers could be a US objective, but that still leaves Fareed Zakaria's question unanswered: then 'what would an acceptable level of influence for China be, given its economic weight in the world? If Washington does not first ask this question, it cannot make serious claims about which uses of Chinese power cross the line'.[22] By turning the natural competition with China that is inherent in international politics into an open-ended strategic rivalry, the US risks bringing about precisely what it seeks to avoid. First, the hawks in Washington reinforce the hawks in Beijing: those in the Chinese strategic establishment who feel that no compromise is possible with the US and therefore do harbour more revisionist designs. Second, if the Sino-American rivalry becomes a systematic cold war-type confrontation, in which both seek to carve out an exclusive sphere of influence and force other states to choose between them, many more are actually likely to fall under Beijing's sway than would be the case if all powers pursued non-exclusive connectivity schemes. Churchill said of the US that 'Their national psychology is such that the bigger the Idea the more wholeheartedly and obstinately do they throw themselves into making it a success. It is an admirable characteristic provided the Idea is good.'[23] The idea that the US and China cannot be but strategic rivals carries strong bipartisan support in Washington. The risk is that this would lead the US to forego exploring the conditions under which both great powers could co-exist within the existing international order, and that instead they would go down a path that would irretrievably lead to a total decoupling of relations.

Meanwhile, it has become less clear what the US stands for: which positive objectives does it pursue? US power is such that America has successfully maintained its central position in international politics, notably in economic and military terms, and it can afford the cost of faulty strategy such as in the Middle East. But American influence has been severely dented. The Trump administration had come to see even America's allies and partners as antagonists that must be cajoled into aligning with US strategy, if necessary by threatening and imposing economic sanctions and US troop withdrawals. At the same time, we have seen the US withdraw from the multilateral architecture. Behind the traditional rhetoric about freedom, democracy and human rights – which to many outside and inside the US did not sound very credible when coming from the Trump administration – what is the positive project that the US pursues and that could mobilise the support of other countries? 'We are not China' will not be enough. On the domestic front, the same question coloured the 2020 presidential campaign: will US policies, at home and abroad, be guided by fear and repression, or by aspiration and investment? Just like the rest of world tries to grasp Chinese domestic politics, so it anxiously follows the currents of the American political debate, since US choices have such enormous global impact.

★★★

Russian grand strategy presents the mirror image of that of China. As a declining rather than a rising power, Russia since at least 2008 has been pursuing an offensive strategy, including the threat and use of force, with the aim of regaining its position as a first-rate power by recreating an exclusive sphere of influence in the former Soviet republics. It has even expanded its territory by force of arms: the veneer of a referendum after the facts cannot obscure that the annexation of the Crimea was the result of plain military conquest. The other side of this proactive strategy has been the ongoing attempts to weaken the coherence of NATO and the EU, and to push the US out of European security affairs, so as to prevent these powers from interfering with Russia's grand design.[24] Russian interventions in countries as far apart as Syria and Libya, the Central African Republic and Venezuela serve both purposes: they are meant to increase Russian prestige and to directly benefit Russian interests, while creating distractions for and putting pressure on the US and the EU.

Russian resources are limited, however. They are sufficient to exercise great nuisance power vis-à-vis Europe and America. But there is a risk of this negative objective coming to overshadow the positive objective (from Moscow's point of view) of creating a Russian sphere, as that project is hitting its limits in the face of public opinion in the countries of the former USSR that has grown accustomed to independence. Russia may score some further successes and expand its sphere of influence. But it will be against the will of the local population, and therefore costly, while absorbing more former Soviet territory would not significantly increase Russia's resources. Yet, as we have seen, the strategy is too tied up with the regime's domestic legitimacy to be easily abandoned, in the absence of a mobilising domestic economic project. As Pericles warned the Athenians: 'Your empire is now like a tyranny; it may have been wrong to take it; it is certainly dangerous to let it go.'[25]

Meanwhile, the various interventions outside the former Soviet Union are costly too, but do not always bring much benefit beyond enhancing Moscow's nuisance capacity. The nature of the Russian economy limits the extent to which it can exploit its successes, except in specific sectors such as energy and arms. A Russian foothold in Libya, for example, can be a base from which to influence the states of the region and steer them in a direction opposed to the EU's interests. It could even be a base from which to weigh in on maritime security in the central Mediterranean. But to what end, unless Russia would seek to escalate tensions with the EU and the US? The same applies, *mutatis mutandis*, to the new naval facilities that Russia opened in Sudan in 2020.[26] Russian grand strategy has been successful in guaranteeing that Russia remains a power to be reckoned with but, to an extent, Russia is doing geopolitics without purpose. In the words of Dominic Lieven: 'imagining that Russia will once again be a great empire if it reabsorbs the east Ukrainian rust belt is moonshine. Ukraine is no longer at the heart of European geopolitics, and Europe is no longer at the centre of the world.'[27] Although it has great nuisance power, Russia is not powerful enough to overturn the existing regional order, let alone the world order, unless by unleashing a great power war that it could never hope to win.

If Russia nonetheless continues to pursue the same grand strategy, then the result will be stalemate. Because of its aggressive strategy, its interference in EU and US domestic politics, and its failure to honour successive diplomatic undertakings on Ukraine, few in the European and American strategic establishment still consider Russia as a potential partner. In the eyes of many, Russia has been 'tarred as unstable and dangerous, paranoid and untrustworthy'.[28] Unable to restore constructive relations with the EU or the US, Russia will have no real alternative to its partnership with China, ideas in some American quarters of recruiting it for an anti-Chinese front notwithstanding. In view of its geopolitical situation, Russia cannot afford to antagonise China. There is little that the US could offer to compensate for the risk, unless Washington would be willing to bypass its European allies and make a deal that would grant Russia the exclusive sphere of interest in Ukraine and elsewhere that it has failed to establish on its own. With Trump in the White House such a deal could be imagined; Biden's victory has made it impossible. The greater risk anyway appears to be the opposite outcome: that in the face of worsening Sino-American tensions, Russia, in spite of its misgivings, would be pushed ever closer into the arms of China, and align with Beijing against the US.

★★★

Of the four great powers that dominate international politics in the 21st century, the EU is the most committed to maintaining a stable rules-based international order as a public good in its own right. A strong awareness has grown that great power rivalry not only risks undermining the international order that the EU needs for its own prosperity, but also threatens to escalate into a new cold war-type confrontation between the US and China, in which the Europeans would inevitably be but secondary players in a secondary theatre. The EU, therefore, has started to carefully reposition itself in international politics. For the first time since the Second World War, the Europeans at the level of grand strategy have set out on a course that no longer runs entirely parallel with the US. The European way of life is, of course, much closer (though far from identical) to that of the US than to that of Russia or China, but on key issues their interests are too divergent for Brussels to simply align with Washington. The EU institutions, in fact, have come to the conclusion that the EU should not align with any power; it should pursue its own distinctive grand strategy, in defence of multilateralism and against unbridled rivalry. Trump's erratic and confrontational manner certainly contributed to pushing the EU down this path; Europeans realised that they had to look out for their own economic interests. But the divergence is more fundamental: the question is whether one can accommodate China as a great power or not. For the EU, the answer so far is positive: China's rise is not problematic per se, if it adheres to the basic rules of the international order. The relationship with China will be a very difficult one, and the EU will need to take firm measures to safeguard its sovereignty in the face of China's economic and political penetration of the continent; but the EU does prefer to maintain a working relationship, cooperating with Beijing when it can while pushing back when it must. EU High Representative Josep Borrell borrowed the title of the Serge Gainsbourg song to describe EU–China relations: *je t'aime, moi non plus* – I love you, me neither.[29]

In a way the EU has come full circle. At the end of the Second World War, leaders like Belgian Foreign Minister Paul-Henri Spaak (who in 1946 chaired the first session of the UN General Assembly, and in 1957 became the second secretary-general of NATO) initially sought an independent strategic role for Europe, aligning neither with the US nor with the USSR. That ambition foundered because of the Cold War and the divisions among the Western Europeans. As the EU enters the 2020s, it has another chance to build a truly independent posture in international politics. All the wiser for having been disillusioned by

Trump, German Chancellor Angela Merkel expressed the state of the European Union in clear terms: 'It is no longer such that the United States simply protects us, but Europe must take its destiny in its own hands, that's the task of the future.'[30] That, concluded French President Emmanuel Macron, gave Europe a choice: 'taking our own destiny in hand', indeed, or 'renouncing a strategy of our own, aligning with whatever power that be'.[31] But once again divisions within the EU, exacerbated by the lack of centralised decision making on foreign and defence policy, greatly handicap Europe. The EU's nascent grand strategy is not equally shared by all EU member states or even by all EU institutions, nor has it yet been incorporated into all relevant strands of EU policy. As a result, even though on key issues Brussels has staked out its position (on China, on Iran, on European defence, and so on), all too often the EU lacks the power to translate that position into common action. Push-back against China is neither strong nor unified enough when it matters; the INSTEX mechanism has failed to keep the Iran nuclear deal alive; and very limited use is being made of the new mechanisms for defence integration that have been launched.

In this way, the EU risks ending up in a permanently ambivalent position: it is more than a satellite of the US, but it is not a really independent power either. The EU has taken sufficient steps to irritate the US, but not to obtain the benefits sought: to further its autonomous capacity to defend the European interest, and to play a stabilising role in great power relations. Such a half-hearted stance threatens to alienate Europe's allies and partners while tempting its adversaries.

★★★

The EU objective of coexistence of all great powers within an agreed set of fundamental rules that prevent natural competition from escalating into systematic rivalry is probably the best that can be achieved in a multipolar world. The EU alone cannot bring it about, even if it were a true great power, able to formulate a global ambition and take decisions to act upon it – which it is not and likely will not be for some time. And yet there are grounds for optimism – there always are. Not because the great powers will suddenly come to see the world in another light, but because their own interests may yet bring the great powers to prevent rivalry from escalating beyond a point that they would all come to regret. There are policies that all current great powers could adopt without abandoning their way of life or denying the core tenets of their grand strategy.

Conclusion: Power to Engage

'Oceania was at war with Eurasia: therefore Oceania had always been at war with Eurasia. The enemy of the moment always represented absolute evil, and it followed that any past or future agreement with him was impossible.'[1] The readers of George Orwell's *1984* know that Oceania had in fact previously been at war with Eastasia, the third great power mentioned in the book, and that the alliance had probably shifted several times before already. But who the enemy is does not matter to the regime of Oceania; what matters is that there is an evil to make war against, in order to legitimise the dictatorship of Big Brother. The war is not meant to be won; waging permanent war has become an end in itself.

Great power politics in the 21st century does not resemble this pattern – yet. But the elements are there that could produce an uncontrollable dynamic leading to permanent open-ended rivalry between the great powers. In 1991, the Soviet Union fell apart and the Cold War ended; only for rivalry to begin anew between the Russian Federation, the US and the EU. Had democracy taken root in Russia and not given way to authoritarianism, rivalry might have been avoided, *if* the democratic regime had accepted a reduced stature in international politics. But would a democratic Russia not also have sought great power status, like its predecessor? Likewise, a hypothetical democratic China would certainly still be a great power, might well uphold the claims to Taiwan and the South China Sea, and would definitely compete globally for markets, resources and influence. Would China and the US end their rivalry then? In fact, tensions arise even between the US and the EU, when the former perceives the latter to be gaining too much power and independence in certain areas, and, vice versa, when Brussels feels that Washington does not respect it as a strategic player. Tensions exist between China and Russia as well. Harmonisation of domestic political systems clearly does not suffice to prevent natural competition between powers from sliding into rivalry. The risk of permanent rivalry arises not because the great powers have different ways of life, but when they cannot accept the existence of peer competitors that pursue their legitimate interests in all the same theatres across the globe.

Having peer competitors forces a great power into greater efforts to maintain its own competitiveness. If, however, the very existence of a peer competitor is seen as a threat and a ground for rivalry, such rivalry cannot be 'won' in any meaningful way. A change of regime would not do. Only if the 'rival' great power voluntarily abandoned its global ambitions or ceased to exist as a power because of military defeat, economic collapse, or revolution and civil war, would rivalry come to an end. As none of these scenarios is very likely for the US, China, Russia or the EU in the near to medium term, the risk is real that a situation of permanent systematic rivalry would evolve if these four cannot accept each other's existence as great powers. Over time, certain powers might settle for such a situation: the need to fight an ever-present rival could be used to justify and legitimise the domestic power structures and the position of the strategic establishment; authoritarian leaders could invoke it to stay in power, democratic leaders to be re-elected. The great powers could also instrumentalise permanent rivalry to maintain leadership over their allies and partners. Eventually, rivalry would come to be seen as the natural condition of international politics. And since one would not expect to win this permanent rivalry, then in the end perhaps it would cease to matter who the rival was and what way of life it had. Thus certain American strategists today can contemplate allying with their former Cold War rival, Russia, against their current rival, China, possibly even at the expense of European security interests, although Russia remains an authoritarian state. Unexpectedly, among those advocating this unlikely partnership are some of the fiercest anti-Soviet 'cold warriors' from the 1980s. Permanent rivalry generates such cynicism. One wonders whether such cynics still believe in the intrinsic value of their own American way of life and its benefits for the citizen. If they do not, then what in their eyes is the point of grand strategy, except for those in power to stay in power? Indeed, in a world marked by permanent rivalry, even the democratic great powers might easily slide into authoritarianism, just like during the Cold War values were often trampled upon for the 'greater good' of fighting communism.[2]

Permanent rivalry entails a permanent risk of war. In the face of nuclear deterrence, no great power may wish for a direct confrontation. But for many years already, the military stand-off between great powers in the South China Sea, the military presence of several powers in the Middle East and North Africa, and their military interference in eastern Europe has meant an ever-present risk of military incidents, with a dangerous potential for escalation. If rivalry between some or all of the great powers were to become systematic and all-encompassing, the risk of war would soar. If it would come to war, who is to say that escalation to nuclear war could be avoided? But even a non-nuclear war between great powers, unlike previous wars, would likely not leave the homeland of any power untouched – something that the hawks in the various strategic establishments may wish to consider.

Twenty-first century great power politics does not have to lead to permanent rivalry, though. In this concluding chapter I put forward four precepts for a grand strategy that the US, China, Russia and the EU could all pursue without abandoning either their way of life or their global ambitions, while at the same time avoiding an escalation of tensions. First, the great powers must accept each other as peer competitors, and see engagement rather than confrontation as the default mode for relations between them. Second, they must invest in the international order and abide by the rules that they agree together. Third, they must respect the sovereignty of all other states, and refrain from seeking exclusive spheres of interest. Fourth, each must strengthen its own sovereignty as a precondition to engage the others. If the four great powers adopted a grand strategy that adhered to these guidelines, friction could be controlled and constructive relations given the best possible chance.

★★★

The first precept, and the key to avoiding rivalry without end (and, ultimately, without purpose), is to accept that one will have peer competitors. Multipolarity, the coexistence of several great powers, is the most common state of affairs in the history of international politics. Short of internal collapse, the current great powers will remain great powers. Fooling oneself into believing otherwise can only lead to frustration, or to confrontation. Rather, the US, China, Russia and the EU ought to recognise that the fact that they are great powers, and even the fact that China is a rising power, is not in itself problematic: all of them have legitimate global interests, and the right to pursue them in legitimate ways. Naturally, this will produce competition, for markets, resources and influence – that is inherent in international politics. But so is cooperation, for in many instances their interests will overlap. Problematising the fact as such that another player is a peer competitor closes off these natural avenues for cooperation, and serves only to instil needless fear. A power can drive a hard bargain even as it cooperates and seeks win–win solutions with other powers; using tough tactics, however, is not the same as pursing zero-sum objectives.

Rather than a logic of confrontation, therefore, each great power should follow a logic of engagement: maintaining working relationships with the other powers, looking to cooperate whenever interests coincide, and taking measures directly against another power only when directly targeted by it. In sum: cooperate when you can, but push back when you must. A great power can legitimately push back when another power moves from natural competition to conscious rivalry against it, and uses its power to pursue its interests in illegitimate ways, through subversion, coercion or aggression. In such cases, a great power *must* push back even, in order to defend its way of life, for which its strategic establishment is accountable to its citizens – it will not want to be seen as tolerating a push-over. Engagement should not be equated with appeasement, therefore. On the contrary, pushing back when another power threatens one's vital interests or breaks the core rules of the international order is necessary in order to maintain the logic of engagement. Otherwise, if those who break the rules perceive that there are no consequences, they will be encouraged to persist in their aggressive strategy and engagement will eventually give way to all-round confrontation. Thus, for example, the EU and the US maintain sanctions while Russia illegally occupies part of Ukraine; thus they offer diplomatic and military support to the coastal states of the South China Sea as long as they continue to resist Chinese encroachment. Push-back must be proportional, however, in order to prevent escalation. Compartmentalisation of relations remains crucial, therefore: the ability to cooperate on one issue while disagreeing on another – but making it clear that the more flagrant the violation of the rules in one domain, the more other domains will be affected by the countermeasures. Unfair economic practices such as dumping, for example, justify economic countermeasures, but will not usually lead to reactions in another domain. Having people murdered on the territory of another power, in contrast, may lead to a wide array of countermeasures across the political, economic and security dimensions of relations between the powers concerned.

The great powers can also push back together against a third state if that threatens peace and security, for example by the proliferation of nuclear weapons. The powers often instrumentalise such an issue for their own purposes: some confront the offending state, while others rally behind it. The latter often do so only to cause nuisance to the former. If, instead, the great powers would effectively cooperate to prevent or halt what eventually might be a threat to them all, that would be a powerful instrument to build mutual trust among them. The Iran nuclear deal was an example of how the great powers could work together, difficult though it was. Until the Trump administration left the deal and destroyed this fragile cooperation. During the 2020 US presidential campaign, Biden announced that he would re-join the nuclear deal, but reforging the required degree of trust to make it work again will take time in any circumstances.

The logic of engagement means that every great power can work with any other great power when interests coincide. This implies independence: that a great power is in a partnership or an alliance with another great power should not prevent it from cooperating with a third power when there is a legitimate opportunity. That indeed would amount to breaking the logic of engagement in favour of creating two blocs: the US and the EU versus China and Russia. There is but a thin dividing line, of course, between, on the one hand, working with another great power for the purpose of distancing it from its partner or ally while staying closely aligned with one's own partner or ally, and, on the other hand, genuine cooperation on an issue of shared interest. But both motivations can very well drive policy simultaneously. The idea of aligning in new constellations only to isolate one of the great powers, such as the US–Russia partnership mentioned above, goes against the logic of engagement as well: isolating China will not strengthen the international order but push Beijing into fully rejecting and therefore undermining it. For engagement to have a chance, therefore, every great power ought to remain sufficiently independent in spirit to explore *all* opportunities for cooperation. Thus the US should see EU–China or EU–Russia cooperation as a way to promote China's and Russia's commitment to the international order rather than as inherently undermining American strategy. Similarly, Russia might see the benefit of finding a way back to normal relations with the EU without weakening its partnership with China.[3]

Engagement does not imply equidistance. Between the European and American ways of life, the resemblances far outweigh the differences, hence interests overlap to a great extent, though not fully; the US and the EU see different, but complementary roles for themselves in international politics. Brussels and Washington are thus likely to stay very close to each other and, in any case, much closer than to Moscow or Beijing. On the condition, that is, that their roles and the grand strategies that follow from them do not become contradictory. If the US were to purposely opt for a strategy of confrontation with China merely in order to maintain its status as the leading power, the EU would be unlikely to simply follow suit. If, on the contrary, China chooses the path of aggression against the US or other states, the EU would definitely align with the US against it. Russia and China are both authoritarian states, but in other aspects their ways of life are rather different, and their interests are often far from complementary, though differences with the EU and the US are far larger. Of their own accord, therefore, Moscow and Beijing are likely to remain partners without growing much closer, unless confrontation with other powers would push them into deepening their cooperation.

Differences between the ways of life of the great powers will remain, and engagement does not demand approval. The EU and the US can legitimately criticise and condemn Russia and China when they violate human rights, for example. From their point of view, indeed, they must do so, in order to uphold the universality of human rights. One does not have to like the other powers, but even as one condemns certain aspects of their way of life, one must respect them as powers with legitimate interests. Grand strategy ought to be driven by reason, not by emotion. One should not frame international politics as a civilisational confrontation.[4] The purpose of grand strategy is to safeguard one's own way of life, not to change the other powers' ways of life. To that end, one can legitimately aspire to affect the other powers' behaviour in international politics; one can also hope in the long term to have influence on their domestic politics by a consistent principled stance in favour of human rights, but ultimately only the Chinese or the Russians can change the Chinese or Russian way of life. If one starts out with the objective of changing the other's way of life, and the ambition to actively interfere in their domestic politics for that purpose, substantial engagement is impossible and confrontation will inevitably ensue. Whereas if one 'embraced a more mixed order and accepted some of the difficult compromises that came with it', one could actually end up wielding more influence than in a world riven by confrontation.[5]

★★★

The second precept is that the great powers must invest in effective multilateralism. All great powers have an interest in a functioning international order: a stable framework with enforceable rules and effective multilateral institutions, which allows them to trade and invest, to address global challenges, to maintain workable political relations, and to protect their interests. In spite of the corona crisis, the global economy remains truly global, and all states remain deeply interconnected. The great powers do realise the importance of the rules-based order – that is why they compete for influence in the multilateral architecture, manoeuvring their candidates into key positions and rallying votes behind them, so that they are better placed to shape the rules. As long as this is done through legitimate means, that is a perfectly legitimate pursuit. But the great powers also regularly undermine the rules because they tend to ignore them and to bypass the multilateral institutions when that suits their interests. Withdrawing from a multilateral organisation because one is dissatisfied with certain malfunctions or with the degree of influence that other powers have gained over it, only aggravates the problem. The more the US, for example, retreated from the multilateral bodies that create some order in our world (such as the WHO), the more it enabled China to do exactly the opposite of what the American (and European) interest demands: to move in, fill the gap, and lean on the other states to re-write the rules to its sole advantage. The EU alone will likely not have sufficient weight to prevent that. Similarly, creating alternative groupings that are directed against a specific great power (such as the 'alliance of democracies' that the Trump administration proposed), will only provoke that power to do likewise, until eventually two or more parallel multilateral systems emerge that are no longer interconnected – and thus become unable to provide effective global governance. Tackling global problems such as the climate crisis then becomes impossible. The Biden presidential campaign specifically announced a return to the WHO; all great powers must embrace multilateralism as a whole for it to be effective.

A degree of buy-in from all of the great powers and a certain level of cooperation between them are at once a precondition to make multilateralism work, and a result of multilateralism if it is successful. It is a fact that the US and the EU remain overrepresented in key multilateral bodies, while China in particular is underrepresented, given its weight in international politics.[6] It is not a law of nature, for example, that the heads of the World Bank and the International Monetary Fund always are American and European, respectively. Rectifying this must be part of any 'grand bargain' for the future of multilateralism.[7] Compared to most other states, including key regional powers, China already has a major stake in the system, though, and it has been quite successful in recent years in mobilising states to vote for its candidates for senior positions in various international organisations – that is just the normal politics of such organisations. The other dimension of the bargain, of course, is that the powers that have the greatest representation must fulfil an exemplary role in upholding the rules. It would not be in the interest of the other powers to accept growing Chinese influence in the multilateral system without further ado unless they would trust China to commit to the core rules.

The core rules that could shape stable and peaceful relations between the great powers are peace, reciprocity and non-exclusivity. First, all great powers should refrain from the threat or use of coercion, by military or non-military means, as a way to pursue their interests. The illegitimate use of force by one great power ought to have consequences in its relations with *all* other great powers, sending a clear message that aggression cannot be tolerated – not even on the part of the power that one is closest to. Second, the great powers must themselves apply the rules that they expect others to adhere to, notably in economic relations. Threatening or using sanctions such as tariffs to coerce other powers into applying reciprocity, however, is an instrument that risks creating more economic pain than the problem it seeks to address. Instead, the powers could foster a dynamic of 'positive reciprocity': making it clear that future economic opening-up to another power would be conditional upon that power first implementing full reciprocity in all existing economic relations. Cutting back existing relations, as the Trump administration did vis-à-vis China, should be an instrument of last resort rather than the first step. Third, the great powers should foster a level economic playing field in other states as well, so that they can all do business everywhere according to the same rules. This would prevent normal economic competition from escalating into geopolitical rivalry and a race to create exclusive spheres of influence.

If they adhered to these three core rules, the great powers could not only avoid rivalry from spinning out of control, they could also establish a basis for cooperation on the global challenges that concern the interests of all of them. The freedom of access to the global commons (the seas, space, air space, and cyber space[8]), the climate crisis, non-proliferation, the global open economy, artificial intelligence, and, of course, the coronavirus pandemic and global health stand out as priorities that demand multilateral management. Without the active participation of the great powers, multilateralism can achieve but little; but the great powers alone, without buy-in from other states, cannot solve the global problems listed above either.[9] Without multilateral cooperation, great power politics can easily slide into rivalry; but if such cooperation does not involve all great powers of the day, multilateralism can be perverted to serve the interests of some of the powers while others attempt to undermine it. Taking into account both the weight of the great powers and the necessity of inclusivity towards and acceptance from the other states, the great powers should collectively take the lead in the multilateral institutions. They could function as a concert of powers embedded within multilateralism.[10]

★★★

The third precept is that the great powers must respect the sovereignty of all other states. Any attempt to create an exclusive sphere of influence and dominate another state is likely to be counterproductive: it will trigger the suspicion of the other great powers, and it will push the targeted state into seeking protection from other powers. Or by forcing the target state to choose between two mutually exclusive allegiances, it will render a country apart, as when Ukraine was torn between Russia and the EU. Ultimately, this dynamic of competing connectivity schemes (notably the BRI, the EAEU, the EU–Asia Connectivity Strategy) and spheres of influence can only lead to the creation of antagonistic blocs. At the same time, connectivity is crucial for the functioning of the global economy, and for each individual great power. The great powers, therefore, must commit to create connectivity by consent: they can entice but must not coerce states to connect their economies with their own, and they cannot in any way block states from developing equally profound connections with other powers as well.

The corona crisis might stimulate the great powers to look for consent rather than coercion. As the resources of both the powers and the target states have been gravely affected by the corona-induced economic recession, it makes less and less economic sense for states to engage in parallel connectivity schemes with different powers, each with their own flagship investment projects. Rather, it would be advisable to decide which are the priority projects from the point of view of the interests of the target states, and to join up efforts to ensure that those are implemented – 'connecting the connectivities', as Anita Prakash calls it.[11] Moreover, in order to ensure a smooth functioning of the flows of people, goods, services and capital, all states have an interest in harmonising norms and standards when it comes to securing travel and transport against the coronavirus. The great powers will naturally continue to compete for influence over norms and standards, but the huge common challenge of COVID-19 ought at least to induce an element of concertation as well.

★★★

The fourth and final precept is that each great power must protect its own sovereignty and maintain a sufficient power base to engage the other powers. Even a strategy of engagement does require power: one obviously cannot confront another great power from a position of weakness, but one cannot constructively engage it from a weak position either – one would risk inviting undue interference. A state that feels vulnerable will not have the confidence to proactively engage with and open up to other states. Finally, therefore, in order to engage each other, to concert within the multilateral system, and to create connectivity, the great powers must preserve their capacity to make their own decisions, independent from the other powers, and the capacity to act upon those decisions and defend their own interests.

Sovereignty and reciprocal connectivity can be combined: each power can identify the specific sensitive sectors of the economy in which it limits or excludes foreign participation, in order to prevent any other power from abusing its presence for subversive purposes, while upholding connectivity as the general rule. These sovereignty issues should be well defined. Invoking vague security concerns to impede natural economic competition (such as Trump declaring car imports into the US a national security threat, for example)[12] destroys mutual trust and connectivity, and risks being self-defeating. Furthermore, sovereignty certainly does not mean autarky: decoupling one's economy from another major world economy will create havoc, not just for the two powers directly concerned, but for the global economy as a whole. In order to maintain sovereignty, it is crucial though that each power achieves a sufficient degree of autonomy in key technologies, in order not to have to rely on foreign suppliers in what really are sensitive sectors of the economy. Artificial intelligence, quantum computing, biotechnology, renewable energy, and 5G are the primary examples, in addition to the classic domain of armaments and military equipment. Every great power logically needs the capacity to defend itself militarily. The corona crisis has demonstrated the vital importance of sufficient autonomy in the health sector as well. At the same time, a vaccine for the coronavirus is a public good. The first state to develop an effective vaccine and to vaccinate its own people does have an advantage: domestically, in returning back earlier than others to a normal functioning of society, and internationally, in sharing the vaccine with allies and partners first. But since every state depends on its connectivity with the rest of the world, every state does have an interest in the global availability of the vaccine, or connectivity would forever remain seriously impeded, not to mention the continued spread of ever new mutations of the virus.

Sovereignty also depends on domestic public support: a strong state is a state whose citizens wholeheartedly support its role in international politics. Oftentimes, states draw citizens' attention away from domestic problems by engaging in prominent foreign enterprises. In some great powers, the public to some extent even appears willing to sacrifice domestic investment and personal prosperity to the benefit of strong armed forces and the international prestige of the state. In the end, however, people everywhere demand sufficient prosperity to fully take part in society. The state can address inequality between citizens via social security, or it can assuage it by fostering optimism and the belief that things will get better even if they are not so good now. Alternatively, inequality can be repressed, and sublimated into a story of national greatness, which outweighs individual poverty, but which is threatened by other states and therefore demands individual sacrifice. Eventually, however, people will come to realise that rather than other states it is their own government that consciously limits their prosperity, and will seek to elect other leaders – thus in 2020 Biden won the popular vote in the US. Where that option is not open to them, the regime will have to fear domestic revolution and regime change – that remains the ultimate angst of the CCP. Disaffected citizens, moreover, become easy targets for subversion by external powers. Domestic equality, on the contrary, generates domestic unity, which is why it is a pillar of sovereignty.

While every great power safeguards its own sovereignty, it also ought to recognise the sovereignty of the other powers, and refrain from any attempts at subverting it. This brings us back to the starting point of this concluding chapter: the very first precondition for a stable world is that the great powers accept the existence of peer competitors and recognise each other's right to pursue their legitimate interests in legitimate ways. Since the turn of the century, there has been no direct military confrontation between the great powers, although the risk of incidents, and the potential for escalation, remains high; the powers have also engaged in proxy wars. But there have been many instances of great powers attempting to subvert, sometimes on a quasi-permanent basis, the political decision making of other powers, notably by interfering in election processes. Perhaps the great powers could formally undertake to abstain from any intervention in the domestic politics of the others, be it in day-to-day decision making or in the selection of the future leadership. Such a 'non-subversion pact' would not entail approval of the way of life of the other powers, and one power could still legitimately criticise another for its domestic violations of human rights and other norms and values. The great powers could remain open to a mutual cultural, academic and political presence, advertising their way of life in strictly legitimate ways. But all powers would accept that the only ones who can legitimately change the way of life of another power are its own people. Then they can confidently engage each other.

★★★

Rivalry can never be entirely excluded from relations between states in general and between great powers in particular. Nor will the precepts outlined above, even if all great powers incorporate them into their grand strategies, settle all outstanding issues, such as the illegal occupation of the Crimea and the South China Sea. But starting from these precepts, future rivalry can be kept to manageable proportions. The first step is to recognise that active rivalry is different from natural competition, and that all states, peer competitors included, have legitimate interests. Hence, when those interests overlap, natural opportunities for cooperation emerge as well. Exploiting those opportunities to the full while limiting the risk of incidents and escalation can be the guiding principle for the grand strategy of all great powers, while each preserves its own way of life and pursues its global interests. The challenge of 21st century great power politics is to maintain one world: one international order to which all states contribute, and in which all states have the opportunity of building stable and mutually beneficial relations with any other state, with a concert of the great powers embedded in strong multilateral institutions in a leading role. The great powers should heed the words of Joseph Nye: 'Leadership is not the same as domination, and it will need to be shared.'[13] The alternative, allowing the world once more to be divided into antagonistic and mutually exclusive blocs, would be destructive for the global economy, and paralyse multilateral decision making, rendering it impossible to solve urgent global challenges such as the climate crisis.

To some, my agenda may seem naïve. Predicting war, including a great power war, is easy, however. One does not predict peace, on the contrary – one builds it. Does not the transformation of Europe, from a set of rival imperialist powers into a European Union that aspires to a mediating role in international politics, prove that positive change is possible?

> Cooperating with the west and the east, contracting the necessary alliances on one or the other side as required, without ever accepting any form of dependence. ... Bringing the states that touch on the Rhine, on the Alps, on the Pyrenees to group together politically, economically, and strategically. Making that organisation into one of the three planetary powers and, if one day necessary, the arbiter between the two Soviet and Anglo-Saxon camps.[14]

The role that De Gaulle outlined for Europe in 1959 is exactly the one it could play today, between the US, Russia and China.

The type of international politics that this book, in the end, argues for is actually best captured by the EU motto: Unity in Diversity. It will not be easy for the EU to play this role, or even to establish internal consensus about it. De Gaulle's wartime relations with Churchill proved that even between comrades in arms, relations often are far from easy. But, giving Churchill the last word: 'Statesmen are not called upon only to settle easy questions. These often settle themselves. It is where the balance quivers, and the proportions are veiled in mist, that the opportunity for world-saving decisions presents itself'.[15]

Notes

Preface and Acknowledgements

1   Dwight D. Eisenhower, *Crusade in Europe*. New York, Doubleday, 1948, p 256.
2   'Les bons diners font des bons dépêches'. Quoted in: Emmanuel de Waresquiel, *Talleyrand. Le prince immobile*. Paris, Fayard, 2006.
3   Alasdair Roberts, 'Grand Strategy Isn't Grand Enough'. In: *Foreign Policy*, 20 February 2018.
4   Hugh Trevor-Roper, *One Hundred Letters. Edited by Richard Davenport-Hines & Adam Sisman*. Oxford, Oxford University Press, 2014, p 139.
5   Michael J. Green, *By More than Providence–Grand Strategy and American Power in the Asia Pacific since 1783*. New York, Columbia University Press, 2017, p 170.
6   Harold Nicolson, *Peacemaking 1919*. London, Constable, 1933, pp 7–8.
7   Steven Runciman, *A History of the Crusades. Volume 1: The First Crusade*. Cambridge, Cambridge University Press, 1951, p xii.

Introduction

1   Lauren Egan, 'Trump calls coronavirus Democrats' "new hoax"'. NBC News, 28 February 2020.
2   Peter Hirschberg, 'Internal Chinese report warns Beijing faces Tiananmen-like global backlash over virus'. Reuters, 4 May 2020.
3   Christopher Frayling, *The Yellow Peril. Dr Fu Manchu & The Rise of Xenophobia*. London, Thames & Hudson, 2014.
4   Mark B. Smith, *The Russia Anxiety. And How History Can Resolve It*. London, Allen Lane, 2019.
5   Michael Pillsbury, *The Hundred-Year Marathon: China's Secret Strategy to Replace America as the Global Superpower*. New York, Henry Holt, 2015.
6   Alastair Iain Johnston, 'Shaky foundations: The "intellectual architecture" of Trump's China policy'. *Survival*, 61(2), 2019, pp 189–202.
7   Andrew A. Michta, 'The building-blocks of a China strategy'. *The American Interest*, 7 May 2020.
8   François Heisbourg, *Le Temps des Prédateurs. La Chine, les États-Unis, la Russie et Nous*. Paris, Odile Jacob, 2020.
9   Herbert R. MacMaster, 'How China sees the world'. *The Atlantic*, May 2020.
10 Fareed Zakaria, 'The new China scare. Why America shouldn't panic about its latest challenger'. *Foreign Affairs*, 99(1), 2020, No. 1, pp 52–69, on p 52.

[11]   Graham Allison, *Destined for War. Can America and China Escape Thucydides's Trap?* Boston, MA, Houghton Mifflin Harcourt, 2017, p 10.

[12]   Hanns W. Maull, 'The once and future liberal order'. *Survival*, 61(2), 2019, pp 7–32, on pp 21–22.

[13]   Winston S. Churchill, *The Second World War. Volume I: The Gathering Storm*. London, Cassell, 1948, p 353.

[14]   Joseph S. Nye, 'The Rise and Fall of American Hegemony from Wilson to Trump'. *International Affairs*, 95(1), 2019, pp 63–80 on p 75.

[15]   European Commission, *EU-China – A Strategic Outlook*. Brussels, European Commission, 12 March 2019.

[16]   UN News, *COVID-19: UN chief calls for global ceasefire to focus on 'the true fight of our lives'*. New York, United Nations, 23 March 2020.

[17]   Maull, 'The once and future liberal order', p 19.

[18]   François Heisbourg, 'From Wuhan to the world: How the pandemic will reshape geopolitics'. *Survival*, 62(3), 2020, pp 7–24.

[19]   Daniel W. Drezner, Ronald R. Krebs and Randall Schweller, 'The end of grand strategy. America must think small'. *Foreign Affairs*, 99(3), 2020, pp 107–117.

[20]   Lucas Kello, *The Virtual Weapon and International Order*. New Haven, Yale University Press, 2017.

[21]   André Barrinha and Thomas Renard, 'Power and diplomacy in the post-liberal cyberspace'. *International Affairs*, 96(3), 2020, pp 749–766.

[22]   Maull, 'The once and future liberal order', p 20.

[23]   Krishan Kumar, *Visions of Empire. How Five Imperial Regimes Shaped the World*. Princeton, Princeton University Press, 2017, p 19.

[24]   Michael Howard, *Captain Professor. A Life in War and Peace*. London, Continuum, 2006, p 208.

[25]   Hew Strachan, 'Strategy in theory; Strategy in practice'. *The Journal of Strategic Studies*, 42(2), 2019, pp 171–190 on p 171.

[26]   Harold Nicolson, *Peacemaking 1919*. London, Constable, 1933, p 137.

[27]   Graham Allison, *The US-China Strategic Competition: Clues from History*. Washington, Aspen Institute Paper, February 2020, p 2.

[28]   Allison, *The US-China Strategic Competition*, p 2.

[29]   Peter Rudolf, *Der amerikanisch-chinesische Weltkonflikt*. Berlin, Stiftung Wissenschaft und Politik, Studie No. 23, October 2019, p 10.

[30]   Xuetong Yan, *Leadership and the Rise of Great Powers*. Princeton, Princeton University Press, p 14.

[31]   Dwight D. Eisenhower, *Crusade in Europe*. New York, Doubleday, 1948, p 475.

[32]   Georgy Zhukov, *The Memoirs of Marshal Zhukov*. London, Jonathan Cape, 1971, p 631.

[33]   Ana Swanson, 'A new red scare is reshaping Washington'. *The New York Times*, 20 July 2019.

[34]   Committee on the Present Danger: China, 'The Mission of the Committee'. www.presentdangerchina.org.

[35]   Hal Brands, 'The Chinese century?'. *The National Interest*, 154, 2018, pp 35–45 on p 37.

[36]   Hal Brands, 'China rivalry may put the US back in the coup business'. New York, Bloomberg, 12 May 2020.

[37]   Joshua R. Itzkowitz Shifrinson, 'Partnership or predation? How rising states contend with declining great powers'. *International Security*, 45(1), 2020, pp 90–126.

38 Stephen M. Walt, 'Europe's future is as China's enemy'. *Foreign Policy*, 22 January 2019.

39 Lawrence Freedman, 'The rise and fall of great power wars'. *International Affairs*, 95(1), 2019, pp 101–117 on p 102.

40 Christopher Coker, *Can War Be Eliminated?* Cambridge, Polity, 2014, p 7.

Chapter 1

1 Carl von Clausewitz, *On War*. London, Penguin Classics, 1984 (translated by J. J. Graham).

2 'Aber im Kriege erweist sich häufig gerade das Einfachste als das Schwerste. Nicht in dem Entschluß and sich, sondern in seiner unbeirrten Durchführung liegen zumeist die wahren Schwierigkeiten.' Erich von Manstein, *Verlorene Siege*. Bonn, Athenäum Verlag, 1955, p 405.

3 'La politique devait être l'action au service d'une idée forte et simple.' Charles de Gaulle, *Mémoires de Guerre. L'appel 1940–1942*. Paris, Plon, 1954, p 219.

4 Lawrence Freedman, *Strategy*. Oxford, Oxford University Press, 2013, p 614.

5 Dominique Enright, *The Wicked Wit of Winston Churchill*. London, Michael O'Mara, 2011.

6 Andrew Roberts, *Masters and Commanders. How Roosevelt, Churchill, Marshall and Alanbrooke Won the War in the West*. London, Allen Lane, 2008.

7 Freedman, *Strategy*, p 141.

8 Office of the Historian, *Kennan and Containment, 1947*. Washington, State Department, 2016.

9 Edward Luttwak, *The Grand Strategy of the Byzantine Empire*. Cambridge, MA, Belknap, 2009, p 409.

10 Colin S. Gray, *Strategy and Politics*. London, Routledge, 2016, p 29.

11 Alasdair Roberts, 'Grand strategy isn't grand enough'. *Foreign Policy*, 20 February 2018.

12 Daniel W. Drezner, Ronald R. Krebs and Randall Schweller, 'The end of grand strategy. America must think small'. *Foreign Affairs*, 99(3), 2020, pp 107–117.

13 Koen Troch and David Manunta, 'Sir, Did you say strategy? Our answer: Foresight!' *Belgisch Militair Tijdschrift – Revue Militaire Belge*, 10(20), 2020, pp 1–12.

14 Colin S. Gray, *Fighting Talk: Forty Maxims on War, Peace and Strategy*. Westport, CT, Praeger Security International, 2007.

15 Andrew Ehrhardt and Maeve Ryan, 'Grand Strategy is no silver bullet, but it is indispensable'. *War on the Rocks*, 19 May 2020.

16 Drezner et al, 'The End of Grand Strategy'.

17 'Fort bien, mais a-t-il de la chance?' Quoted in: Jean Tulard, *Napoléon Chef de Guerre*. Paris, Tallandier, 2012.

18 Colin S. Gray, *Strategy and Politics*. London, Routledge, 2016, p 25.

19 Freedman, *Strategy*, p 611.

20 Freedman, *Strategy*, p ix.

21 Richard K. Betts, 'The grandiosity of grand strategy'. *The Washington Quarterly*, 42(4), 2019, pp 7–22 on p 8.

22 Christian Hartmann, Thomas Vordermayer, Othmar Plöckinger and Roman Töppel, *Hitler, Mein Kampf. Eine kritische Edition*. Munich, Institut für Zeitgeschichte, 2016.

23 Colin Gray, *Strategy and History. Essays on Theory and Practice*. London, Routledge, 2016.

24 Ian Morris, *War: What is it Good for? The Role of Conflict in Civilisation, from Primates to Robots*. London, Profile Books, 2014, p 342.

25 Guy Verhofstadt, *The United States of Europe*. London, The Federal Trust, 2006.

26 Walter Scheidel, *Escape from Rome. The Failure of Empire and the Road to Prosperity*. Princeton, NJ, Princeton University Press, 2019.

27 Betts, 'The grandiosity of grand strategy', p 7.

28 Dominic Lieven, *Towards the Flame. Empire, War and the End of Tsarist Russia*. London, Allen Lane, 2015, p 367.

29 Josep Borrell, Speech at the Raisina Dialogue 2020 in New Delhi. Brussels, European External Action Service, 16 January 2020.

30 Richard Aldous, *Schlesinger – The Imperial Historian*. New York, Norton, 2017, p 342.

31 Arthur Harris, *Bomber Offensive*. London, Collins, 1947, p 42.

32 Winston S. Churchill, 'The sinews of peace'. Speech delivered at Fulton College, Westminster, Missouri, 5 March 1946.

33 Vladimir Putin, Speech and the Following Discussion at the Munich Conference on Security Policy. Moscow, The Kremlin, 10 February 2007.

34 Ronald Asmus, *A Little War That Shook the World: Georgia, Russia, and the Future of the West*. London, St. Martin's Press, 2010.

35 Federica Mogherini, *Shared Vision, Common Action: A Stronger Europe. A Global Strategy for the European Union's Foreign and Security Policy*. Brussels, European External Action Service, 28 June 2016.

36 The Kremlin, *National Security Strategy*. Moscow, The Kremlin, December 2015.

37 Olga Oliker, *Unpacking Russia's New National Security Strategy*. Washington, Center for Strategic and International Studies (CSIS), Commentary, 7 January 2016.

38 Gregory Carleton, *Russia. The Story of War*. Cambridge, Belknap, 2017, p 34.

39 Hillary Clinton, 'America's pacific century'. *Foreign Policy*, 11 October 2011.

40 The White House, *National Security Strategy of the United States of America*. Washington, The White House, December 2017.

41 Stephen M. Walt, 'The myth of American exceptionalism'. *Foreign Policy*, 11 October 2011.

42 Stockholm Peace Research Institute, *Global military expenditure sees largest annual increase in a decade*. Stockholm, SIPRI, 27 April 2020.

43 Thomas G. Mahnken, *Forging the Tools of 21st Century Great Power Competition*. Washington, Center for Strategic and Budgetary Assessments, 2020, p 4.

44 Elizabeth C. Economy, *The Third Revolution. Xi Jinping and the New Chinese State*. New York, Oxford University Press, 2019, p 188.

45 Xi Jinping, *Secure a Decisive Victory in Building a Moderately Prosperous Society in All Respects and Strive for the Great Success of Socialism with Chinese Characteristics for a New Era*. Report Delivered at the 19th National Congress of the Communist Party of China. Beijing, Xinhua News Agency, 18 October 2017.

46 Bonnie S. Glaser and Matthew P. Funaiole, *Xi Jinping's 19th Party Congress Speech Heralds Greater Assertiveness in Chinese Foreign Policy*. Washington, Center for Strategic and International Studies (CSIS), Commentary, 26 October 2017.

47 M. Taylor Fravel, *Active Defense. China's Military Strategy since 1949*. Princeton, Princeton University Press, 2019, pp 275–276.

48 Stephen R. Platt, *Autumn in the Heavenly Kingdom. China, the West, and the Epic Story of the Taiping Civil War*. London, Penguin, 2012.

49 Douglas MacArthur, *Reminiscences*. New York, McGraw-Hill, 1964, p 367.

[50] Javier Solana, *A Secure Europe in a Better World. European Security Strategy*. Brussels, Council of the EU, 12 December 2003.

Chapter 2

[1] Quoted in: Richard Toye, *The Roar of the Lion. The Untold Story of Churchill's World War II Speeches*. Oxford, Oxford University Press, 2013, p 18.

[2] Bernard Law Montgomery, *The Memoirs of Field-Marshal Montgomery*. London, Collins, 1958, p 191.

[3] Edward N. Luttwak, *The Grand Strategy of the Roman Empire from the First Century AD to the Third*. Baltimore, MD, Johns Hopkins University Press, 1976.

[4] Francis Fukuyama, *The End of History and the Last Man*. New York, Free Press, 1992.

[5] Charles Krauthammer, 'The unipolar moment'. *Foreign Affairs*, 70(1), 1991, pp 23–33.

[6] Paul Kennedy, *The Rise and Fall of the Great Powers. Economic Change and Military Conflict from 1500 to 2000*. London, Unwin Hyman, 1988, p xxi, p 413.

[7] Barry Gewen, *The Inevitability of Tragedy. Henry Kissinger and his World*. New York, Norton, 2020, p 338.

[8] Hal Brands and Eric Edelman, 'The upheaval'. *The National Interest*, 150, 2017, pp 30–40.

[9] International Institute for Strategic Studies, *The Military Balance 2020*. London, IISS, 2020.

[10] Hanns W. Maul, 'European policies towards China and the United States: Can they support a strategic triad?' *European Foreign Affairs Review*, 21, Special Issue, 2016, pp 29–46 on p 31.

[11] Kerry Brown, *China's World. What Does China Want?* London, I.B. Tauris, 2017, p 35.

[12] Josep Borrell, Speech at the Raisina Dialogue 2020 in New Delhi. Brussels, EEAS, 16 January 2020.

[13] Mark Leonard, Jean Pisani-Ferry, Elina Ribakova, Jeremy Shapiro and Guntram Wolff, *Redefining Europe's Economic Sovereignty*. Brussels, Bruegel, Policy Contribution No. 9, June 2019, p. 9.

[14] Paul Stronski and Richard Sokolsky, *The Return of Global Russia. An Analytical Framework*. Washington, Carnegie, December 2017, p 30.

[15] Erik Brattberg and Philippe Le Corre, *The Case for Transatlantic Cooperation in the Indo-Pacific*. Washington, Carnegie, 18 December 2019, p 3.

[16] Lee Hsien Loong, 'The endangered Asian century. America, China, and the perils of confrontation'. *Foreign Affairs*, 4 June 2020.

[17] Xuetong Yan, *Leadership and the Rise of Great Powers*. Princeton, NJ, Princeton University Press, p. 199.

[18] Evan A. Feigenbaum, 'China and the world. Dealing with a reluctant power'. *Foreign Affairs*, 96(1), 2017, pp 33–40 on p 39.

[19] Fidel Sendagorta, *The Triangle in the Long Game. Rethinking Relations Between China, Europe, and the United States in the New Era of Strategic Competition*. Cambridge, MA, Harvard Kennedy School, Belfer Center Report, June 2019, p 57.

[20] Xuetong Yan, *Leadership and the Rise of Great Powers*, pp 88–90.

[21] Hanns Günther Hilpert, 'Values and orders: Ideological conflicts and challenges'. In: Barbara Lippert and Volker Perthes (eds), *Strategic Rivalry Between United*

States and China. Causes, Trajectories, and Implications for Europe. Berlin, Stiftung Wissenschaft und Politik, Research Paper No. 4, April 2020, pp 35–38 on p 35.

[22] Nele Noesselt, 'The European Union and China's multidimensional diplomacy: Strategic triangulation?'. *European Foreign Affairs Review*, 21, Special Issue, 2016, pp 11–28 on p 14.

[23] John Maynard Keynes, *The Economic Consequences of the Peace.* New York, Harcourt, Brace and How, 1920, p 11.

[24] Odd Arne Westad, 'The sources of Chinese conduct. Are Washington and Beijing fighting a new cold war?'. *Foreign Affairs*, 98(5), 2019, pp 85–95.

[25] Hal Brands and Zack Cooper, 'After the responsible stakeholder, what? Debating America's China strategy'. *Texas National Security Review*, 2(2), 2019, pp 68–81 on p 77.

[26] Giovanni Grevi, *The Interpolar World: A New Scenario.* Paris, EU Institute for Security Studies, Occasional Paper No. 79, June 2009.

[27] Norman Angell, *Europe's Optical Illusion.* London, Simpkin, Marshall, Hamilton, Kent & Co., 1909.

[28] Graham Allison, 'The new spheres of influence. Sharing the globe with other great powers'. *Foreign Affairs*, 99(2), 2020, pp 30–40.

[29] Thomas G. Mahnken, *Forging the Tools of 21st Century Great Power Competition.* Washington, Center for Strategic and Budgetary Assessments, 2020.

[30] Joseph S. Nye, 'The rise and fall of American hegemony from Wilson to Trump'. *International Affairs*, 95(1), 2019, pp 63–80.

[31] Derek Grossman and John Speed Meyers, 'Minding the gaps: US Military strategy toward China'. *Strategic Studies Quarterly*, 13(4), 2019, pp 105–121.

[32] Brands and Cooper, 'After the responsible stakeholder, what?', p 69.

[33] Sulmaan Wasif Khan, *Haunted by Chaos. China's Grand Strategy from Mao Zedong to Xi Jinping.* Cambridge, MA, Harvard University Press, 2018, pp 2–3.

[34] Gregory Carleton, *Russia. The Story of War.* Cambridge, MA, Belknap Press, 2017, p 22.

[35] Dmitri Trenin, 'Russia has grand design for the international order'. *Moscow Times*, 26 October 2017.

Chapter 3

[1] Winston S. Churchill, *The Second World War. Volume III: The Grand Alliance.* London, Cassell, 1950, p 536.

[2] Geoffrey Parker, *The Grand Strategy of Philipp II.* New Haven, CT, Yale University Press, 2000.

[3] Stephen G. Fritz, *The First Soldier. Hitler as Military Leader.* New Haven, CT, Yale University Press, 2018.

[4] Herbert P. Bix, *Hirohito and the Making of Modern Japan.* New York, Harper Collins, 2000.

[5] 'L'optimisme va bien à qui en a les moyens.' Charles de Gaulle, *Mémoires de Guerre. L'unité 1942–1944.* Paris, Plon, 1956, p 237.

[6] Herbert R. McMaster, *Dereliction of Duty. Lyndon Johnson, Robert McNamara, the Joint Chiefs of Staff and the Lies that Led to Vietnam.* New York, HarperCollins, 1997.

[7] Robert S. McNamara, *In Retrospect. The Tragedy and Lessons of Vietnam.* New York, Times Books, 1995.

[8] Rik Coolsaet, *Anticipating the Post-Daesh Landscape.* Brussels, Egmont Institute, Egmont Paper No. 97, October 2017.

9   Churchill, *The Second World War. Volume III*, p 536.

10 Robert Person, *Four Myths about Russian Grand Strategy*. Washington, Center for International and Strategic Studies (CSIS), 22 September 2020.

11 Timothy Snyder, *The Road to Unfreedom. Russia, Europe, America*. New York, Tim Duggan Books, 2018, p 91.

12 Lawrence Freedman, *The Future of War. A History*. London, Allen Lane, 2017, p 225.

13 Eugene Rumer, Richard Sokolsky, Paul Stronski and Andrew S. Weiss, *Illusions vs Reality. Twenty-Five Years of US Policy Toward Russia, Ukraine, and Eurasia*. Washington, Carnegie, 2017, p 36.

14 Snyder, *The Road to Unfreedom*, p 54.

15 Józef Czapski, *Inhuman Land. Searching for the Truth in Soviet Russia 1941–1942*. New York, New York Review Books, 2018, p 126.

16 Lawrence Freedman, 'Who wants to be a great power?' *Prism*, 8(4), 2020, pp 3–14 on p 9.

17 Kishore Mahbubani, *Has the West Lost It? A Provocation*. London, Allen Lane, 2018, p 14.

18 Ian Johnson, 'The flowers blooming in the dark'. *The New York Review of Books*, 67(5), 2020, pp 46–48 on p 46.

19 Sulmaan Wasif Khan, *Haunted by Chaos. China's Grand Strategy from Mao Zedong to Xi Jinping*. Cambridge, Harvard University Press, 2018, p 154.

20 Xuetong Yan, *Leadership and the Rise of Great Powers*. Princeton, NJ, Princeton University Press, p 138.

21 Yan, *Leadership and the Rise of Great Powers*, pp 132–134.

22 Bill Hayton, *The Invention of China*. New Haven, Yale University Press, 2020.

23 Fidel Sendagorta, *The Triangle in the Long Game. Rethinking Relations Between China, Europe, and the United States in the New Era of Strategic Competition*. Cambridge, Belfer Center Report, Harvard Kennedy School, June 2019, p 59.

24 Khan, *Haunted by Chaos*, p 238.

25 Michael J. Mazarr, 'Rethinking restraint: Why it fails in practice'. *The Washington Quarterly*, 43(2), 2020, pp 7–32.

26 George Orwell, *Notes on Nationalism*. London, Penguin Classics, 2018.

27 William Slim, *Defeat into Victory*. London, Cassell, 1956, p 182.

28 Athanassios G. Platias and Constatinos Koliopoulos, *Thucydides on Strategy. Grand Strategies in the Peloponnesian War and Their Relevance Today*. London, Hurst, 2010, p 125.

29 Snyder, *The Road to Unfreedom*, p 79.

30 Gregory Carleton, *Russia. The Story of War*. Cambridge, The Belknap Press, 2017, p 235.

31 Nadezhada Arbatova, 'Three faces of Russia's neo-Eurasianism'. *Survival*, 61(6), 2019, pp 7–24 on p 19.

32 Rosemary Foot, 'Remembering the past to secure the present: Versailles legacies in a resurgent China'. *International Affairs*, 95(1), 2019, pp 143–160.

33 Yong Deng, *China's Struggle for Status: The Realignment of international relations*. Cambridge, Cambridge University Press, 2008, p 8.

34 Yuen Foong Khong, 'Power as prestige in world politics'. *International Affairs*, 95(1), 2019, pp 119–142.

35 Slim, *Defeat into Victory*, p 64.

36 Peter Rudolf, *Der amerikanisch-chinesische Weltkonflikt*. Berlin, Stiftung Wissenschaft und Politik, SWP Studie No. 23, October 2019, p 14.

[37] Graham Allison, *Destined for War. Can America and China Escape Thucydides's Trap?* Boston, New York, Houghton Mifflin Harcourt, 2017, p 10.

[38] Christopher R. Hill, 'What does Washington want from China? Pique is not a policy'. *Foreign Affairs*, 11 May 2020.

[39] Tony Judt, *Postwar. A History of Europe Since 1945*. London, Penguin, 2005, p 793.

[40] Robert Kagan, *The Jungle Grows Back. America and Our Imperilled World*. New York, Knopf, 2018, p 56.

[41] Harold Nicolson, *Peacemaking 1919*. London, Constable, 1933, p 193.

Chapter 4

[1] Alex Danchev and Daniel Todman (eds), *Field Marshal Lord Alanbrooke. War Diaries 1939–1945*. London, Phoenix, 2002, p 680.

[2] Sean Kay, *America's Search for Security. The Triumph of Idealism and the Return of Realism*. Lanham, Rowman & Littlefield, 2014, p 129.

[3] Steve Coll, *Directorate S. The CIA and America's Secret Wars in Afghanistan and Pakistan*. New York, Penguin, 2018.

[4] Abigail Green, 'Prophetic chronoscape'. *London Review of Books*, 42(6), 2020, pp 13–14.

[5] Yauheni Preiherman, *Unsettled Union: The Future of the Belarus-Russia Relationship*. London, European Council on Foreign Relations, Commentary, 21 January 2020.

[6] Xuetong Yan, *Leadership and the Rise of Great Powers*. Princeton, Princeton University Press, 2019, p 41.

[7] Brian G. Carlson, *Vostok-2018: Another Sign of Strengthening Russia-China Ties*. Berlin, Stiftung Wissenschaft und Politik, Comment No. 47, November 2018.

[8] Ian Bond, *The EU, the Eurasian Economic Union and One Belt, One Road. Can They Work Together?* London, Centre for European Reform, March 2017, p 7.

[9] Bradley Jardine and Edward Lemon, *In Russia's Shadow: China's Rising Security Presence in Central Asia*. Washington, Wilson Center, Kennan Cable No. 52, May 2020.

[10] Valbona Zeneli and Nataliia Haluhan, 'Why China is setting its sights on Ukraine'. *The Diplomat*, 4 October 2019.

[11] Giorgio Cafiero, *China Plays the Long Game on Syria*. Washington, The Middle East Institute, 10 February 2020.

[12] Andrey Kortunov, *Will Russia Return to Europe?* Moscow, Russian International Affairs Council, 6 November 2018.

[13] Sergey Karaganov, 'The new cold war and the emerging Greater Eurasia'. *Journal of Eurasian Studies*, 5(2), 2018, pp 85–93 on p 86.

[14] Dmitri Trenin, *How Russia Can Maintain Equilibrium in the Post-Pandemic Bipolar World*. Moscow, Carnegie, 1 May 2020, p 1.

[15] Bobo Lo, *A Wary Embrace. What the China-Russia Relationship Means for the World*. Sydney, Penguin – Lowy Institute, 2017, p 60.

[16] Sergey Lukonin, 'Redefining Russia's pivot and China's peripheral diplomacy'. In: Lora Saalman (ed), *China-Russia Relations and Regional Dynamics. From Pivots to Peripheral Diplomacy*. Stockholm, Stockholm International Peace Research Institute, March 2017, pp 3–7 on p 3.

[17] Jacob Stokes and Julianne Smith, 'Facing Down the Sino-Russian Entente'. *The Washington Quarterly*, 43(2), 2020, pp 137–156 on p 143.

[18] Trenin, *How Russia Can Maintain Equilibrium*, p 1.

[19] Bobo Lo, *A Wary Embrace*.

20 Winston S. Churchill, *The Second World War Volume IV: The Hinge of Fate*. London, Cassell, 1951, p 120.
21 'Rester alliés avec les Etats-Unis, mais pas nécessairement alignés'. Michel Barnier, *L'affirmation stratégique des européens. Discours à la Sorbonne*. Paris, 21 January 2019.
22 Mark Leonard, Jean Pisani-Ferry, Elina Ribakova, Jeremy Shapiro and Guntram Wolff, *Redefining Europe's Economic Sovereignty*. Brussels, Bruegel, Policy Contribution No. 9, June 2019, p 9.
23 Hal Brands and Evan Braden Montgomery, 'One war is not enough: Strategy and force planning for great power competition'. *Texas National Security Review*, 3(2), 2020, pp 80–92.
24 Douglas Barrie, Lucie Béraud-Sudraeau, Henry Boyd, Nick Childs, Bastian Giegerich, James Hackett and Meia Nouwens, *European Defence Policy in an Era of Renewed Great-Power Competition*. London, International Institute for Strategic Studies, February 2020, p 1.
25 Brands and Montgomery, 'One war is not enough', p 85.
26 Bernard Law Montgomery, *The Memoirs of Field-Marshal Montgomery*. London, Collins, 1958, p 512.
27 Douglas Barrie, Lucie Béraud-Sudraeau, Henry Boyd, Nick Childs, Bastian Giegerich, James Hackett and Meia Nouwens, *European Defence Policy in an Era of Renewed Great-Power Competition*. London, International Institute for Strategic Studies, February 2020, p 17.
28 Jolyon Howorth, *Autonomy and Strategy: What Should Europe Want?* Brussels, Egmont, Security Policy Brief No. 110, April 2019.
29 Barry Posen, *Restraint: A New Foundation for US Grand Strategy*. Ithaca, NY, Cornell University Press, 2014.
30 Kathleen H. Hicks, Joseph P. Federici, Seamus P. Daniels, Rhys McCormick and Lindsey Sheppard, *Getting to Less? The Minimal Exposure Strategy*. Washington, Center for Strategic and International Studies, February 2020.
31 Lawrence Freedman, *Ukraine and the Art of Strategy*. Oxford, Oxford University Press, 2019, p 16.
32 Luis Simón, Alexander Lanoszka and Hugo Meijer, 'Nodal defence: The changing structure of US alliance systems in Europe and East Asia'. *Journal of Strategic Studies*, 43(2), 2019, pp 1–29.
33 Michael R. Pompeo, *Communist China and the Free World's Future. Speech at the Richard Nixon Presidential Library and Museum*. Washington, State Department, 23 July 2020.

Chapter 5

1 'La diplomatie, sous des conventions de forme, ne connaît que les réalités.' Charles de Gaulle, *Mémoires de Guerre. L'unité 1942–1944*. Paris, Plon, 1956, p 186.
2 Joseph S. Nye, *The Future of Power*. New York, PublicAffairs, 2011.
3 Thomas E. Ricks, *Fiasco. The American Military Adventure in Iraq*. London, Allen Lane, 2006, p 128.
4 Bernard Barrera, *Opération Serval. Notes de guerre, Mali 2013*. Paris, Éditions du Seuil, 2015.
5 Isaiah Wilson III and Scott Smitson, 'Solving America's gray-zone puzzle'. *Parameters*, 46(4), 2016, pp 55–67.

6 Geoffrey Gertz and Miles M. Evers, 'Geoeconomic competition: Will state capitalism win?' *The Washington Quarterly*, 43(2), 2020, pp 117–136.

7 Lawrence Freedman, *The Future of War. A History*. London, Allen Lane, 2017, p 225.

8 Jean-Vincent Holeindre, *La Ruse et la Force. Une Autre Histoire de la Stratégie*. Paris, Perrin, 2017.

9 Lucas Kello, *The Virtual Weapon and International Order*. New Haven, Yale University Press, 2017, p 199.

10 Geraint Hughes, 'War in the grey zone: Historical reflections and contemporary implications'. *Survival*, 62(3), 2020, pp 131–158.

11 Dmitri Trenin, *It's Time to Rethink Russia's Foreign Policy Strategy*. Moscow, Carnegie, 25 April 2019, p 2.

12 Richard K. Betts, 'From Cold War to hot peace: The habit of American force'. *Political Science Quarterly*, 127(3), 2012, pp 353–368 on p 354.

13 Robert Gates, 'The overmilitarization of American foreign policy'. *Foreign Affairs*, 99(4), 2020, pp 121–132 on p 122.

14 Robert D. Blackwill and Jennifer M. Harris, *War by Other Means. Geoeconomics and Statecraft*. Belknap Press, Cambridge, MA, 2016, p 230.

15 James B. Steinberg, 'What went wrong? US-China relations from Tiananmen to Trump'. *Texas National Security Review*, 3(1), 2020, pp 119–133.

16 Markus Brunnermeier, Rush Doshi and Harold James, 'Beijing's Bismarckian ghosts: How great powers compete economically'. *The Washington Quarterly*, 41(3), 2018, pp 161–176.

17 Alessandro Nicita, *Trade and Trade Diversion Effects of United States Tariffs on China*. Geneva, United Nations Conference on Trade and Development, UNCTAD Research Paper No. 37, 2019.

18 Tom McTague, 'The decline of the American world'. *The Atlantic*, 24 June 2020.

19 Alex Danchev, *Alchemist of War. The Life of Basil Liddell Hart*. London, Weidenfeld & Nicolson, 1998, p 65.

20 Karen E. Smith, 'The end of civilian power Europe: A welcome demise or a cause for concern?' *The International Spectator*, 35(2), 2000, pp 11–28.

21 Hew Strachan, *The Direction of War. Contemporary Strategy in Historical Perspective*. Cambridge, Cambridge University Press, 2013, p 127.

22 Jolyon Howorth, 'The EU as a global actor: Grand strategy for a global grand bargain?' *Journal of Common Market Studies*, 48(3), 2010, pp 455–474.

23 Christophe Gomart, *Soldat de l'ombre. Au cœur des forces spéciales*. Paris, Tallandier, 2020, pp 158–159.

24 Ian Manners, *Europe and the World*. London, Palgrave, 2009.

25 Anu Bradford, *The Brussels Effect. How the European Union Rules the World*. Oxford, Oxford University Press, 2020.

26 Abdolrasool Divsallar and Marc Otte, *Reviving the Security Function: EU's Path to Save the JCPOA*. Brussels, Egmont Institute, Security Policy Brief No. 113, July 2019.

27 Bernard Law Montgomery, *The Memoirs of Field-Marshal Montgomery*. London, Collins, 1958, p 524.

28 Elie Perot, *The Aachen Mutual Defence Clause: A Closer Look at the Franco-German Treaty*. Brussels, Egmont Institute, Security Policy Brief No. 105, February 2019.

29 Lawrence Freedman and Jeffrey Michaels, *The Evolution of Nuclear Strategy. Fourth Edition*. London, Palgrave Macmillan, 2019, p 678.

30 Sulmaan Wasif Khan, *Haunted by Chaos. China's Grand Strategy from Mao Zedong to Xi Jinping*. Cambridge MA, Harvard University Press, 2018, p 227.

31 Michael Paul and Marco Overhaus, 'Security and security dilemmas in Sino-American relations'. In: Barbara Lippert and Volker Perthes (eds), *Strategic Rivalry Between United States and China. Causes, Trajectories, and Implications for Europe*. Berlin, Stiftung Wissenschaft und Politik, Research Paper No. 4, April 2020, pp 20–24.

32 Sven Biscop (ed), 'COVID-19 and the future of Asia-Europe relations. Inaugural Asia-Europe policy forum'. *Asia Europe Journal*, 18(2), 2020, pp 195–258.

Chapter 6

1 Jeffrey W. Meiser, 'Ends + ways + means = (bad) strategy'. *Parameters*, 46(4), 2016, pp 81–91.

2 William Slim, *Defeat into Victory*. London, Cassell, 1956, p 295.

3 Winston S. Churchill, *The Second World War Volume III: The Grand Alliance*. London, Cassell, 1950, p 236.

4 Hew Strachan, *The Direction of War. Contemporary Strategy in Historical Perspective*. Cambridge, Cambridge University Press, 2013, p 103.

5 Carl von Clausewitz, *On War*. London, Penguin Classics, 1984 (translated by J. J. Graham).

6 Bernard Law Montgomery, *The Memoirs of Field-Marshal Montgomery*. London, Collins, 1958, p 38.

7 François Heisbourg, 'The emperor vs the adults: Donald Trump and Wilhelm II'. *Survival*, 59(2), 2017, pp 7–12.

8 Edward Luttwak, *The Grand Strategy of the Byzantine Empire*. Cambridge, Belknap, 2009, p 415.

9 André Beauffre, *Le Drame de 1940*. Paris, Perrin, 2020.

10 Benn Steil, *The Marshall Plan: Dawn of the Cold War*. Oxford, Oxford University Press, 2018.

11 'Comme cela est humain, l'idéalisme y habille la volonté de puissance.' Charles de Gaulle, *Mémoires de Guerre. L'unité 1942–1944*. Paris, Plon, 1956, p 238.

12 Hal Brands and Eric Edelman, 'The upheaval'. *The National Interest*, 150, 2017, pp 30–40.

13 Hanns W. Maull, 'The once and future liberal order'. *Survival*, 61(2), 2019, pp 7–32 on p 11.

14 Robert Tombs, *The English and their History*. London, Allen Lane, 2014, Chapter 14.

15 Mark Leonard, Jean Pisani-Ferry, Elina Ribakova, Jeremy Shapiro and Guntram Wolff, *Redefining Europe's Economic Sovereignty*. Brussels, Bruegel, Policy Contribution No. 9, June 2019, p 7.

16 Henry Nau, 'What Trump gets right about US foreign policy'. *The National Interest*, 30 April 2020.

17 G. John Ikenberry, 'The next liberal order. The age of contagion demands more internationalism, not less'. *Foreign Affairs*, 99(4), 2020, pp 133–142 on p 134.

18 Amit Gupta, 'Global strike vs. globalization: the US-China rivalry and the BRI'. In: Francisco Leandro and Paulo Duarte (eds), *The Belt and Road Initiative. An Old Archetype of a New Development Model*. Singapore, Palgrave Macmillan, 2020, p 46.

19 Steven Runciman, *A History of the Crusades. Volume III: The Kingdom of Acre*. Cambridge, Cambridge University Press, 1954, p 248.

20 Andrew Chatzky and James McBride, *China's Massive Belt and Road Initiative*. New York, Council on Foreign Relations, January 2020.

21 Jasper Roctus, *Remolding China's 'Empty' Belt and Road Initiative: An Opportunity for the EU*. Egmont Institute, Brussels, Security Policy Brief No. 128, June 2020.

22 Tanguy Struye de Swielande and Dorothée Vandamme, 'The new silk roads: Defining China's grand strategy'. In: Leandro and Duarte (eds), *The Belt and Road Initiative*, pp 6–7.

23 Sulmaan Wasif Khan, *Haunted by Chaos. China's Grand Strategy from Mao Zedong to Xi Jinping*. Cambridge, MA, Harvard University Press, 2018, p 231.

24 Thomas P. Cavanna, 'Unlocking the gates of Eurasia: China's Belt and Road Initiative and its implications for US grand strategy'. *Texas National Security Review*, 2(3), 2019, pp 10–37 on p 16.

25 Jordan Calinoff and David Gordon, 'Port investments in the Belt and Road Initiative: Is Beijing grabbing strategic assets?' *Survival*, Vol. 62(4), 2020, pp 59–80.

26 Munza Mushtaq, 'Sri Lanka piles on more Chinese loans amid virus and debt crisis'. *Nikkei Asian Review*, 15 May 2020.

27 Mikko Huotari, Jan Gaspers, Thomas Eder, Helena Legarda and Sabine Mokry, *China's Emergence as a Global Security Actor. Strategies for Europe*. Berlin, MERICS, Papers on China No. 4, July 2017, p 73.

28 Evan A. Feigenbaum, 'China and the world. Dealing with a reluctant power'. *Foreign Affairs*, 96(1), 2017, pp 33–40 on p 39.

29 Jisi Wang, '*Marching Westwards': The Rebalancing of China's Geostrategy*. Beijing, Peking University, International and Strategic Studies Report, 7 October 2013.

30 Timothy Snyder, *The Road to Unfreedom. Russia, Europe, America*. New York, Tim Duggan Books, 2018, p 82.

31 Nadezhada Arbatova, 'Three faces of Russia's neo-Eurasianism'. *Survival*, 61(6), 2019, pp 7–24 on p 20.

32 Ian Bond, *The EU, the Eurasian Economic Union and One Belt, One Road. Can They Work Together?* London, Centre for European Reform, March 2017.

33 Richard Ghiasy, 'Eurasian Economic Union Policies and Practice in Kyrgyzstan'. In: Lora Saalman (ed), *China-Russia Relations and Regional Dynamics. From Pivots to Peripheral Diplomacy*. Stockholm, SIPRI, March 2017, pp 25–27 on p 26.

34 Elaine Kurtenbach, 'US woos Asia with plan to rival China's 'Belt and Road''. *Associated Press*, 5 November 2019.

35 Tobias Gehrk-e, *Redefining the EU-China Economic Partnership: Beyond Reciprocity Lies Strategy*. Brussels, Egmont Institute, Security Policy Brief No. 104, February 2019.

Chapter 7

1 'Kein Operationsplan reicht mit einiger Sicherheit über das erste Zusammentreffen mit der feindlichen Hauptmacht hinaus.' Helmuth von Moltke the Elder, *Militärische Werke. Volume 2*. Berlin, Mittler & Sohn, 1900, p 291.

2 William Slim, *Defeat into Victory*. London, Cassell, 1956, p 295.

3 Winston S. Churchill, *Great Contemporaries*. London, Thornton Butterworth, 1937, p 130.

4 Hal Brands, Peter Feaver, William Inboden and Paul D. Miller, *Critical Assumptions and American Grand Strategy*. Washington, Center for Strategic and Budgetary Analysis, 2017, pp 2–3.

5 Winston S. Churchill, *The Second World War. Volume I: The Gathering Storm*. London, Cassell, 1948, p 107.

6 Dwight D. Eisenhower, *Crusade in Europe*. New York, Doubleday, 1948, p 36.

7 Alex Danchev and Daniel Todman (eds), *Field Marshal Lord Alanbrooke. War Diaries 1939–1945*. London, Phoenix, 2002, p 581.

8   Bernard Law Montgomery, *The Memoirs of Field-Marshal Montgomery*. London, Collins, 1958, p 521.

9   Dwight D. Eisenhower, *Crusade in Europe*. New York, Doubleday, 1948, p 48.

10   Alex Danchev and Daniel Todman (eds), *Field Marshal Lord Alanbrooke*, p 306.

11   David Stahel, *The Battle for Moscow*. Cambridge, Cambridge University Press, 2015.

12   Rachel Kleinfeld, *Do Authoritarian or Democratic Countries Handle Pandemics Better?* Washington, Carnegie Endowment, 31 March 2020.

13   Volker Ullrich, *Adolf Hitler. Die Jahre des Untergangs*. Frankfurt am Main, Fisher, 2018, p 671.

14   Winston S. Churchill, *The Second World War Volume I: The Gathering Storm*, p 107.

15   Jolyon Howorth, *Security and Defence Policy in the European Union. 2nd Edition*. Basingstoke, Palgrave, 2014, p 69.

16   John Bolton, *The Room Where it Happened. A White House Memoir*. New York, Simon and Schuster, 2020.

17   Daniel W. Drezner, Ronald R. Krebs and Randall Schweller, 'The end of grand strategy. America must think small'. *Foreign Affairs*, 99(3), 2020, pp 107–117.

18   Minxin Pei, 'China's coming upheaval. Competition, the coronavirus, and the weakness of Xi Jinping'. *Foreign Affairs*, 99(3), 2020, pp 82–95.

19   Edward N. Luttwak, *The Grand Strategy of the Roman Empire. From the First Century AD to the Third*. Baltimore, MD, Johns Hopkins University Press, 1976, p 127.

20   Timothy Snyder, *The Road to Unfreedom. Russia, Europe, America*. New York, Tim Duggan Books, 2018, p 29.

Chapter 8

1   Thomas E. Ricks, *The Gamble. General Petraeus and the Untold Story of the American Surge in Iraq, 2006–2008*. London, Allen Lane, 2009, p 92.

2   'C'est un mot métaphysique et politique qui signifie à peu près la même chose qu'intervention.' Emmanuel de Waresquiel, *Talleyrand. Le Prince Immobile*. Paris, Fayard, 2006, p 576.

3   Winston S. Churchill, *The Second World War Volume II: Their Finest Hour*. London, Cassell, 1949, p 102.

4   Edward Spears, *Assignment to Catastrophe. Volume I. Prelude to Dunkirk July 1939 – May 1940*. London, William Heinemann, 1954, p 29.

5   Churchill, *The Second World War Volume II*, p 477.

6   Winston S. Churchill, *The Second World War Volume I: The Gathering Storm*. London, Cassell, 1948, p 438.

7   Lawrence Freedman, *Ukraine and the Art of Strategy*. Oxford, Oxford University Press, 2019, p 168.

8   Athanassios G. Platias and Constatinos Koliopoulos, *Thucydides on Strategy. Grand Strategies in the Peloponnesian War and Their Relevance Today*. London, Hurst, 2010, p 128.

9   Geoffrey Parker, *Emperor. A New Life of Charles V*. New Haven, NJ, Yale University Press, 2019, p 496.

10   David G. Chandler, *The Campaigns of Napoleon*. London, Weidenfeld and Nicolson, 1966.

11   Fredrik Logevall, *Embers of War. The Fall of an Empire and the Making of America's Vietnam*. New York, Random House, 2012.

[12] Barry Gewen, *The Inevitability of Tragedy. Henry Kissinger and his World*. New York, Norton, 2020.

[13] Theo Farrell, *Unwinnable. Britain's War in Afghanistan 2001–2014*. London, Bodley Head, 2017.

[14] 'Vous êtes un homme! Car vous savez dire: "J'ai eu tort".' Charles de Gaulle, *Mémoires de Guerre. L'unité 1942–1944*. Paris, Plon, 1956, p 213.

[15] Colin S. Gray, *Strategy and Politics*. Abingdon, Routledge, 2016, p 77.

[16] Christopher Coker, *Rebooting Clausewitz. 'On War' in the Twenty-First Century*. Oxford, Oxford University Press, 2017, p 40.

[17] Hew Strachan, 'Strategy in theory; Strategy in practice'. *The Journal of Strategic Studies*, 42(2), 2019, pp 171–190 on p 176.

[18] Donald Stoker, *Why America Loses Wars. Limited War and US Strategy from the Korean War to the Present*. Cambridge, Cambridge University Press, 2019, p 8.

[19] Halford J. MacKinder, 'The geographical pivot of history'. *The Geographical Journal*, 23(4), 1904, pp 421–444 on pp 428–429.

[20] Rupert Smith, *The Utility of Force. The Art of War in the Modern World. 2nd Edition*. London, Penguin, 2019, p 425.

[21] Beatrice Heuser, *The Evolution of Strategy. Thinking War from Antiquity to the Present*. Cambridge, Cambridge University Press, 2010, p 505.

[22] Basil H. Liddell Hart, *Strategy. Second Revised Edition*. London, Faber & Faber, 1967.

[23] Sean McFate, *Goliath. Why the West Doesn't Win Wars. And What We Need to Do about it*. London, Michael Joseph, 2019.

[24] Kishore Mahbubani, *Has the West Lost It? A Provocation*. London, Allen Lane, 2018, p 91.

[25] Mikko Huotari, Jan Gaspers, Thomas Eder, Helena Legarda and Sabine Mokry, *China's Emergence as a Global Security Actor. Strategies for Europe*. Berlin, MERICS Papers on China No. 4, July 2017, p 28.

[26] Nikolay Kozhanov, *Russian Policy across the Middle East. Motivations and Methods*. London, Chatham House, Research Paper, February 2018, p 8.

[27] Paul Stronski and Richard Sokolsky, *The Return of Global Russia. An Analytical Framework*. Washington, Carnegie, December 2017, p 27.

[28] Niklas Swanström, 'Redefining Russia's pivot and China's peripheral diplomacy'. In: Lora Saalman (ed), *China-Russia Relations and Regional Dynamics. From Pivots to Peripheral Diplomacy*. Stockholm, SIPRI, March 2017, pp 10–13 on p 12.

Chapter 9

[1] Jean-Michel Veranneman de Watervliet, *Belgium in the Second World War*. Barnsley, Pen & Sword Books, 2014.

[2] Winston S. Churchill, *The Second World War Volume VI: Triumph and Tragedy*. London, Cassell, 1954, p 257.

[3] Henry Kissinger, *World Order*. New York, Penguin, 2015, pp 235–236.

[4] Institute for Crime and Justice Policy Research, *World Prison Brief*. London, Birkbeck College, 2020.

[5] Christopher R. Hill, 'What does Washington want from China? Pique is not a policy'. *Foreign Affairs*, 11 May 2020.

[6] 'Point n'est besoin d'espérer pour entreprendre ni de réussir pour persévérer.'

[7] G. John Ikenberry, 'The end of liberal international order?' *International Affairs*, 94(1), 2018, pp 7–23 on p 9.

[8] Joseph S. Nye, 'The rise and fall of American hegemony from Wilson to Trump'. *International Affairs*, 95(1), 2019, pp 63–80 on p 74.

[9] John Lewis Gaddis, *George F. Kennan. An American Life*. New York, Penguin, 2011, p 417.

[10] 'Tout peut, un jour, arriver, même ceci qu'un acte conforme à l'honneur et à l'honnêteté apparaisse, en fin de compte, comme un bon placement politique.' Charles de Gaulle, *Mémoires de Guerre. Le Salut 1944–1946*. Paris, Plon, 1959, p 73.

[11] Harold Nicolson, *Peacemaking 1919*. London, Constable, 1933, p 193.

[12] John Bew, *Realpolitik: A History*. Oxford, Oxford University Press, 2016.

Chapter 10

[1] Quoted in Chris Wrigley, *A.J.P. Taylor. Radical Historian of Europe*. London, I.B. Tauris, 2006, p 143.

[2] Karl-Heinz Frieser, *Blitzkrieg-Legende. Der Westfeldzug 1940*. Munich, Oldenbourg, 2012.

[3] Athanassios G. Platias and Constatinos Koliopoulos, *Thucydides on Strategy. Grand Strategies in the Peloponnesian War and Their Relevance Today*. London, Hurst, 2010, p 132.

[4] Barry Eichengreen, 'Versailles: The economic legacy'. *International Affairs*, 95(1), 2019, pp 7–24 on p 8.

[5] Winston S. Churchill, *The Second World War Volume VI: Triumph and Tragedy*. London, Cassell, 1954, p 183.

[6] Galeazzo Ciano, *Journal Politique 1939–1943. Volume I*. Neuchatel, Editions de la Baconnière, 1948, p 21.

[7] Joseph S. Nye, 'What is a moral foreign policy?' *Texas National Security Review*, 3(3), 2019, pp 96–108 on pp 107–108.

[8] Paul Kennedy, *The Rise and Fall of the Great Powers. Economic Change and Military Conflict from 1500 to 2000*. London, Unwin Hyman, 1988, p xviii.

[9] M. Taylor Fravel, *Active Defense. China's Military Strategy since 1949*. Princeton, NJ, Princeton University Press, 2019, p 276.

[10] Sulmaan Wasif Khan, *Haunted by Chaos. China's Grand Strategy from Mao Zedong to Xi Jinping*. Cambridge, MA, Harvard University Press, 2018.

[11] Herbert R. MacMaster, 'How China sees the world', *The Atlantic*, May 2020.

[12] Fareed Zakaria, 'The new China scare. Why America shouldn't panic about its latest challenger'. *Foreign Affairs*, 99(1), 2020, pp 52–69.

[13] Nele Noesselt, 'The European Union and China's multidimensional diplomacy: Strategic triangulation?'. *European Foreign Affairs Review*, 21, Special Issue, 2016, pp 11–28 on p 24.

[14] Andrew S. Erickson, 'China'. In: Thierry Balzacq, Peter Dombrowski and Simon Reich, *Comparative Grand Strategy. A Framework and Cases*. Oxford, Oxford University Press, 2019, pp 73–98.

[15] Graham Allison, *The US–China Strategic Competition: Clues from History*. Cambridge, MA, Belfer Center, Harvard Kennedy School, February 2020, p 16.

[16] Dominic Lieven, *Towards the Flame. Empire, War and the End of Tsarist Russia*. London, Allen Lane, 2015, p 367.

[17] Joseph S. Nye, 'The rise and fall of American hegemony from Wilson to Trump'. *International Affairs*, 95(1), 2019, pp 63–80 on p 74.

[18] Jisi Wang, 'China's search for a grand strategy. A rising great power finds its way'. *Foreign Affairs*, 90(2), 2011, pp 68–79 on p 77.

[19] Evan A. Feigenbaum, 'China and the world. Dealing with a reluctant power'. *Foreign Affairs*, 96(1), 2017, pp 33–40 on p 33.

[20] Hanns Günther Hilpert and Gudrun Wacker, 'Chinese narratives about the United States'. In: Barbara Lippert and Volker Perthes (eds), *Strategic Rivalry Between United States and China. Causes, Trajectories, and Implications for Europe*. Berlin, Stiftung Wissenschaft und Politik, Research Paper No. 4, April 2020, pp 12–15 on p 13.

[21] Graham Allison, *Destined for War. Can America and China Escape Thucydides's Trap?* Boston and New York, Houghton Mifflin Harcourt, 2017, p 109.

[22] Zakaria, 'The new China scare', p 61.

[23] Winston S. Churchill, *The Second World War Volume V: Closing the Ring*. London, Cassell, 1952, p 494.

[24] Henrik Larsen, *Neo-Containment: A Strategy Toward Russia*. Zürich, Centre for Security Studies, ETH Zürich, Policy Perspectives No. 1, January 2020.

[25] Athanassios G. Platias and Constatinos Koliopoulos, *Thucydides on Strategy. Grand Strategies in the Peloponnesian War and Their Relevance Today*. London, Hurst, 2010, p 53.

[26] Andrew Osborn, 'Putin, Extending Russian Footprint, Approves New Naval Facility in Sudan'. In: *Reuters*, 16 November 2020.

[27] Dominic Lieven, *Towards the Flame. Empire, War and the End of Tsarist Russia*. London, Allen Lane, 2015, p 367.

[28] Gregory Carleton, *Russia. The Story of War*. Cambridge, MA, Belknap Press, 2017, p 79.

[29] Josep Borrell, 'Chine: Les éléments d'un front uni européen'. Paris, Institut Montaigne, 3 September 2020.

[30] Angela Merkel, *Speech at the Ceremony Awarding the International Charlemagne Prize to French President Emmanuel Macron*. Aachen, 10 May 2018.

[31] 'Une reprise en main de notre destin ou celui, renonçant à toute stratégie propre, d'un alignement sur quelque puissance que ce soit.' Emmanuel Macron, *Discours du Président sur la stratégie de défense et de dissuasion devant les stagiaires de la 27ième promotion de l'Ecole de Guerre*. Paris, 7 February 2020.

Conclusion: Power to Engage

[1] George Orwell, *1984*. London, Secker and Warburg, 1949, p 119.

[2] Michael J. Boyle, 'America and the Illiberal Order after Trump'. In: *Survival*, 62(6), 2020, pp 510–76.

[3] Dmitri Trenin, *How Russia Can Maintain Equilibrium in the Post-Pandemic Bipolar World*. Moscow, Carnegie, 1 May 2020.

[4] Jeff Rathke and Yixiang Xu, *A Transatlantic China Policy Can Succeed Where the US and Europe Would Fail Separately*. Washington, AICGS, 13 February 2020.

[5] Michael J. Mazarr, 'The once and future order. What comes after hegemony?' *Foreign Affairs*, 96(1), 2017, pp 25–32 on p 30.

[6] Barry Eichengreen, 'Versailles: The economic legacy'. *International Affairs*, 95(1), 2019, pp 7–24 on p 23.

[7] Mark Leonard, Jean Pisani-Ferry, Elina Ribakova, Jeremy Shapiro and Guntram Wolff, *Redefining Europe's Economic Sovereignty*. Brussels, Bruegel, Policy Contribution No. 9, June 2019.

[8] Chuanying Lu, 'Forging stability in cyberspace'. *Survival*, 67(2), 2020, pp 125–136.

9 Hanns W. Maull, 'Die internationale Ordnung: Bestandsaufnahme und Ausblick'. *Sirius – Zeitschrift für Strategische Analysen*, 4(1), 2020, pp 3–23 on p 17.

10 Pamela Aall, Chester A. Crocker and Fen Osler Hampson, 'A New Concert? Diplomacy for a Chaotic World'. In: *Survival*, Vol. 62(6), 2020, pp 77–94.

11 Anita Prakash, 'Connecting the connectivities: It's time for regional initiatives to work together'. In: Shada Islam (ed), *Rethinking Global Governance*. Brussels, Friends of Europe Discussion Paper, Winter 2020, pp 18–21.

12 David Shepardson, 'Trump declares some auto imports pose national security threat'. *Reuters*, 17 May 2019.

13 Joseph S. Nye, 'The Rise and Fall of American Hegemony from Wilson to Trump'. *International Affairs*, 95(1), 2019, pp 63–80 on p 75.

14 'Collaborer avec l'Ouest et l'Est, au besoin contracter d'un côté ou bien de l'autre les alliances nécessaires, sans accepter jamais aucune espèce de dépendance. ... Amener à se grouper, aux points de vue politique, économique, stratégique, les États qui touchent au Rhin, aux Alpes, aux Pyrénées. Faire de cette organisation l'une des trois puissances planétaires et, s'il le faut un jour, l'arbitre entre les deux camps soviétique et anglo-saxon.' Charles de Gaulle, *Mémoires de Guerre. Le Salut 1944–1946*. Paris, Plon, 1959, p 179.

15 Winston S. Churchill, *The Second World War Volume I: The Gathering Storm*. London, Cassell, 1948, p 284.

Index

inefficiency and inagility of 73,
141–142
invoking of collective defence
guarantee 87
maritime operations around
Libya 163–164
reorientation in 1990s 152
and Russia 27–28, 55–58, 64–66, 85,
97–98, 111
and United States 74, 81–82, 84–90,
92–93, 110–111, 150–151
Navalny, Alexei 56
navy bases 6, 59, 60, 171–172, 207
Netherlands 46, 134, 186
neutrality 175–176, 178
New Zealand 91
Nicolson, Harold xi, 11, 71, 189
Niger 164
9/11 terrorist attacks 30, 122, 152–153,
204
Nitze, Paul 17
Nixon, Richard 38, 61, 80, 160,
172, 185
non-state actors 10
Nordstream 2 pipeline 106
North American Free Trade
Agreement 123
North Atlantic Treaty
Organization *see* NATO
North Korea 41, 70, 76, 105, 155,
170–171
North Macedonia 65
Norway 65
nuclear weapons 13, 40–41, 70, 76,
112–113
Nye, Joseph S. 48, 96, 187, 197, 222

O

Obama, Barack, and administration 29,
30, 73–74, 82, 105, 153, 164
O'Brien, Robert 133
Orbán, Viktor 150, 151
Orwell, George 66, 211

P

Pakistan 41, 74, 90, 129, 160
Palmerston, Lord 90
'partnership diplomacy' 137
patriotism 66–71
Pei, Minxin 154
Pericles 206
Philip II of Spain 53, 159
Philippines 63, 104
Pillsbury, Michael 4–5
Poland 85, 111, 143, 144, 151, 189, 196
political power, defined 95
Pompeo, Mike 91, 191

Portugal 75, 185
Posen, Barry 89
Prakash, Anita 219
precepts for grand strategy
engagement with peer
competitors 213–216
investment in effective
multilateralism 216–218
respect for sovereignty of other
states 218–219
safeguarding of own
sovereignty 219–221
Putin, Vladimir
and authoritarianism 6
confrontational stance 57–58, 60
cooperation between EAEU and
BRI 132–133
coronavirus aid to Italy 114
on dissolution of USSR 67
meeting Trump 21, 82, 153
speeches 27, 39
and succession 155
and Syria 180

Q

Qadhafi, Muammar 60, 97, 142,
163, 164
Quadrilateral Security Dialogue
(the Quad) 90–91
Quezon, Manuel 32

R

Reagan, Ronald 172, 191
Realpolitik 190
Ricks, Thomas E. 96
Roberts, Alasdair x, 17
Rochau, Ludwig von 190
Roctus, Jasper 126, 134
Roman Empire 36–37, 155
Romania 120, 143, 198
Roosevelt, Franklin D. 16, 67, 121
rules-based international order 187–188
Runciman, Steven 125
Russia
overview of grand strategy 28–29
allies and alliances 75–76, 90
and authoritarianism 6, 37
and Belarus 56, 75–76, 173
buffer zone on western borders 55, 66,
144, 180, 181
and Central African Republic 11, 59,
76, 206
and China 42, 77–80, 92, 174, 201
Churchill dictum on 8
civil war 74–75
clarity of strategic aims 60
and Cold War 12